A Greater Commission:
A Theology for
World Missions

A Greater Commission:
A Theology for
World Missions

by

Robert Duncan Culver

MOODY PRESS
CHICAGO

All Scripture quotations, except those noted otherwise, are from
the *New American Standard Bible,* © 1960, 1962, 1963, 1968,
1971, 1972, 1973, 1975, and 1977, by the Lockman Foundation
and are used by permission.

Library of Congress Cataloging in Publication Data

Culver, Robert Duncan.
    A greater commission.

    Bibliography: p.
    Includes index.
    1. Missions—Biblical teaching. I. Title.
BV 2073.C85   1984   266'.001   84-20746
ISBN: 0-8024-3302-2 (pbk.)

1 2 3 4 5 6 7 Printing/LC/89 88 87 86 85 84

Printed in the United States of America

Contents

PART 3
PAUL'S MANDATE FOR GOING AND SENDING
(Rom. 10 and 15)

PART 4
JESUS' POST-RESURRECTION SAYINGS

Preface

What is the Christian's guide to missionary evangelism? The Bible, of course, is the obvious answer. The Bible, however, is a large book; so the next question is, What texts relate specifically to the mission of world evangelism? Where does one read to find a mandate for missions, a description of practice in the great effort, and principles to shape and guide it? Where can one read about power to effect a successful mission?

Faithful teachers speak about such things whenever the topic or a pertinent text comes up in process of sermon or lecture. There are important pivotal texts that treat nearly every important aspect of doctrine: Philippians 2, Hebrews 2 on the incarnation, and Romans 5 on the imputation of sin come immediately to mind. Missionary promotional literature usually features so-called Great Commission texts from Jesus' post-resurrection ministry. Formal textbooks on missionary theology properly and necessarily find mandate, practice, and principle in the whole Bible, although the same Great Commission texts tend to be emphasized, sometimes being called the "marching orders of the church."

Unfortunately, some of the most pertinent scriptural passages have been passed by or treated only lightly in preaching, promotion, and theological literature. The biblical teachings and texts that moved the early church to action are not the ones usually employed today and apparently have not been widely used at any point in the nearly two centuries of modern missionary history. The purpose of this book is to bring renewed attention to the mandate for the Christian mission of world evangelism as found in Christian history and the Bible and to direct fresh consideration to important passages of the New Testament that previously have not been placed anywhere near the center of a biblical theology of principles and practices for disciples taking part in the mission of world evangelism.

Moving these four rather large texts—Matthew 10 and 13, and Romans 10 and 15—to center perhaps will give a more substantial basis for uprooting some from workplace, home, and family, to go away on a mission than was previously thought to exist. Perhaps a firmer demand upon all the rest to join in sending and supporting will also stand forth. Perhaps Matthew 28:19-20 and the other Great Commission texts in the last chapters of the gospels mean simply and compellingly that all Christians must take the gospel along wherever they go, as obviously all the visitors present at the first Christian Pentecost did, while Matthew 10 and 13 tell believers how to do that task and what to expect when they do it. And perhaps Romans 10 and 15 direct believers to do something still more and provide the scriptural basis for missions in the biblical theology of the apostle Paul. Perhaps these Pauline texts are the strongest possible source of the *greater commission* sometimes phrased: "If you cannot go yourself, then send someone else."

Introduction

Mandate for Mission in the Ancient and Modern Church

When William Carey, the father of modern missions, sought to convince his Christian brethren of their duty to evangelize the world, he faced formidable opposition and entrenched complacency. The complacency is understandable, but for some of the finest theological minds, in an age of biblical conviction, to have been utterly opposed, is puzzling.

In Carey's day serious, sustained effort to carry the name of Christ to regions where that name was not pronounced in saving belief had not prevailed in the church for a long time. Whatever the causes for this apparent neglect, Protestant Christians simply had not been aroused in numbers either to go as missionaries to the pagan world or to send others if they should volunteer to go.

Carey was not the first to be aroused to the call and duty of missionary evangelism. Yet, says Robert Hall Glover, he

> has been justly called "the father of modern missions." His career constituted an epoch indeed. It brought about a veritable revolution in missionary planning and thinking. Hitherto missionary undertakings had been mere isolated and spasmodic efforts on the part of individuals or little groups, while the mass of the churches, ministers and members alike, remained utterly indifferent and apathetic toward the condition of the pagan world. It was through Carey that there came an outburst of general missionary zeal and effort such as had not been since the days of the apostles, inaugurating a new era of united, organized, and systematic operations which have continued without abatement and with ever-widening reach and increasing force to the present day.[1]

Never in the history of any religion, Christian or otherwise, has there been a century like the nineteenth century of Protestant missions. Kenneth Scott Latourette's seven-volume *A History of The Expansion of Christianity* devotes three volumes to that period of one hundred years and aptly calls it "The Great Century." Herbert Kane affirms:

---

1. Robert Hall Glover, *The Progress of World-Wide Missions,* p. 59.

The emissaries of the cross were to be found in all parts of the habitable globe, from the frozen wastes of Greenland to the steaming jungles of Africa. Churches, chapels, schools and hospitals were scattered with great profusion from Turkey to Tokyo, from Cairo to Cape Town, from Monterrey to Montevideo, from Polynesia to Indonesia.[2]

The twentieth century has witnessed no abatement, generally considered, in the explosive missionary expansion of Christianity, though there have been shifts to new agencies and important changes in some tactics and strategies. On the negative side, theological liberalism has resulted in a spectacular collapse of support and effort in sending countries among many older established denominations. This collapse has been reflected in a corresponding withdrawal of forces from foreign fields and, of course, departures from *bona fide* Christianity among many of the workers still sent out. Latent universalism has destroyed the very reason for preaching to the pagan multitudes. Yet much that is positive is occurring. There are still armies of missionaries on the fields. Smaller and newer denominations, less affected by liberalism and consequent spiritual apathy, are filling the slack caused by the weakness in the older denominations. Dozens of interdenominational and independent mission organizations continue to send new thousands of "overseas" missionary evangelists. Though "faith missions" have been in existence for more than a century, some of the ones most active now came into existence after World War II (several future founders and early promoters of faith missions were among the veterans of World War II and the Korean conflict who attended my seminary classes). There is even much relief today from the physical hardships and peril to life once suffered by western missionaries in foreign service.

The stream of going and sending has not been channeled only through evangelists, pastors, and teachers. Some of the most powerful radio stations in the world are missionary stations broadcasting the Good News in about every major language and in many sub-languages and dialects. Never in the history of the human race have so many languages been reduced to written form with subsequent Bible translation and publication.

Why did this mighty effort arise at the time it did—late in the 18th century? What reason or reasons were given by the first modern missionary propagandists? A cautious answer will recognize that divine Providence caused it to arise. No particular branch of the Protestant Reformation devoted prime attention to the heathen world for more than two centuries. Moravians and German Pietists (Spener, Francke, Zinzendorf, and others) were forerunners of *the* "forerunner," William Carey. A Baptist among Baptist ultra-Calvinists, he wrestled with the notion that Providence intends "the Obligations of Christians to Use Means for the Conversion of the Heathens." He concluded that God does so intend, wrote a book to prove it, convinced his church associations and went out to India, as Herbert Kane remarks, "accompanied by a reluctant wife, four children, and two companions"[3] on June 13, 1793. Within a few years all Protestant denominations

---

2. J. Herbert Kane, *Understanding Christian Missions,* p. 159.
3. Ibid., p. 148.

were sending out missionaries. The great movement was on. The means Carey had fiercely advocated (human associations, fund raising, etc.) were falling into place and being vigorously employed.

Back to the earlier question: What reasons did Carey give? Significantly, he based his argument squarely on those sayings of Jesus during His post-resurrection appearances to the apostles that in recent decades have come to be called the Great Commission. To Carey, the command in Matthew 28:19 and Mark 16:15 to "Go" was an imperative that applied to Christians through the ages. It was an imperative that called forth a response either of obedience or disobedience and it was the essential basis of foreign missions. Today Carey's view is widely shared. Harry R. Boer observes that "it is clear that the Great Commission has been the dominant motivation to missionary witness during the . . . period in the century and a half since Carey published his *Enquiry* in 1792."[4]

But when Carey first published his views they were regarded as bizarre and new. The men of Carey's day thought that the issue raised by the command in Matthew 28:19 and Mark 16:15 was not one of obedience or disobedience but rather one of identification: To whom did the command apply? They saw the command as applying only to Jesus' immediate apostles. Boer's valuable studies of the subject led him to believe that this idea was inherited from the Protestant Reformers,[5] who held similar views, but it probably had a much earlier origin. Studies of interpretation through the centuries indicate that the idea was to some degree constant throughout the entire Christian era, including the earliest period of the church. The Reformers were thus following a lead of some authority. They, like the church generally in the centuries before them, simply did not base any of their views on what is today called the Great Commission.

The sharp contrast in the views of Carey and the views of the men who went before him raises yet another question: Is it possible that the unquestioning reliance today upon Matthew 28 and other post-resurrection sayings of Jesus about a mission of world evangelism is in part a strong reaction to long held contrary assumptions? Is the historical emphasis a *biblical* emphasis? Does the history of missionary activity in apostolic times and in the first three centuries support the thesis that the main scriptural support for a worldwide mission of evangelism is properly derived from Jesus' statements in His post-resurrection appearances? It can be argued that in the years since Carey the focus has been too sharply on the commission in the verses in the gospels and Acts concerning the post-resurrection appearances, and that in other New Testament passages Jesus actually had much to say on the subject that is certainly and directly applicable today. If this thesis is true, those other New Testament texts warrant some of the attention that has been lavished on the narrower range of truth. A good starting point is the early church and its understanding of the biblical basis of the missionary mandate.

The first Christians did not immediately sense that a new epoch in redemption and salvation history had dawned. They did not seem to have known that Chris-

---

4. Harry R. Boer, *Pentecost and Missions*, pp. 15-27.
5. Ibid., p. 27.

tianity (as their faith has since been named) is a missionary faith by its very constitution. Yet, once the true state of affairs struck home a zeal took over among them that has never been surpassed. In some respects the first three centuries live up to Roland Allen's trenchant description of the period as *The Spontaneous Expansion of the Church*.[6] Though not without specific missionary organization and propaganda, the church did not have a missionary society; it was one.

Glover calls attention to "the remarkable progress of the gospel during this period" and "the widespread and profound influence exerted by its devoted adherents."[7] The Christians were quite aware that they were in a campaign of world conquest for their Lord. There was no limit to their ambitions and goals in this regard. Less than 30 years after the ascension and after little more than a decade in the mission to eastern Mediterranean lands Paul wrote to Rome in the West, "from Jerusalem and round about as far as Illyricum [Israel to Yugoslavia] I have fully preached the gospel. . . . not where Christ was already named" (Rom. 15:19-20).

Justin Martyr (110-165), native of Palestine, martyred during the reign of Marcus Aurelius, wrote,

> There is no people, Greek or Barbarian or any other race by whatsoever appellation or manner they may be distinguished, however ignorant of art and agriculture, whether they dwell in tents or wander about in covered wagons, among whom prayers and thanksgiving are not offered, in the name of the crucified Jesus, to the Father and creator of all things.[8]

Tertullian (160-240), North African preacher, churchman, and theologian, wrote a lengthy, spirited defense of Christianity citing more than once the numerical spread of "God's school," i.e., the Christians, reporting that Christians were spread abroad in greater numbers than the emperor's soldiers and that if they were all to resort to arms they could defeat the Roman armies! And the missionary success had all occurred in a relatively short time. Christians were a "race that covers the whole world! We are but of yesterday, and we have filled everything you have—cities, islands, forts, towns, exchanges, yes! and camps, tribes, decuries [town councils] palace, senate, forum. All we have left to you is the temples!"[9]

Eusebius of Caesarea (266-340), first great church historian, also lived in this early era. One of his best paragraphs relates to the missionary zeal and technique that eventually led to the Christianization of the Empire and legalization of Christianity where it had formerly been unlawful to be a Christian. He wrote:

> These, as the holy disciples of such men [the apostles] also built up the churches where foundations had been previously laid in every place by the apostles. They

---

6. Roland Allen, *The Spontaneous Expansion of the Church*.
7. Glover, p. 21.
8. Justin Martyr, as quoted in Glover, p. 21.
9. Tertullian *Apology* 37. 3-4. See also 1. 7.

augmented the means of promulgating the gospel more and more, and spread the seeds of salvation and of the heavenly kingdom throughout the world far and wide For most of the disciples at that time, animated with a more ardent love of the divine word, had first fulfilled the Saviour's precept by distributing their substance to the needy. Afterwards leaving their country, they performed the office of evangelists to those who had not yet heard the faith, whilst with a nobel ambition to proclaim Christ, they also delivered to them the books of the holy gospels. After laying the foundation of the faith in foreign parts as the particular object of their mission, and after appointing others as shepherds of the flocks, and committing to these the care of those that had been recently introduced, they went again to other regions and nations, with the grace and cooperation of God.[10]

The disciples did not, however, become missionaries immediately after Jesus' ascension. Their Lord had said early in His ministry that He was sent only to "the lost sheep of the house of Israel" (Matt. 10:6). Nothing He said later seems to have modified the disciples' acceptance of that limitation for their own life and ministry. Modern Christians are puzzled at the reluctance of the apostolic group at Jerusalem to move out into the world preaching the gospel and establishing new congregations of believers. It seems to us that given the resurrection, the ascension, and Pentecost the result should have been an immediate push outward. But Luke's narrative in Acts is careful to show that such was not the case. Several years passed before anything like that took place.

True, Philip, called the Evangelist, one of the seven "deacons" of Acts 6, evangelized Samaria (Acts 8). The Samaritans, however, though not quite ortho-dox, practiced the Mosaic religion and were genetically related to the Jews. Jesus, whom Paul calls a "minister of the circumcision," (Rom. 15:8, KJV) once lodged in one of their towns, ate their food, and talked freely with one of their women (John 4). Jesus' own evangelistic work there was prelude to Philip's. There is also the case of the Ethiopian eunuch (Acts 8). Yet he was a God-fearer—not quite a proselyte with full membership in the Jewish nation, but a zealous adherent to Judaism—or else he would not have traveled from distant upper Egypt to observe a Jewish ritual feast.

There were two changes in the disciples themselves that had to be made before the mission to all the world could begin. First, they had to become aware that their Lord's redemptive work had been intended for the entire human race. In other words, they had to see that the divinely prescribed Jewishness of Old Testament religion had now evolved into a divinely intended universal offer of salvation for all mankind. They had to see that Old Testament particularism was only a preparation for New Testament universalism. They had always believed that Gentiles could worship God truly but only by becoming Jews first (circumci-sion, Mosaic ritual observance, etc.). The disciples needed *insight* into the full meaning of Christ's redemptive work.

Second, there had to be a great increase of spiritual and psychic power among the apostles and their company. They had to lose both their social dependence on

10. Eusebius *Ecclesiastical History* 3. 37.

one another and a similar attachment for the familiar scenes of their Savior's short sojourn among them. They were in acute need of some great inward power and inspiration to wake them up, get them up, and move them out. This power was provided at Pentecost and will be treated briefly later. But they still lacked *enlightenment* on the universal redemption of Christ and on the universal offer of salvation.

Writers on the subject frequently suppose necessary *insight* was furnished by the immediate *enlightenment* provided when the risen Jesus "opened their minds to understand the Scriptures, . . . that repentance for forgiveness of sins should be proclaimed in His name to all the nations" (Luke 24:45-47). The supposition might be accepted as correct if those apostles had not for several years remained essentially inert, as far as any mission of evangelism among Gentiles was concerned. Luke tells their story and how change came about in Acts 3 to 11.

Some of the most significant points for this inquiry are that *first,* by a miracle of revelation, Peter, the leader, was compelled to believe that non-Jews could be saved and enter into all the benefits of Christianity, without first becoming Jews (i.e., by circumcision, ritual practice, etc.). It took extreme measures, all reported in Acts 10 and 11. So strange did the new order seem to Peter that he felt it necessary to have six men, who witnessed part of the miracle, corroborate his story when he later reported it. *Second,* and just as important, the miracle of revelation was accepted by the Jewish believers at Jerusalem who "glorified God, saying, 'Well then, God has granted to the Gentiles also the repentance that leads to life' " (Acts 11:18).

As will be discussed at length later, the Old Testament had indicated that the purpose of God in having a "chosen people" was that salvation might ultimately be secured for and preached to all the nations. But somehow none of the Jews of Jesus' time got the point, not even His most intimate followers. During the forty days (Acts 1:3), Jesus had spoken of their being "witnesses . . . even to the remotest part of the earth" (Acts 1:8), of their making "disciples of all the nations" (Matt. 28:19), and of their proclaiming "repentance for forgiveness of sins . . . in His name to all the nations" (Luke 24:47). But those most favored eleven men still did not understand that Jesus was intending a worldwide mission of evangelism to Gentiles.

Peter had grasped the point by the time the gospel of Mark was composed. Eusebius (fourth-century church historian) is the authority for asserting that Mark was Peter's companion and that Peter was the source and authority for the gospel that Mark wrote. Long after the revelatory events of Acts 10 they (Peter and Mark) commented on the story of Mark 7:14-23 that "Thus He declared all foods clean" (v. 19), because by then they recognized that the Mosaic laws regarding kosher foods were obsolete. There is now no Jewish diet with biblical sanction. But in Acts 10 Peter had not yet understood the point. All his Jewish convictions about the necessity of Jewishness for a right relation to God remained intact. They were shattered only by the thrice-given vision (Acts 10:16) and the manifest gift of the Spirit to Gentiles *as Gentiles* (Acts 10:44-48).

There is not even awareness of a universal Christian mission in Peter's account

in Acts 10 of the Lord's post-resurrection command to preach. Peter tells Cornelius's household that after the resurrection Jesus appeared "not to all the people";
instead, he appeared to a select few, who were then "ordered . . . to preach to the
people" (Acts 10:41-42). Such was apparently Peter's understanding of the Great
Commission at the time of the events of Acts 10. "The people" had not seen the
risen Christ but were to be told about Him. Who are "the people" (*to lao*, Gr.)?
Harry R. Boer has laid the matter out clearly:

> The word *laos* (of which *to lao* is the dative with the article) is a favorite word with
> Luke. He uses it 36 times in the Gospel and 47 times in Acts, a total of 83 times, thus
> far more than half of the 140 times the word is used in the New Testament. It is
> Luke's favorite designation for the people of Israel as God's people. In designating
> groups of non-Jewish people he constantly avails himself of *ochlos*, which means crowd
> or multitude. Luke uses *laos* (i.e., people) as a parallel expression to *ethne* (gentiles)
> but only in the plural [i.e., peoples]. In 10:42 its singular use clearly indicates the
> Jewish people. Whatever intimations Peter may have had concerning a universal
> significance of the gospel, in a concrete confrontation with gentiles he cannot hide the
> fact of his particularistic conception of the *preaching* of the gospel. Even in the flesh
> and blood presence of gentiles to whom he had been supernaturally called for the
> explicit purpose of speaking words whereby Cornelius would be saved, he and all his
> house, 11:14, it does not occur to Peter that the command to preach the gospel which
> the Lord had given had reference to the gentiles.[11]

It is remarkably plain that the leaders of the Jerusalem church were both
offended that Peter had been consorting with Gentiles (Acts 11:1-3) and astound-
ed at his report of how God had compelled him to acknowledge that Gentiles now
had equal access to God, in Christ, with Jews (Acts 11:18).

The church at Jerusalem was certainly aware of no general commission to
evangelize Gentiles. Peter, its leading exponent, was aware of no such commission. How about Paul? The first hint of Paul's vocation as missionary to Gentiles
came in a revelation to Ananias, the first man to minister to his need for
enlightenment after the Damascus road experience: "Go, for he is a chosen
instrument of Mine to bear My name before the Gentiles" (Acts 9:15). The
narrative proceeds with revelation of the openness of the gospel invitation to
Gentiles (Acts 10-11). Meanwhile, disciples became active as evangelists in Phoe-
nicia, Cyprus, and Antioch (of Syria) but first only to Jews (Acts 11:19), then to
Greeks (Acts 11:20). After that Barnabas looked for Saul at Tarsus and, finding
him, brought him to Antioch. From that mainly Gentile church, a year or so later,
the two set out on what has come to be called Paul's first missionary journey. The
formal Christian mission of world evangelism had begun. It has never ceased to
the present day.

What does Paul say about why he gave his life to the mission? Was he aware of
some general commission that commands every Christian, "Go and preach the
gospel in the unevangelized places; if you cannot go send someone else"? It does

---

11. Boer, p. 39. See also the article on *laos* in *TDNT.*

not seem so. Quoting Isaiah 49:6, Acts 13:47 says: "For thus the Lord has commanded us,

'I HAVE PLACED YOU AS A LIGHT FOR THE GENTILES,
THAT YOU SHOULD BRING SALVATION TO THE END OF THE EARTH.' "

So there were two parts to Paul's mandate. The first part was a special revelation from God delivered by Ananias at Damascus. Perhaps he also received some special revelation of his own. At that time there were no gospels—no Matthew 28:19-20, no Mark 16:15. So he did not read his commission there. Anyway, Paul emphatically rejected the notion that he received his message from older Christians of the Jerusalem church (Gal. 1:11-22). He said instead that he had been set apart by God to preach Christ among Gentiles (v. 16) and that in connection with his earliest Christian experiences he was taught by "revelation" (v. 12). Paul claimed he "did not consult with flesh and blood [with other human beings] . . . but I went away to Arabia" (vv. 16-17).

It is therefore evident that no conscious awareness of a formal verbal order, such as the Great Commission, constrained Paul and his friend Barnabas to staff the first known organized effort at world evangelism. Neither was there any such awareness in the Gentile church at Antioch. There was certainly no such awareness in the Jewish church at Jerusalem before whom the mission had to be defended. Later, certain Jewish Christians continued in the opinion that despite Peter's experience in the Cornelius affair and his subsequent report, the Gentile believers needed to become practicing Jews as a part of becoming Christians. Acts 15 tells how the church put an end to that. Still later there were errorists and heretics who would have impeded the efforts at evangelism among Gentiles by imposing Jewish customs and scruples on them. But they were misrepresenting the gospel and Paul wrote Galatians to correct their errors.

The second part of Paul's mandate was a necessary inference drawn from the whole Bible as it existed in his time, what Christians today call the Old Testament. This inference was that since the Bible predicted in many ways the extension of the gospel to the heathen and since Jesus came to make a universal redemption some men ought to go tell mankind everywhere and others ought to send them. It was and is as simple as that. These two parts of Paul's, and the church's, mandate will be considered later on. First, what Jesus had to say in two long "seminars" with His apostles on the subject of the Christian mission of world evangelism will be considered.

PART 1

PRACTICE IN THE MISSION OF WORLD EVANGELISM:

(Matt. 9:35—10:42)

Evangelization of the Roman world was already well along when Matthew wrote his gospel. About A.D. 180, writing in the third book of his five-volume *Against Heresies,* Irenaeus of Lyon wrote of the missionary setting of Matthew's gospel as follows:

> It was through those from whom the Gospel came to us that we have learnt the plan of our salvation. For what they preached they afterwards handed down to us by the will of God in the Scriptures, to be "the foundation and pillar" of our faith. It is not right to say that they preached before they had perfect knowledge, and some say, who boast that they are the revisers of the Apostles. For after our Lord rose from the dead, they were filled with the power of the Holy Spirit, who came upon them from above, and acquired perfect knowledge, and went to the ends of the earth proclaiming the good things we have from God, and announcing to men the heavenly peace. Matthew edited a writing of the Gospel among the Hebrews in their own language,[1] while Peter and Paul were preaching the Gospel in Rome and founding the Church.[2]

The Hebraic cultural frame and the missionary setting mentioned clearly by Irenaeus will aid in understanding Matthew's unique interest in the mission of world evangelism. Ancient Hebrew writers of prose essays usually wrote of their theme and purpose last. Modern authors also usually write a statement of theme or purpose after their book is finished but then they set these brief addresses to the reader at the beginning of the book and call it a *preface.* The ancient Jewish author was likely to set such a thing at the point where he concluded his writing—near the end of his book. A clear case of such a statement of purpose or theme is the last chapter of Ecclesiastes. The gospel of John has such a statement at the end of chapter 20.

Matthew also did this but much more subtly. He closed his book with a final post-resurrection appearance of the Lord. At that occasion the disciples worshipped Jesus

---

1. Eusebius (about A.D. 325) quotes Papias (about A.D. 100) to this effect.
2. Irenaeus *Against Heresies* 3. 1. 1.

and He, claiming all authority in the universe, announced the familiar Great Commission. With this the author implicitly stated what had been his theme and purpose right along.

From the very beginning Matthew marshalled his materials toward this announcement at the end. There are two long chapters (10 and 13) especially concerned with the coming mission of world evangelism. Matthew made it a point, without denigrating the body, to emphasize some of Jesus' words about the importance of one's soul. At least a dozen times, aside from chapters 10 and 13, the missionary theme is explicit, beginning with the naming of the child of Mary by the angel: "and you shall call His name Jesus, for it is He who will save His people from their sins" (Matt. 1:21). The call to missionary discipleship comes only seven verses from the end of the temptation story: "Follow Me, and I will make you fishers of men" (Matt. 4:19). A reading of the following partial listing will demonstrate that this theme is sustained to the end: 5:29-30; 8:11; 9:35-38; all of chapter 10; 11:25-30; 12:46-50; all of chapter 13; 18:9-14; 19:28-30; 21:42-43; 24:13-14; 25:31-46; 26:13; 28:16-20.

Two of these sections are long. The first in literary order (actually not in point of time in Jesus' ministry) is 9:35-38 and all of chapter 10. In both sections Christ imparts information on the practice of missionary evangelism by means of a series of parables and parabolic explanations. His subjects include how the gospel operates, what the future results will be, and what the probable expectations of success or failure are. Chapter 10 mainly treats *procedures,* chapter 13, *principles.*

1

The Great Harvest Field: Vision of World Evangelism

(Matt. 9:35-38)

This passage is unique to Matthew, having no parallel in the other gospels. Like a similar passage at Matthew 4:35-25, which introduces the Sermon on the Mount, these verses are a preface to the almost unique following chapter on the mission of the twelve. They had been accompanying Jesus now for some time and He wished them to catch glimpses of the great harvest field of the world as He saw it. He also wanted them to feel with some of the depth of His great heart the need of mankind as He felt it. It cannot be doubted that all the mission fields of all times to follow, down to the last tribe, were in the scope of His vision. Therefore, it would not be stretching too much the *intent* of Christ's words to say that He also desires His people today to feel for the needs of mankind.

As this juncture Jesus saw the people as neglected by their official civil and religious leaders. To Him they appeared not only as needy, but as stolen from God. He knew which ones were His and He longed for them even then. In telling these things, this vivid and touching paragraph places the human emotions of Jesus Christ on display. In that passion He craved the sympathy of His disciples and needed their sharing of the burden of prayer (v. 38). At that time He saw in the twelve whom He had chosen the very agents who would begin to bring His Father's purposes in redemption to pass—out in the spiritual harvest fields of the world.

There is a connection not only with chapter 10, immediately to follow, but with the parables of chapter 13. This is the first occurrence in any of the gospels of Christ's favorite figure for the evangelistic task, the planting of seed and, after growth, the gathering of harvest. Chapter 13 opens with the parable of the four soils. It continues with a story of good seed and evil seed in the parable of the tares, plus the parable of the seed that, once planted, grows "by itself" (omitted by Matthew but after the four soils in Mark 4:26-29). Mustard seed and leaven continue the simile. This figure also reappears twice in the writings of John (the supplementer of the synoptic gospels), who reports Jesus' vision of the Samaritans of Sychar as a harvest field (John 4:35-36) and the magificent vision of the harvest at the consummation of the ages (Rev. 14:14-19).

There are some fine Christians who think the primary purpose of Jesus for His apostles was to offer the promised kingdom to Israel. Others see only the purpose of founding the church. This difference is not of great importance ultimately, as is seen when the qualifications each places on his interpretation are exposed. The former readily acknowledge that "God had foreseen the rejection of His Son, and His sacrificial death was the very foundation of the divine plan of blessing for the world, but that did not lessen Israel's responsibility, as Peter declared (Acts 2:23)."[1] The latter see only the founding of a worldwide church in our Lord's plan for the first advent, even though they readily acknowledge that it was necessary for the Jews to hear about the Messiah first. John Calvin states that Christ

> had been sent by the Father as a minister of the Circumcision, to fulfil the promises which had once been given to the fathers—cf. Rom. 15:8. God had made a peculiar alliance with the stock of Abraham. Naturally Christ began by continuing the grace of God to the chosen people, until the time was ripe to publish it abroad. From the resurrection, we may definitely see the second stage, the blessing promised to all nations being shed forth, even as the veil of the temple was rent, the partition wall of strife pulled down.[2]

The differences between these two views is not to be belittled. Advocates of the former expect a national restoration of Israel in which the twelve apostles shall have a part; the latter specifically reject any such program. With few exceptions, they affirm to the contrary that the church *is* the promised kingdom of God. Later, in these pages, a more comprehensive view, which finds both the present church and restored Israel within the kingdom Jesus came to establish, will be presented.

The emphatic point on which most agree is that it was always God's plan to use the apostles to found the church of Christ and that our Lord had this specifically in mind when He called them. Furthermore, the same Paul who sets forth Christ as the sole foundation of a fruitful Christian life (1 Cor. 3:11) declared of the church, the household of God, that it is being "built upon the foundation of the apostles and prophets, Christ Jesus Himself being the corner stone" (Eph. 2:20). History and the New Testament unite in telling us that this is true—Jesus chose His apostles to serve as founders of the church.

1. H. A. Ironside, *Expository Notes on the Gospel of Matthew,* p. 119.
2. John Calvin, *Calvin's Commentaries: A Harmony of Matthew, Mark and Luke,* 1:291.

2

The Twelve Apostles:
Workers in the Harvest

(Matt. 10:1-4)

It is not likely that the great importance of these twelve men to Jesus' plan for the ongoing mission of world evangelism can be overemphasized. A comparison of the account in Matthew with passages in Mark and Luke shows that at least several of the apostles were chosen at an earlier point in Jesus' ministry (Mark 3:13-15; cf. 6:6-13; Luke 6:12-16; cf. 9:1-2). It suited Matthew's purpose to list their names for the first time in conjunction with Jesus' vision of the field and the first apostolic preaching mission. In certain respects the men were unique. They alone had the permanent conferral of the supernatural powers described in verse 1. They alone accompanied Jesus "from the beginning" (John 15:27) and, as eyewitnesses of His resurrection, reported that event to the nations (Acts 1:1-4; 2:32; 10:39). Yet in other ways, both they and their work were representative of what all God's servants in the project of world evangelism must be.

Since the "names of the twelve apostles" (Matt. 10:2) are highlighted, it is appropriate to ask who these men were. They are listed in pairs: Peter and his brother Andrew; James and John, brothers and sons of Zebedee; Philip of Beth-saida and Bartholomew, also known as Nathaniel; Thomas and Matthew, or Levi; James, the son of Alphaeus, and Thaddaeus, also known as Judas or Lebbaeus; and finally Simon the Cananaean, or Zealot, and Judas Iscariot. All were residents of the Galilean area of north Palestine except Judas the traitor who was from Kerioth (Iscariot means man of Kerioth) in the far south. Four or more were fishermen, one was a tax clerk. The occupations of the rest are not known. None of them was from the highly educated, ruling, or wealthy classes. It is reasonably certain from the personal anecdotes with which the gospels are well supplied that none of the apostles was a man of unusually acute mental or spiritual powers. There is really nothing especially notable about them singly or in aggregate to distinguish them from other men of their time.

What then can be learned from these verses about the true laborers in the harvest of souls in the great mission of world evangelism? Many things.

THE SIGNIFICANCE OF TWELVE

First, there is a significant use of a symbolic number twelve—the usual numerical emblem of the Old Testament people of God. There were twelve sons of Jacob and the twelve corresponding tribes of the "children of Israel." That number reappears in many symbolical representations in Hebrew religion and history: "twelve pillars for the twelve tribes of Israel" at Mount Horeb (Ex. 24:4), twelve precious stones on the "breastplate" of Aaron's "ephod" (Ex. 28:21; 39:14), twelve cakes of bread on the table of "show bread" (Lev. 24:5), twelve princes (Num. 1:44), twelve oxen drawing six wagons, and twelve silver platters, bowls, and golden spoons (Num. 7:3, 84), twelve bullocks, rams, lambs, and kids for the dedication of the Tabernacle in the wilderness (Num. 7:87). Sometimes this number is employed in the New Testament to stand for Israel, the Old Testament people of God (Matt. 19:28; Luke 22:30; James 1:1; Rev. 12:1; cf. Gen. 37:5-11). It is not surprising therefore that in John's vision of the coming city of God, in which shall dwell the redeemed of the ages, there are twelve gates, each attended by one of twelve angels. The gates have "names . . . written on them, which are those of the twelve tribes of the sons of Israel" (Rev. 21:12). It is also not surprising that Israel's Messiah should have foreseen a time when His twelve apostles will sit on twelve thrones ruling the twelve tribes (Matt. 19:28; Luke 22:30).

Twelve also stands for the New Testament people of God, the ones to be drawn from all the nations. The twelve apostles were the designated founders of and missionaries to the worldwide church, as well as the first leaders of it. Matthew began to hint at their mission early in his book as will be seen, and progressively revealed more as he went along. The worldwide mission was always on Jesus' schedule for the future, as Matthew 10 clearly indicates. So it should not be surprising to find the names of "the twelve apostles of the Lamb" written on the twelve foundations of the coming city (Rev. 21:14) where the redeemed of all the ages shall dwell. The "elders" John saw in heaven who speak for the redeemed of all the ages and represent them in John's vision quite logically, then, number exactly twenty-four, twelve for the old dispensation and twelve for the new (Rev. 4:4, 10-11; 5:8-10).

Thus, though Jesus saw clearly the worldwide dimension of redemption and thought of Himself and His public ministry always with that in mind, it is quite natural that while still moving wholly in Jewish circles, the missionary founders of the church should have numbered exactly twelve.

THE SIGNIFICANCE OF FAMILIAL AND COMMUNITY RELATIONSHIPS

A second matter of great significance to the evangelical mission is the special value of social relationships as exemplified by the connections among the twelve. There are at least two pairs of brothers—Andrew and Peter, sons of Jona, and John and James, sons of Zebedee. All four of them worked as fishermen in the Capernaum-Bethsaida area. James the Less (Little) and Matthew may also have been brothers inasmuch as each is said to be the son of Alphaeus. This Alphaeus may be Cleopas (the same in Aramaic), if so, then their mother stood at the cross as another member of a large family group. Thomas also may be their brother. There is evidence that the mother of the sons of Zebedee and Jesus' mother were sisters; if so, they were first cousins of Jesus. Philip was another resident of Bethsaida, hence a neighbor of the first four and a close friend of Nathaniel (or Bartholomew) as well. Except for Judas, who was of the distant Kerioth all, including Jesus Himself, were Galileans. And it must not be forgotten that five or six of the twelve were disciples of John the Baptist before they became disciples of Jesus.

Most things good and evil among men are promoted by primary social relationships of family and friendship. Former ages have found that easier to understand. Nowadays, diplomas, degrees, courses, seminars, textbooks, committees, caucuses, meetings, books, articles, and speeches seem to be of preeminent importance. Yet it is the primary social relationships that always have been and always will be vehicles for the promotion of every kind of significant human enterprise. Parents will always seek to promote their own children and will expect care in their old age. So it is and ought to be. Propaganda and advertisement are useful, but when the best possible person for a secretary, a physician, a lawyer, or a counselor is desired, an ad is run in the newspaper only as a last resort. Almost invariably a relative, friend, or neighbor is asked for advice. Saving truth is always best obtained at mother's knee, over the back fence, or at the nearest place of quiet talk between neighbors.

THE SIGNIFICANCE OF PREPARATION

A third principle is that men worthy of being laborers in the great harvest must be prepared by God. First the Spirit of God leads men to become Jesus' disciples. Then they advance to become apprentice "fishers of men." Only after that do they become special agents in the harvest. The twelve had individually long awaited the consolation of Israel; several heard John and, as John insisted, they prepared the way of the Lord in their own hearts by repentance. When John said of Christ, "Behold, the Lamb of God! . . . they followed Jesus" (John 1:36-37, KJV). Later, when Jesus said "Follow Me, and I will make you fishers of men" (Matt. 4:19), the record says they left all and did just that. This is the significance of the initial call of five or six back in the spring of the first year of His ministry (John 1:35-51), the call of a year later (Matt. 4:18-22), and the fact that the "twelve disciples" of Matthew 10:1 became the "twelve apostles" (sent ones) of Matthew 10:2 and 5.

Apprenticeship, testing, and training are necessary. They all had to be indoctrinated with the principles of Christ. That is why several of the twelve were called to be disciples as long as three years before Jesus' death. They also had to be endued with divine power as Matthew 10:1 and 8 indicate and as the Lord's parting instructions after the resurrection made specific (Acts 1:4-5). They needed to be told what to expect in the world where their witness was to be given. This He proceeded immediately to do (Matt. 10:5-42). Finally, they needed instruction in the specific principles of evangelism. This also He began immediately to do as shall be seen in the rest of the tenth chapter of Matthew.

THE SIGNIFICANCE OF INSIGNIFICANCE

Of greatest importance is that no particular mental cast, intellectual attainment, or worldly advantage is necessary to be one of the fishers of men. The disciples were distinguished by no illustrious ancestry. They had no splendid prizes of university scholarships to offer. As far as the social, political, and religious elite were concerned, the twelve were all unlettered men, like their new Master.

But was there not perhaps some unusual talent, genius, natural gift, or attainment that distinguished some and made them worthy? Hardly. They were distinguished rather by the lack of these qualities. One of their number was rash, unsteady, quick to speak, and slow to think. Jesus made him their leader-designate—but there is not the slightest evidence that these qualities dictated Jesus' decision. Another was thoughtful and affectionate; others skeptical, pessimistic, gossipy, cowardly, brave, or taciturn. God used everything that every one of them had and was, but only after God transformed them and their natural qualities.

God can and does use such men in His great harvest of the souls of men. Paul does not say that there are no wise, no mighty, no noble who are employed by God in this great project, but he does affirm that "not many wise according to the flesh, not many mighty, not many noble; but God has chosen the foolish . . . the weak . . . the base . . . and . . . the things that are not, that He might nullify the things that are; that no man should boast before God" (1 Cor. 1:26-29). True, God does sometimes use the men of highest genius, of most refined taste, and of most extensive education. But then, as always, God's servants were mainly men of no distinguished attainment until after the Lord got hold of them. Under God's transforming power no man is of insufficient worldly or personal value to be useful in the Lord's great mission of world evangelism.

There is a question that must yet be answered. Does not the Lord's choice of Judas, from among His professed disciples, to be an apostle, place all affirmations about these men—their training, position, and function—in doubt?

It is assumed that Jesus was aware of Judas's true character both in appointing him and in tolerating his annoying presence among the close followers at all (John 6:64, 70-71; 13:2, 27; 17:12). Based on this, one can then be certain that Jesus had purposes in so doing and that the purposes were accomplished. Indeed, it can truly be said, if these inferences are correct, that Judas served the purposes for which he was chosen as well as any of the twelve.

This can be seen by reasoning backward from the fact that it was Judas who said at the last, "I have sinned by betraying innocent blood," i.e., a just person (Matt. 27:4). In Jesus' own time and onward to the present, ungodly men have sought to find ground for some charge of immorality, impurity, bad character, or bad action in Him. The charges of those Jewish leaders contemporaneous with

Jesus are familiar—He committed blasphemy by claiming God for His Father; He broke the Sabbath by healing the sick; He ate and drank too much. In recent generations writers have made snide suggestions that there was impurity in His relationship with Mary Magdalene, that He was intemperate and uncompassionate in His tirade against the Pharisees and others (Matt. 23), that He was ill-tempered with the Syrophoenician woman (Matt. 15:21-28; Mark 7:24-30), or simply unreasonable when He cursed the fig tree (Matt. 21:18-20; Mark 11:12-14, 20-24). If such suspicions as these could ever have become charges capable of being successfully sustained men would long ago have destroyed the Savior's unflawed reputation. Thus, the best testimonies to His righteous character, from the nature of the case, would be from His enemies, especially if one of them was known to have been intimately associated with Him for a long time. Just such a person was Judas. He had been admitted to the inmost circle of Jesus' friends. He had seen Him in every situation of day-to-day living, eating, sleeping, walking, talking, together with the other eleven, almost without interruption for about two years—if Judas's call took place about the time of the opening of the long Galilean ministry. It was this man who, moved by motives of greed and who knows what else, said, "I have sinned by betraying innocent blood" (Matt. 27:4). It is therefore impossible, on the basis of the gospel records or legitimate inferences drawn from them, to entertain the slightest doubt of the righteousness of Jesus' life and character.

Judas was, therefore, as useful to the Lord as any member of the twelve, though in a special way. It has rightly been said, in view of these things, that not only does Christianity require a Judas, but that Christ knew that He needed a Judas for the sake of future generations. Judas, along with Annas, Caiaphas, Pilate, Herod, and the others, was a part of the "predetermined plan and foreknowledge of God" (Acts 2:23) foreseen in prophecy, as Jesus said, "I know the ones I have chosen; but it is that the Scripture may be fulfilled, 'HE WHO EATS MY BREAD HAS LIFTED UP HIS HEEL AGAINST ME' " (John 13:18; cf. Ps. 41:9; also John 6:70-71; 17:12; Acts 1:15-20; 4:27-28).

The next part of the chapter that will be looked at, Matthew 10:5-42, is divided into three distinct portions by divisions indicated at the close rather than at the beginning of each section. This is common in Scripture as in the case of the five books of Psalms, (1-41; 42-72; 73-89; 90-106; 107-150) the close of each being a formal benediction; and the three parts of Isaiah 40-66 (40-48; 49-57; 58-66), each of which is closed by 'there is no peace,' says my God, 'for the wicked' or a similar statement. In like manner, the three portions of Matthew 10:5-42 are indicated by "truly I say to you" (vv. 15, 23, and 42).

3

The First Mission:
Application Then and Now

(Matt. 10:5-15)

There are a number of questions that might be treated before plunging into the rest of this great chapter. Most of them, however, will be treated as they occur in the course of actual exposition. At this point, only some facts about the passage will be observed in a general way.

It is clear that the first section (5-15) relates primarily to the mission immediately before the disciples and from which they returned in a few weeks. Mark (6:30) and Luke (9:10) tell of the apostles' return though inexplicably Matthew does not. The next section (16-23) relates primarily to their ministry after the ascension and until the Christians left the area a short time before the time of the destruction of Jerusalem, A.D. 70. Yet there is hardly anything said that does not apply with equal, if secondary, force to all believers until the end of time. This will be discussed in connection with verse 23. Beginning with verse 24 and onward to verse 42, the end of the chapter, the instruction relates in its primary application to believers of this entire epoch. Older writers (Alford, Edersheim, Ellicott) agree in main with this interpretation and bring primary and secondary references of prophetic passages to bear. More recently, William Hendriksen simply stated: "A single reading of the charge shows that from verse 16 to the end, the One who addresses the Twelve is predicting the future. He is describing what is going to happen when the church brings Christ's message to those lost in sin."[1] Whether the address is a unit, all delivered on one occasion, or if the predictions of martyrdom and severe persecution come from a period late in Jesus' ministry or were invented by the author or early church has been debated in the literature. It is not necessary on any factual grounds to reject the unity of the address. Hendriksen presents the views and summarizes reasons for rejecting the notion of combination of addresses (see Hendriksen, pp. 447-49).

THE MESSENGERS (v. 5a)

Though the twelve are in focus here, Jesus' instructions are no more restricted to them alone than a general's field orders can be said to apply only to the ones

1. William Hendriksen, *Matthew: New Testament Commentary Series*, p. 446.

receiving the orders or only to men directly under his command. They are for all who are or shall be under his command in one way or another unless and until the orders are rescinded. Jesus' orders are, in principle, for all Christians.

This will be seen more clearly as this section (10:5-42) is seen in connection with the whole theological purpose of Matthew. Everything in the book leads up to the final sentence, a formal announcement of a worldwide mission of evangelism. But that happens to be only the last of over a dozen places where Matthew comments that Jesus' mission was both to provide a redemption sufficient for all people of all time and to equip an initial corps of men who would begin the mission of world evangelism. These men were then to pass on both their mission and passion to the new disciples. Following are a few of these critical junctures in Matthew's story.

The first such passage is the initial call of the first four to be permanent followers, accompanying Jesus wherever He went henceforth, "Follow Me, and I will make you fishers of men" (4:19). Within a few weeks of the opening of His ministry, immediately after the striking manifestation of faith by a Gentile (Roman army officer) at Capernaum, Jesus' disciples heard Him say, "Many shall come from east and west, and recline at the table with Abraham, and Isaac, and Jacob, in the kingdom of heaven" (8:11). There has already been comment on Jesus' missionary vision of the multitudes (9:35-38). The current passage (10:5-42), in such language as His apostles in their primer stage could understand, several times presents a world horizon. The lengthy passage 12:46—13:58 is dealt with later. Other passages worth attention are 14:13-14, 18:7-14, and 19:23-30. There is a distinct prophecy of the mission to the Gentile world: "The kingdom of God will be taken away from you [Jews], and be given to a nation producing the fruit of it" (21:43); "And this gospel of the kingdom ["the gospel," Mark 13:10 parallel] shall be preached in the whole world for a witness to all the nations, and then the end shall come" (24:14). The latter passage is an amazingly distinct statement of Jesus' plans and a clear window on the purpose of Matthew in selecting some of the materials he did for his gospel.

Even more amazing and equally revealing is the report of Matthew (and of Mark) of Jesus' words to the guests at the house of Simon the leper, at Bethany, on the Sabbath evening nearly a week before His betrayal. Mary of Bethany had anointed Jesus' head and feet with a very valuable ointment. Some had censured her act as a waste. Then came Jesus' famous reply, "For when she poured this perfume upon My body, she did it to prepare Me for burial. Truly I say to you, wherever this gospel ["the gospel," Mark 14:9] is preached in the whole world, what this woman has done shall be spoken of in memory of her" (Matt. 26:12-13). There can be scarcely any doubt, on the basis of this passage alone, that Jesus intended the gospel offer of salvation to be carried to the whole world. It is equally certain that Matthew wrote with the clear purpose of conveying that to his readers. The formal announcement of the mission, which Matthew strategically placed at the very close of his book (a very Hebraic thing to do), is then only the capstone of a pyramid.

Bringing this to bear on Matthew's tenth chapter, it seems clear that all that Jesus says therein has meaning for the world mission. It will become clear in the

following pages that there is increasing immediacy of application to disciples on
the mission of world evangelism in all epochs as the discourse moves to its close.

THE FIELD (VV. 5b-6)

The reasons why the initial stage of the worldwide evangelistic mission was
limited to the Jewish people are plain enough. That God "has visited us and
accomplished redemption for His people" (Luke 1:68) had been announced already by the father of Jesus' forerunner. Messiah's coming was no longer a mere
prediction. The beginning of fulfillment had taken place. The future tense, "Messiah shall come," changed emphatically to present tense when the forerunner
proclaimed, "Behold, the Lamb of God who takes away the sin of the world" (John
1:29). "The Law and the Prophets were proclaimed until John; since then the
gospel of the kingdom of God is preached" (Luke 16:16). Jesus the Messiah had
only crumbs from the messianic table for Gentiles (Mark 7:24-30); except the
"grain of wheat falls into the earth and dies, it remains by itself alone" said Jesus
(John 12:24). He was exclusively Israel's Messiah until "by the predetermined
plan and foreknowledge of God" He should be rejected and slain by Israel (Acts
2:23), Gentiles witlessly assisting (Acts 3:13-15) and doing thereby what God's
"hand and . . . purpose predestined to occur" (Acts 4:27-28). Until redemption
was finished, the proclamation had to be to Israel.

There are other reasons why Jesus limited His entire ministry to Israel. One
was the disciples' state of mind. Jesus might give aid to a Caesarean centurion or
a Syrophoenician mother but the twelve Jewish apostles-to-be were not ready for
any ministry to Gentiles. Jesus spoke of "other sheep, which are not of this fold"
(John 10:16) and three times He told Peter to feed them (John 21:15-17), but
even after Jesus' post-resurrection prediction of a future Christian witness in
"Samaria" and on to "the uttermost parts of the world," it finally took persecution
to drive some of the twelve out of Jerusalem. Peter, himself, never fully understood until God gave a very special vision to him on the subject (Acts 10:9-16).
Perhaps he did not fully understand it even then. So the worldwide mission of
evangelism must be listed among the things Jesus had in mind in His words: "You
cannot bear them now" (John 16:12). This, of course, must be related to Pentecost, the opening of the minds of the apostles to their worldwide mission (Acts
10-11), and the special calling of Paul.

Furthermore, given that Jewish generation's almost totally nationalistic understanding of the Old Testament promises, there would not have been any reception
at all for messengers of a claimant Messiah who would send the messengers of
His reign equally to Samaritans and Gentiles. Likely, if Jesus had given Himself
freely to Gentiles there would have been none of the enthusiastic crowds of Jews,
miracles or not. They would never listen to a Jewish rabbi who consorted with
Gentiles.

God was in no way limiting the field of mission to the Jewish people; He was
only putting them on the schedule first by way of pledge to their ancestors, by
way of sovereign choice, and by historical necessity. Paul's missionary party

customarily gave attention to the scattered Jewish communities before turning to Gentiles (Acts 13:5, 14; Rom. 1:16). The same precedence of Jewish evangelism prevailed throughout the book of Acts.

THE EXAMPLE OF STRATEGY (v. 6)

Deeper lessons appear when considering the strategy Christ gave to His disciples. "Go to the lost sheep of the house of Israel." There are two features, at least, of necessary Christian evangelistic strategy in these words: (1) go first to the ones the witnessing disciple is most fitted, by reason of personal history and ability, to win; (2) go first to the people nearest at hand.

With regard to the first, the twelve apostles were in every regard Jewish. Not only so, they were provincials of their country, regarded by Jews of Judea—the national center—as rude outlanders. This appears in quite a number of New Testament incidents. The authentic messengers of God (the prophets) to the Jews from earliest times had been "from your countrymen" (Deut. 18:15, 18). So far as is known, no Edomite or Moabite ever preached to Israel for Jehovah God. Ultimately, when an effective mission to Gentiles was launched, it was by Paul who, though Jewish by ancestry and religion, was Greek by culture, residence, language, and outlook. Knowledgeable writers of the life of Christ generally observe how thoroughly everything about Jesus' entire career breathes the atmosphere of Judaism. All efforts to make of Him an urbane, cosmopolitan citizen of the world must fail. His discourses, as well as the narrative—except for the entrance of an occasional Roman official—are entirely within a Jewish-oriental world.[2]

This lesson must be learned. Everything human beings say and do is specifically culturally related. It is not incorrect to say that in a measure every man is culturally bound and is necessarily so if life is to have social meaning at all. If so, then the Christian message must always be culturally related. Even language itself is a cultural phenomenon. The gospel will always find a better reception if the missionary understands the culture and ways of the people he hopes to reach. He must, as far as possible, adapt his own personal life-style to theirs. He cannot and likely should not fully do so, but in trying he is at least showing respect for the people, their customs and culture.

In the second place the missionary who plans to work overseas must prove to himself, to his supporters, and ultimately to his remote future audience that his faith, hope, and love—his wisdom, too—are genuine. He can best do so by proving them first at home. Sending churches or agencies should see missionary capacity and zeal displayed in the home situation first. It is foolishness to outfit and send an untried missionary 10,000 miles away before he has shown himself a missionary at home.

This applies equally to the largesse of churches and Christians who aspire to be honorable supporters of distant missions. "This law is not an arbitrary impost; it is

2. Robert Duncan Culver, *The Life of Christ*, pp. 189-92.

founded in the truest love and wisdom. Genuine love says, If you have a favor to bestow, offer it first to those of your own kin and neighborhood. Home first, is the dictate of a true philanthropy. That feeling which induces man to cross seas, and to traverse islands and continents, to offer blessings which he has never presented to his own neighbors, who stand in equal need, is the simpering sentiment of a morbid and diseased mind, not the manly love of a true heart. The law is the dictate of wisdom as wisdom as well as love."[3] These words have great weight inasmuch as they come from the pen of a man who was a promoter of foreign missions as well as the sacred art of preaching.

THE MESSAGE OF THE MISSION (V. 7)

This is indicated very briefly: "And as you go, preach, saying, 'The kingdom of heaven is at hand' " (v. 7). Or this might be paraphrased simply: "The king has arrived!" or "Jesus Christ is Lord!" for that is what the good news of the kingdom really means. One theory says that Jesus meant, "I am offering you the kingdom, accept it and all the Old Testament promises about the coming messianic reign will immediately ensue. Reject it and I will withdraw the offer and present it on another day. Meanwhile I will substitute a different program, the church, a unique new thing."

There is a better way of looking at the matter that is fully compatible with the conviction of many that the church is unique and new, not simply a new Israel or a substitute heir of Israel's promises. This can be seen by looking at "kingdom" in the context of the New Testament where it means kingly rule rather than territory. It means "reign" in most of the contexts. "The kingdom" is God's kingship working salvation, "His government as a living and powerful Divine action, revealing itself in ever new forms of self-manifestation, in the course of many dispensations and periods."[4] Though the reign of God will ultimately take visible form on earth, it is not simply a future Millennial kingdom. In Scripture the Old Testament rule of God in Israel was termed "kingdom of God." But the special sphere of God's saving action was taken away from the nation of Israel because of their unbelief (Matt. 21:43) and given to others. The new "nation producing the fruits" of the kingdom (Matt. 21:43) is no particular nation at all, but all of the nations, i.e., the Gentiles. During the present age, the church—the instrument of extension of God's reign in saving power—is called "the kingdom of God." The eternal heavenly kingdom that sinners will not inherit is also called "the kingdom of God" (Gal. 5:21).

Thus "all members of the body of Christ belong to the kingdom and all true citizens of the kingdom belong to the church; they are citizens of that kingdom"[5] (Eph. 2:19; Phil. 3:20; Col. 1:13). Those who are Christians only by profession are referred to by Christ as being in the spiritual kingdom (Matt. 7:21-23; 13:41;

---

3. David Thomas, *The Genius of the Gospel*, p. 151.
4. Erich Sauer, *From Eternity to Eternity*, p. 89.
5. Ibid., p. 91.

22:11-14). Yet sometimes the New Testament acknowledges only the genuine believers as members of that spiritual kingdom (John 3:5). Both the *true* and the *professing* church can be referred to as the kingdom of God if it is kept in mind that this is not permanent.

In the future, the church will inherit the kingdom of glory and power (Matt. 25:34; cf. 1 Cor. 6:10; Gal. 5:21; Eph. 5:5); they will enter into it (Acts 14:22). It is the goal of the pilgrimage to which they have been called (1 Thess. 2:12) and it is their reward (2 Thess. 1:5). If the future kingdom of God, when He is "all in all" (1 Cor. 15:25-28), is thought of as the perfected kingdom of God, the church will be a sphere within the larger sphere. The idea is so fluid in the New Testament that in one chapter, Matthew 19, the kingdom is roughly equated with "eternal life" (v. 16), "treasure in heaven" (v. 21), "enter[ing] the kingdom of heaven" (v. 23), "enter[ing] the kingdom of God" (v. 24), "be[ing] saved" (v. 25), and "inherit[ing] eternal life" (v. 29)—all with no sense of inconsistency with a future visible reign of Christ from a throne (v. 28).

This argument forms at least a possible basis for affirming that the gospel of grace as found in Romans 1:16-17, 1 Corinthians 15:1-8, and throughout the New Testament is accurately described as the good news of the kingdom of God. Paul undoubtedly so understood it (see Acts 20:24-25; 28:31; see also pp. 58 & 59). There *is* a reign of God in the here-and-now, God's present kingdom of grace in the church, but there also *will be* a future manifest kingdom and hence Christians can be "fellow workers for the kingdom of God" (Col. 4:11).

A Basic Principle of Evangelism (v. 8)

"Freely you received, freely give" (Matt. 10:8). Care must be taken in understanding this. "Freely" does not mean copiously or without obstruction as with the running of water; but it means without charge, without expectation of payment to the messenger from those who receive it. *Dōrean* is the Greek word. It is used of how God justifies sinners (Rom. 3:24) and how the Spirit of God in the very last invitation in the Bible offers salvation to sinners: "And whosoever will, let him take the water of life freely" (Rev. 22:17, KJV).

Not all those who hear the gospel and profess to believe it truly understand that principle. Such was the case in the first church established outside of Judea, at Samaria. One of the newly baptized there, Simon by name, after he saw the power of Christ in the apostles' ministry of preaching, sought to buy the power for money in order to use it for his own enrichment. He was soundly rebuked (Acts 8:18-24). To suppose, as some whom Timothy met, that "godliness is a means of gain," is a dangerous error (1 Tim. 6:5), even though in business "honesty" truly "is the best policy." There ought to be a better reason than policy for being honest.

The point need not be labored that this is not in contradiction with Jesus' dictum that "the worker is worthy of his support" (Matt. 10:10). Paul makes this saying of Jesus the basis of his own policy for support of the pastors in the churches he founded (1 Cor. 9:14).

The principle of freely giving that which was freely received is to be the motive for doing gospel preaching. It is, to use some good old words, disinterested benevolence. Christians have something good that came to them *gratis*. They have power to pass it on and should do so without thought of special gain from it.

It is only as pagan peoples have seen this motive demonstrated by their missionary informers that Christianity has gained wholehearted acceptance by large numbers of a population. And, in such a case, the new believers have become genuine new believers, believers in grace, living in grace. They have not received the new religion simply as a means to get themselves up in the world or in better health or to live in a more peaceful community—even though all those blessings usually come. In the lands of Christendom evangelism has usually been weakened by the lack of this distinterested benevolence, for the mission enterprises have seldom been free from sectarian ambition, proselytizing zeal, and lust for power! New believers must not be treated like trophies or scores for publication on the sports page of the newspaper. It must be clear to all that motives are right.

The Preparations (vv. 9-10)

The thrust of these verses is simply "Go as you are." Extra money and extra clothing for that journey was unnecessary. They were not to worry about them. The Lord would provide through generous-hearted people wherever they went. That specific instruction was rescinded after a short while (see Luke 22:35-36). Missionaries would have travel outfits and Paul would even send for missing articles (2 Tim. 4:11-13). The principle, however, that one brings the gospel to his neighbor without special educational or material preparation must always apply. Charlotte Elliott's song is sung in inviting men to Christ and, when turned around, explains how lost men much be reached: "Just as I am, without one plea, But that Christ's blood was shed for me [and thee]." The opportunity comes when the neighbor has a need, or question, or when he opens the door to witness. The verses from courses in "soul-winning" or the formula of some "four things" or "four laws" are seldom quite adequate and sometimes not even appropriate. In the time of the death of a neighbor's child, one goes to him with love and sympathy. That will either be in the heart already or it will not be. The occasion will be cultivated by friendship, but one goes as-is when the occasion arrives.

The Reception of the Message (vv. 11-13)

This is closely related to the reception of the messenger. "Inquire who is worthy... and abide there.... let your greeting of peace come upon [the house]" (Matt. 10:11-13). These words relate to being worthy hosts, not worthy of salvation, of course. The person who responds with hospitality is among those likely to be saved. This is because hospitality is an identifying characteristic of biblical religion and it flourishes wherever biblical religion flourishes (Rom. 12:13; 1 Tim. 3:2; 5:10; Titus 1:8; Heb. 13:2. See also Gen. 18:1-8; 24:25; Ex. 2:20;

Judg. 13:15; 2 Kings 4:8-10; Job 31:31-32; Matt. 9:10; Luke 5:29; 19:5, 7; John 12:1-2; Acts 16:14-15; 18:26; Rom. 16:1-2; 2 Tim. 1:16; Philem. 2, 22; 3 John 5-6). The cities of Sodom and Gomorrah, which were scandalously inhospitable to God's messengers, were also scandalously corrupt and merited the judgment they received (Gen. 13:13; 18:20; 19:1-25; Jude 7).

Paul's experiences exemplify this very well. When he, in obedience to divine guidance, came to Philippi, the missionary knew of no one in the city who would receive him, but there was one known to God who was ready. Luke told the story of what happened when they arrived in the strange new "district":

> And we were staying in this city for some days. And on the Sabbath day we went outside the gate to a riverside, where we were supposing that there would be a place of prayer; and we sat down and began speaking to the women who had assembled. And a certain woman named Lydia, from the city of Thyatira, a seller of purple fabrics, a worshipper of God, was listening; and the Lord opened her heart to respond to the things spoken by Paul. And when she and her household had been baptized, she urged us, saying, "If you have judged me to be faithful to the Lord, come into my house and stay." And she prevailed upon us (Acts 16:12-15).

This illustrates how the Lord prepares people to receive the gospel. It also perfectly illustrates the previous discussion of the way in which messengers' needs were to be supplied (Matt. 10:9-10).

Those who hear and believe the gospel are sometimes the only support the messenger has, as far as food and shelter are concerned. When churches are founded their members are obligated to provide for the material needs of those who minister the Word to them. That obligation is not only a teaching of this passage, where it indicates a proper response to messengers of the gospel, but a teaching of the entire Bible. The Old Testament Law provided this for priests and Levites. The New Testament does the same for its apostles and evangelists (1 Cor. 9:7-14). How they support their ministers is a good index of a group's spiritual condition.

The precise place of preparation of the receptive hearer in the divine order of things, including the eternal counsels of God, is told in another of Luke's stories about Paul's missionary activity. The great apostle had just stopped preaching in Jewish synagogues because of their invincible unbelief, and he had turned to the Gentiles for a more receptive field of work (Acts 13:44-47). The results were that "when the Gentiles heard this, they began rejoicing and glorifying the word of the Lord; and as many as had been appointed to eternal life believed" (Acts 13:48).

Some Negative Effects (vv. 14-15)

A second look at the passage before us will emphasize that a believing response to God's message is a solemn duty; likewise, a hospitable reception of God's messenger's. Failure in either case has fearful, eternal consequences. Jesus said, "And whoever does not receive you, nor heed your words, as you go out of that house or that city, shake off the dust of your feet. Truly I say to you, it will be more tolerable for the land of Sodom and Gomorrah in the day of judgment, than for that city" (Matt. 10:14-15).

What should the evangelist do when both he and his message are overtly rejected by people in a given place? He has no choice but to join the messengers of Matthew 10:14-15 and God the sovereign Lord of the hearts of men in abandoning them, if only for a time. God gave up the ancient heathen world for many ages: "just as they did not see fit to acknowledge God any longer, God gave them over to a depraved mind" (Rom. 1:28; cf. 22-24, 26). But later God sent them the light of the knowledge of life and immortality, through the coming of Christ and the work of His missionaries. There must be times of giving men up to their own obdurate unbelief while the missionary, having once done his duty, officially (if not with some visible symbolic action) abjures himself of further present responsibility and moves on.

Luke's narrative of Paul's actions on his first missionary journey illustrates exactly what Jesus meant. Still at Antioch of Pisidia (in South Asia Minor, Acts 13:14) and no longer preaching to the Jews there but to the now believing Gentiles: "The Jews aroused the devout women of prominence [i.e., female proselytes of the ruling class] and the leading men of the city, and instigated a persecution against Paul and Barnabas, and drove them out of their district. But they shook off the dust of their feet in protest against them and went to Iconium" (Acts 13:50-51). That action is one of the exasperatingly insulting gestures oriental people use to this present day. Jesus approved of such things and that type of action is still valid today. There is no place for dialogue with the prophets of Baal and of the groves (1 Kings 18:19; cf. v. 40) and it was Jesus Himself who spoke out against the repeated and persistent rejection of all God's servants by Jerusalem (Matt. 23:37-39). So also did Stephen, even though he prayed that God would forgive the city (Acts 7:51-60), and Paul, in a measure, did likewise (1 Thess. 2:14-17).

Missionaries and preachers can be so politely civilized that no one pays any attention to them. They excite neither opposition nor approbation. One man's politeness may be another man's nausea and one man's crudeness may be another's lucidity. How would James fit into the present ambiance of civility? He called wicked women adulteresses, told rich men to weep and howl, and equated friendship with the world to enmity with God. How would Jeremiah fare? Or Jesus (Matt. 23), John Knox, or Martin Luther?

The text answers another question: What will God do? He will (even though it is an "age of grace") destroy them—sometimes in the here-and-now, certainly in the world to come (Matt. 10:28). The wreckage of old Jerusalem and the unmarked graves where the thousands of her dead lie slaughtered by the exasperated soldiers of the Roman general Titus, A.D. 70, bear witness to that. Paul foresaw that destroying wrath on Jerusalem only a short time before it fell (1 Thess. 2:16) and utter destruction by divine wrath in the age to come as well (1 Thess. 1:10).

These are solemn things to think about; terrifying to preach but unavoidable. They must be spoken. The Word of God, the gospel, is a two-edged sword (Rev.

1:16; 19:11-15), cutting two ways. It both saves and damns, depending on how men respond to it. Paul says of himself as apostle on the mission of world evangelism, "We are a fragrance of Christ to God among those who are being saved and among those who are perishing; to the one an aroma from death to death, to the other an aroma from life to life. And who is adequate for these things?" (2 Cor. 2:15-16).

4

The Apostolic Mission: Instruction for Today

(Matt. 10:16-23)

There are not, strictly speaking, parallels in the other gospels to Matthew 10:16-42, even though words similar to these reappear in Matthew's account of the Olivet Discourse and the parallels of it in Mark and Luke (cf. Matt. 24:9-10; Mark 13:9-13 and Luke 21:12-19).

The center section of Matthew 10:5-42 is clearly set off in thought (as will be seen) and in form from the first and third. Jesus' "truly I say" sentences in verses 15 and 23 assure that.

Jesus' statement that "it is the Spirit of your Father who speaks in you" (v. 20) suggests a time following the Pentecostal effusion of the Spirit. It must surely be interpreted in the light of John 14:16 in which Christ said, "I will ask the Father, and He will give you another Helper." Jesus also spoke of experiences that did not come to the missionary evangelists until some time after His ascension (vv. 17-18). As fully as was possible at the time, Jesus was enlightening His messengers as to how their mission would proceed when His physical absence from them became permanent.

Writers on this chapter remind variously of three considerations that render these words applicable in all ways (except for the local and specifically circumstantial) to all Christian times. First, Jesus specifically directed the twelve to pass on all His commandments to future generations of disciples as binding upon them (Matt. 28:20). Second, since this is prophetic, a special feature of much biblical prediction becomes applicable: biblical prediction usually lays greater emphasis on kinds of events than on specific occurrences. These "kinds" of events can recur many times. Third, in the Bible the past and present are often a figure for the future. The specific situation of the ancient believers is not unlike those of believers in all times. This is one reason why the Bible is in one way or another invariably applicable and helpful to believers today and in all times before us.

The Olivet Discourse (specifically Matt. 24:8-9; Mark 13:9-13; Luke 21:12-19) repeats a good bit of this section (Matt. 10:19-22). This is with good reason, for in that great prophecy Jesus specifically dealt with the future as consummated in two great future crises. The first was the agonies of Judea leading up to the destruction of Jerusalem by the Romans in A.D. 70. The second will be the second advent of the Lord at the consummation of the present age. These same two crises form the background for the eight verses that will now be examined.

THE SENDER ON EVERY MISSION OF EVANGELISM (v. 16)

The personal pronoun does not appear as the subject of a Greek verb except when emphasis on the subject is intended and such is the case here. The sense is "Behold, I, Myself, send you forth."

This is both an assurance of their ultimate safety and dignity as well as of their responsibility as delegates of the Son of Man. Their authority is involved, too.

The person of the sender makes all the difference in the world as to assurance of the missionary. Though the world abounds with fiery trials, none is more fierce than the fires of Nebuchadnezzar's furnace. As the three Hebrew men said to that pagan king, missionaries can say, "Our God whom we serve is able to deliver us . . . and He will deliver us" (Dan. 3:17), if not from death, then through it. That Person who sends also lends dignity and responsibility to the messengers. They dare not betray their mission: "Everywhere I send you, you shall go" (Jer. 1:7). Jesus, in essence, repeated what was said to Jeremiah: "Do not be dismayed before them, lest I dismay you before them" (Jer. 1:17). This is why Jeremiah never backed down before a whole succession of apostate kings, an assortment of impudent false prophets, blustering but weak-kneed citizens, and several pugnacious prominent people.

Likewise, the authority of the sent one comes entirely from the authority of the sender. It is this note of authority in the Christian religion that has caused it to prevail wherever the Christian message has been truly preached. If the authority of the messenger becomes too prominent, men will ignore him; but if the authority of the ascended Christ is proclaimed, men must take note and decide, for or against Him. How quickly Peter found that out! His very first Christian sermon ended on this note: "Therefore let all the house of Israel know for certain that God has made Him both Lord and Christ" (Acts 2:36, see also vv. 37-41). It was followed by 3,000 positive decisions.

THE NECESSARY MENTAL AND SPIRITUAL QUALITIES OF THE MESSENGERS (v. 16b)

The Bible abounds with symbolism involving animals. Paul called certain false teachers dogs and some particularly fierce opponents wild beasts, while Peter thought of hypocrites in the church as vomiting dogs and wallowing sows! Messiah, in Psalm 22, referred to His tormentors at least six times in such a way. In a manner quite exceptional, Jesus drew from popular lore to compare enemies of the gospel to fierce wolves, and messengers of the kingdom of God with snakes and doves: "In the midst of wolves . . . be shrewd as serpents, and innocent as doves" (Matt. 10:16).

Wolves are certainly fierce, but there is no reason at all for supposing snakes to be particularly intelligent. However, in both ancient popular lore and the Bible, the serpent had cunning imputed to him. Perhaps it was its ability to elude pursuit by hiding under stones and plants that gave the snake that reputation, or its use of its physical disadvantages to stalk small prey. At any rate, ancient literature, both pagan and Jewish, has many references to the fabulous cunning of snakes. The word in recent usage for this sort of wisdom is "strategy." Paul used such cunning when, by raising the question of the resurrection, he diverted the enmity of the Pharisees and Sadducees away from himself and toward one another (Acts 23:6-10). He used it again when he appealed to the poets of classical Greece in his Athenian address (Acts 17:28-29) and when he cited Roman law to his Roman jailors (Acts 16:37; 22:23-25).

The behavior of the dove, especially its gentle cooing sounds, suggests harmless, gentle behavior and guileless purposes. Sometimes violent tyrants see danger to their reign in the quiet prayers and propaganda of innocent, religious people, but usually they do not until too late. This is the story of victory in Christian missions.

An older author, famous both for learning and piety, has written of these two qualities:

> In view of the dangerous circumstances in which they would be placed, Jesus asks of them to combine (a combination to be realized under the direction of the Holy Spirit, as in verse 19) prudence (in the recognition of danger, in the choice of means for counteracting it, in regard to their demeanor in the midst of it . . .) with uprightness, which shuns every impropriety into which one might be betrayed in the presence of the dangers referred to, and therefore refrains from thinking, choosing, or doing anything of a questionable nature in connection with them. The loftiest example of this combination is Jesus Himself; while among the apostles, so far as we know them, the one who ranks highest in this respect is Paul.[1]

It is eminently important to note, however, that the "dove" quality can be exaggerated to being silly (Hos. 7:11). Sometimes Christians must stand up and be counted. Also the serpent-like wisdom can be carried to the point of wicked deceit or destructive subversion of others. In some cases there is danger of the serpent swallowing the dove! (2 Cor. 11:3).

The wolves who will attack the messengers (Matt. 10:16) are identified in verse 17: "beware of men." In Reformation times it was still customary for cultivated Christian controversialists to refer to their adversaries as if they were wild animals. Luther and Calvin published such harsh language, referring to their opponents as asses, dogs, and snakes. Perhaps the two men may be regarded as simply more honest than present public usage allows. At any rate, Psalm 22 characterizes Messiah's enemies as gaping bulls of Bashan, ravening and roaring lions, dogs, and wild oxen. Paul, who certainly was a civilized man, referred to the threatening mob at Ephesus as wild beasts (1 Cor. 15:32; see also 2 Pet. 2:22 and the beast of Revelation). Jesus once compared Gentiles to dogs (Matt. 15:22-27)

1. H. A. W. Meyer, *Critical and Exegetical Commentary on the New Testament*, 1:212.

and false prophets to wolves in sheep's clothing (Matt. 7:15), and Paul compared false teachers to savage wolves (Acts 20:29).

Paul has just been cited as the one who ranks high with respect to the qualities attributed to serpents and doves. It seems likely that he was fully aware of the saying of Jesus in verses 16-17, for once he seemed to allude to it. In the closing paragraphs of the epistle to the Romans, Paul admonished the believers to shun the turbulent people of their assemblies and to eschew any turbulence in their own behavior (Rom. 16:17-18). Then after commenting on their obedience, said to be widely known, he added the sentence that seems clearly to show his acquaintance with Jesus' saying: "I want you to be wise in what is good, and innocent in what is evil" (Rom. 16:19). Thus these mental and spiritual qualities commanded by Jesus for the believers of the apostolic age were exemplified by Paul and others of that age and are held up for our emulation.

THE CHIEF PHYSICAL ENEMIES OF THE MESSENGERS (VV. 17-18)

"Beware of men . . ."—men in general but particularly the Jews in their many local councils of judgment (sanhedrins) and local religious centers (synagogues). Like their Lord, they were to be persecuted by governors and kings such as Pilate and Herod. From the second chapter of Acts onward, the history of the movement revolves about stories of such dangers and conflicts. The arrest of Peter and John, the later imprisonment of Peter, the martyrdoms of Stephen and James, the harassment of Paul in Iconium, Philippi, Thessalonica, Corinth, Ephesus, Jerusalem, Caesarea, and Rome—sometimes by fanatical Jewish mobs, occasionally by furious heathen, and finally in the hands of Imperial Rome—and the persecutions of thousands whose names are unknown today continued without permanent abatement throughout the first three centuries. Persecution has been revived in various forms from time to time up to the present. The twentieth century has its share of martyred missionaries and converts. It was no different with the Old Testament prophets. Stephen, seconding the several passionate outbursts of Jesus on this subject (see Matt. 23:34-35), accurately charged the Jews on the occasion of his martyrdom: "You men who are stiffnecked and uncircumcized in heart and ears are always resisting the Holy Spirit; you are doing just as your fathers did. Which one of the prophets did your fathers not persecute? And they killed those who had previously announced the coming of the Righteous One" (Acts 7:51-52). A new *Fox's Book of Martyrs* could be written about the witness of the many generations of missionary martyrs throughout the Christian centuries. The blood of martyrs will evidently always be the seed of the church.

THE CHIEF RESOURCES OF THE MESSENGERS UNDER ATTACK (VV. 19-20)

The resources of the disciple under unfair, undeserved attack by men cannot be primarily other men, for he has already been told to "beware of men" (v. 17), even though men need not be afraid (vv. 26-31). The resources must be spiritual. Being born of the Spirit of God and indwelt by Him, He may be relied on to bring to our minds in that hour the particular words appropriate to the situation. The man so led truly combines "spiritual thoughts with spiritual words" (1 Cor. 2:13). In the case of a disciple well-trained in orthodox Judaism, such as Stephen, those words were a recital from biblical history, applying it all to the present crisis (Acts 6-7). In the case of those unschooled Galileans, Peter and John, it was a simple confession: "We cannot stop speaking what we have seen and heard" (Acts 4:20). Paul on one occasion cited ancient Greek poets to his unfriendly inquirers and Roman law to his jailor. The disciples, by the Spirit, sometimes spoke boldly (Eph. 6:19), sometimes deeply (1 Cor. 2:10), sometimes sharply (Titus 1:13) or otherwise, but always with wisdom Jesus, on one occasion, said: "So make up your minds not to prepare beforehand to defend yourselves; for I will give you utterance and wisdom which none of your opponents will be able to resist or refute" (Luke 21:14-15).

When brought before their judges (and, in extreme cases, before their executioners), the speeches of many of the great saints of the past stand as examples of what Jesus predicted. Luther's terse sentences at the Diet of Worms (1521) are well known. They came at the end of a two-hour reply to charges. "Will you or will you not retract"? asked the chancellor of Treves, indignantly. To this Luther replied:

> If then, Your Majesty and rulers ask for a simple answer, I will give it without horns and without teeth, as follows: Unless I am shown by the testimony of Scripture and by evident reasoning (for I do not put faith in pope or councils alone, because it is established that they have often erred and contradicted themselves), unless I am overcome by means of the scriptural passages that I have cited, and unless my conscience is taken captive by the words of God, I am neither able nor willing to revoke anything, since to act against one's conscience is neither safe nor honest. God help me, amen![2]

Savonarola was a reformer, preacher, and martyr of Florence, Italy. "He was sentenced to be hanged and burned. He was thus executed with and between two of his friends, May 23, 1498. At the foot of the scaffold he had administered the eucharist to himself and to his two friends. 'My Lord was pleased to die for my sins; why should not I be glad to give up my poor life out of love to Him?' With such words he . . . yielded to the gibbet and the flames." The Dominicans tried unsuccessfully later to canonize him. Luther remarked that God had already done so![3]

John Hus has been called "the Morning Star of the Reformation." After months of imprisonment and torture, all in violation of fair promises of just judgment and safe return from Constance to Prague, Hus wrote to his friends in Prague: " 'I write this . . . in prison and in chains, expecting to-morrow [sic] to receive

2. Martin Luther, as cited in Robert Herndon Fife, *The Revolt of Martin Luther,* p. 666.
3. *McClintock and Strong's Encyclopedia of Biblical, Theological and Ecclesiastical Literature,* s.v. "Savonarola."

sentence of death, full of hope in God that I shall not swerve from the truth, nor abjure errors imputed to me by false witness.' After he had been tied to the stake and the faggots had been piled, he was once more urged to recant. His reply was, 'God is my witness that I have never taught or preached that which false witnesses have testified against me. He knows that the great object of all my preaching and writing was to convert men from sin. In the truth of that gospel which hitherto I have written, taught and preached, I now joyfully die.' The fire was then kindled, and his voice as it audibly prayed in the words of the *Kyrie Eleison* was soon stifled in the smoke."[4]

As long as human languages are spoken those noble testaments will encourage and inspire mankind. It should be added that the Spirit supplies both *what* to say and *how* to say it. The human qualities of sarcasm, pathos, meekness, boldness; the whole range of emotion, tone, and apparent intent are everything in contests of words and when most forceful, either for good or evil, must come from the heart. Here also the Holy Spirit must be the beleagured evangelist's teacher.

THE CHIEF SOURCE OF PERSONAL ATTACK ON THE MESSENGERS (VV. 21-22)

They are indeed "men" (verse 17), especially kinsmen and the close social group. True, "we wrestle not against flesh and blood, but against principalities . . . against spiritual wickedness" (Eph. 6:12, KJV), but the attacks invariably come through men. God is in charge of nature. Demon-mongers and demon spirits have no real power over nature. That form of alleged Christian warfare that plays on man's primitive fear of strange occult powers and "things that go bump in the night" is unworthy of the name. Much rubbish has poured out of the popular religious press on the subject.

So *men* are the enemies of the messengers, taking out on Christ's disciples their rejection and hate of Christ and the humiliating news of salvation by a crucified carpenter. "And you will be hated by all on account of My name" (Matt. 10:22). Where the messenger arouses no hate he must be thought of as being false, in some aspect at least, in his message. This idea is amplified later (see vv. 24-39).

Strangely, the same human relationships that provided the Lord with His messengers also furnished His severest opposition. Ancient households were usually extended families, including three or more generations and extended "in-law" relatives. Earlier it was seen that several sets of brothers and cousins furnished the Lord with most of the twelve apostles. These relations also furnished His fierce enemies as well. Christianity, capturing the heart of only one of a social group, inevitably breaks the solidarity of it, for common religious conviction is necessarily at the heart of every thoroughly sound, full social group such as the family. The others resent the irruption of individuality and will suspect traitorous thinking at least, and disloyalty at worst.

It will be easier to understand and accept this unhappy result of a true commit-

4. *Encyclopedia Britannica*, s.v. "John Huss."

ment to Christian faith as not unusual by examining the way in which the families and neighbors of two famous Old Testament prophets responded to their ministry. Since the passages are not familiar, they will be reviewed and presented in their entirety.

The first is the case of Jeremiah. He hailed from the priestly town of Anathoth, an hour and a half's walk northeast of Jerusalem (Jer. 1:1). He entered upon his prophetic ministry there when still very young (1:4-6) and quickly transferred his residence and ministry to Jerusalem (2:1-2). In that place *men* threatened his life many times, but chiefly they of his own village and family. The threat took the form of a plot on his life and it would have succeeded except for divine intervention. Now for a look at the passage where the prophet speaks for himself:

> Moreover, the LORD made it known to me and I knew it;
> Then Thou didst show me their deeds.
> But I was like a gentle lamb led to the slaughter;
> And I did not know that they had devised plots against me, saying,
> "Let us destroy the tree with its fruit,
> And let us cut him off from the land of the living,
> That his name be remembered no more."
> But, O LORD of hosts, who judges righteously,
> Who tries the feelings and the heart,
> Let me see Thy vengeance on them,
> For to Thee have I committed my cause.

Therefore thus says the LORD concerning the men of Anathoth, who seek your life, saying, "Do not prophesy in the name of the LORD, that you might not die at our hand" (Jer. 11:18-21).

The second case is that of Ezekiel. His own apostate people were in foreign captivity where they formed a community and where the prophet ministered to them. Their enmity took the form of tolerant, rejecting amusement, not so dangerous as violent intentions but just as harmful to the mission of the prophet. God speaks to Ezekiel of these persons:

> "But as for you, son of man, your fellow-citizens who talk about you by the walls and in the doorways of the houses, speak to one another, each to his brother, saying, 'Come now, and hear what the message is which comes forth from the LORD.' And they come to you as people come, and sit before you as My people, and hear your words, but they do not do them, for they do the lustful desires expressed by their mouth, and their heart goes after their gain." (Ezek. 33:30-31)

These people were really using their minister for entertainment. They had not "turned him off," as the saying goes; they had never given him a truly listening heart. Thus God went on to say: "And behold, you are to them like a sensual song by one who has a beautiful voice and plays well on an instrument; for they hear your words, but they do not practice them" (v. 32). But the prophet will be vindicated at last: "The one who has endured to the end . . . will be saved" (Matt.

10:22), for God comforted him, saying, "So when it comes to pass [i.e. Ezekiel's predictions of Jerusalem's destruction]—as surely it will—then they will know that a prophet has been in their midst" (Ezek. 33:33).

So those on the mission of world evangelism have experienced throughout the centuries the fact that the severest personal attacks have come from the messengers' own community, including their families. Sometimes it has taken the form of social ostracism upon becoming a believer. Family solidarity, especially that of the extended family—household, kinsmen, tribe, nation—consistently builds a wall against conversion to Christ. This is true in primitive cultures, but is even more evident where one of the more highly civilized religions—such as Islam, Buddhism, and Hinduism—prevails. Even the solidarity of the messenger's own Christian family has often been an obstacle to service for Christ in faraway and primitive places, especially in former times when travel was slow, dangerous, and expensive; communication was difficult; and living conditions were both harsh and perilous. Parents were (and still are!) loath to give up their children.

On the other hand, family and kinship of any sort can be a great help to the missionary. In this connection, Paul found comfort and aid in his family connections. True, the Jews persecuted him and as a nation gave him cause for anguish, as is seen in the central chapters of his epistle to the Romans (9:1-15; 10:1-3). Yet many of the greetings in the last chapter of Romans include warm words to or from six of Paul's "kinsmen." Two of them, like him, had spent time in prison for Jesus' sake. They had been believers before Paul was and were known among the apostles (16:7, cf. 11). He seems to say that at the time of writing Romans, three of them, Lucius, Jason, and Sosipater, were traveling with him as fellow missionaries (16:21).

PROPER RESPONSE TO REJECTION AND PERSECUTION (V. 23)

"But whenever they persecute you in this city, flee to the next; for truly I say to you, you shall not finish going through the cities of Israel, until the Son of Man comes" (v. 23). The first part of that verse is good advice to missionaries when push comes to shove. Paul employed it many times, beginning with the first of his journeys reported in Acts. When circumstances became too hot in Antioch (Pisidia) he moved on to Iconium. When his life was threatened there, he and Barnabas moved on to Lystra. At Lystra he was stoned by Jews from Antioch and Iconium, but survived to move on to Derbe. Afterward he preached again in all those places (Acts 13:14—14:21). Later the same sort of thing took place successively in the missions to Philippi, Thessalonica, Berea, Athens, and Corinth (Acts 16:12—18:18); still later at Ephesus (Acts 19). So the saying of Jesus was not only good counsel, it was prophetic of the future. Farmers do not plow in thunderstorms. They take shelter and do something else until the storm passes.

The latter part of the verse constitutes one of the greatest problems of gospel interpretation for all who accept Matthew's gospel as having any historical order of reporting. Of course if one's faith allows this to be a fragment of one of Jesus' last discourses placed here to teach some tendentious point of theology (redaction criticism), then there is no problem. But most will want to know what Jesus meant by "you shall not finish going through the cities of Israel, until the Son of Man comes." There are several views of the matter. Some have thought He meant that He would catch up with them before the twelve heralds of His approach had finished their immediate mission to northern Israel (Galilee, see Matt. 10:5-6). But the words seem too weighty to bear such slight freight. Besides, there are substantial reasons for applying the section to missionary evangelism in the apostolic age following Jesus' ascension.

Jesus' puzzling statement may be regarded as the very first prophecy to the apostles that His coming as prophet, healer, and crucified redeemer was to be followed by another coming in power and unveiled glory. He had hinted at such a thing in the Sermon on the Mount (Matt. 7:21-23). The very language of Jesus' sentence seems to be shaped by Daniel 7:13-14, which speaks of a glorious visible coming.

There have been interpreters who held that at this point Jesus was pointing to a period in the coming Great Tribulation after the rapture of the church when a Jewish remnant shall do the very things described here. "It is important to note that this mission is looked upon as continuous, right on 'till the Son of man be come' (verse 24). No doubt it was interrupted at the Cross, and from then until the church period is over, it will continue to be so. But when the Church is rapt to the glory, Messiah's messengers will again go forth with the Kingdom Gospel [said to differ from the gospel of grace today], and Messiah Himself will appear to establish His kingdom in power."[5] This view has current supporters, though it has been modified somewhat to allow a meaningful application of verses 16-23 to the present.[6]

There is some basis for thinking of this reference to the coming of the Son of Man as that providential coming that took place with the coming of the Roman armies to destroy Israel's capital city, Jerusalem, in A.D. 70. The coming at the end of the age and the events of A.D. 70 are brought together in a very remarkable way in Matthew 24, the first part of the Olivet Discourse. The same is true in Mark's report (chapt. 13). Though Luke 21 may provide basis for separating some of Jesus' remarks about the coming destruction of Jerusalem from the advent at the end of this age, it still remains true that Matthew and Mark do not. Furthermore, there are other passages in the gospels that specifically refer to the providential destruction of Jerusalem as a "coming" of Christ or of God. For example, in one of His last parables, Jesus spoke of how the "husbandmen" (Jewish leaders) of the vineyard (Israel) slew the son (Jesus) of a certain man (God) who had planted the vineyard and hired the husbandmen. "He shall come and destroy these husbandmen" (Luke 20:16, KJV; see vv. 9-19). It was specifically spoken against the Jewish leaders (Luke 20:19), as they, themselves, perceived. In Matthew's account the story ends: "Therefore . . . the kingdom of God will be taken away from you, and be given to a nation producing the fruit of it"

5. L. Laurenson, *Messiah the Prince, An Outline of Matthew's Gospel*, pp. 48-49.
6. C. I. Scofield et al, eds., *The New Scofield Reference Bible*, p. 1008.

(Matt. 21:43); in the next verse Jesus goes on to speak of breaking and scattering (v. 44).

This parable, given on the last day of Christ's public ministry, was immediately followed by another in which the climax comes when Caesar's armies are identified (in divine providence) with God's armies, as follows: "But the king [God] was enraged and sent his armies, and destroyed those murderers, and set their city on fire" (Matt. 22:7, see vv. 1-8).

So there is impressive evidence to assert that the destruction of Jerusalem in A.D. 70 was, in providence, a second advent of Christ, perhaps even a type of the eschatological second advent. It is on this basis, in large part, that many reliable commentators take the view held here that Jesus was in a cryptic way indicating that the distinctly Jewish period of world evangelism would be over within the lifetime of the apostles. This matter is important enough, seeing that many remain puzzled about it, to cite from the probably most widely read and thoroughly competent English-language commentator:

> In order to understand these words it is necessary to enter into the nature of our Lord's prophecies respecting the coming, as having an *immediate literal* and a *distant foreshadowed* fulfillment. Throughout the discourse and the great prophecy of ch. xxiv, we find the first apostolic period used as a type of the whole ages of the Church; and the vengeance on Jerusalem, which historically put an end to the old dispensation, and was in its place with reference to that order of things, the coming of the Son of Man, as a type of the final coming of the Lord. These two subjects accompany and interpenetrate one another in a manner wholly inexplicable to those who are unaccustomed to the wide import of Scripture prophecy, which speaks very generally not so much of *events themselves, points of time,*—as of *processions* of events, all ranging under one great description. Thus in the present case there is certainly direct reference to the destruction of Jerusalem.[7]

These remarks of Henry Alford so long ago have been widely quoted. Alford was, incidentally, an Anglican and a foremost premillenarian.

There is another kind of coming of the Son of Man before the missionaries have finished their task of world evangelism. Again and again He specially comes spiritually in the crises of Christian life. This is one of the nuances of the words of Jesus about the sending of the Spirit. Of that Pentecostal event Jesus once said: "And I will ask the Father, and He will give you another Helper . . . He abides with you, and will be in you. I will not leave you as orphans; I will come to you" (John 14:16-18). In that Holy Spirit the Lord came and "stood by" Paul when he was imprisoned in the tower at Jerusalem (Acts 23:11); likewise in the heavenly messenger who "stood before me" as Paul reported to the storm-tossed passengers on their prison ship (Acts 27:23).

Jesus comes again and again to stand by His own in the crises of life while they journey through this world between spiritual death, new birth, and eternal life.

---

7. Henry Alford, *The New Testament for English Readers,* p. 71.

5

The Age-long Mission: The Disciples' Relation to Christ

(Matt. 10:24-33)

A saying of Jesus was passed over lightly in the previous section, but will now be considered: "But it is the one who has endured to the end who will be saved" (v. 22b). It reminds the missionary evangelist that he must guard his own heart and not become so deeply involved with personal interests that he forgets the day of final accounting to God. It is only the good and faithful servants who enter into the joy of their Lord. Supposing the salvation of these servants as persons but failure as servants, it is only what is done for eternity that survives until then. Even Paul, in discussing self-discipline under the figure of athletic competition, states: "I buffet my body and make it my slave, lest possibly, after I have preached to others, I myself should be disqualified" (1 Cor. 9:27).

Jesus' warning about the necessity for endurance also imparts a certain reserve of judgment about recruits for the task. True soldiers are known only when the healthy survivors of the battle count the bodies and the wounded left on the field. Battle casualties are heavy. Loss from desertion can be even heavier at times. Paul did not hesitate to insist on leaving John Mark behind until he should grow up into constancy (he was one who quit under fire) and at the very end of his life, he wrote with great pathos of one Demas, another disappointment in the moment of truth: "Demas, having loved this present world, has deserted me" [presumably at the time of Paul's Roman trial] (2 Tim. 4:10).

To resume the text (Matt. 10:24-33), from verse 24 onward Jesus spoke of the missionary task in the period following the specifically Jewish part of the mission, after every vestige of Judaism, as such, had fallen away. The change was fast taking place when Matthew wrote his gospel. Less than a decade before the fall of Jerusalem, Paul—the leading missionary apostle, the one who opened the Gentile world to the gospel and who spoke most forcefully of God's intention from the very beginning of Hebrew history as being to save Gentiles through Jews (Rom. 15)—was still consorting with Jews, eating kosher food, taking Jewish vows, observing the outward signs, and, on his last known pilgrimage to Jerusalem, he entered the temple precincts intending to offer sacrifice. (See Acts 21, esp. verses 23-27.) After Matthew 10:23 Jesus spoke of a time when such a situation would no longer prevail. Gentile missionaries would be taking the gospel to the Gentile world. All of the chapter contains primary information of timeless application. The first disciples were instructed to pass that information down to later generations, of course (Matt. 28:19-20). But henceforth in the passage, though the Jewishness of Jesus and His immediate auditors is plain enough in the language employed, there is nothing particularly Jewish in the message itself.

Jesus first addressed His remarks to four essentially practical matters of concern to coming generations of disciples on their great mission: Conflicts (vv. 24-25), Duties (vv. 26-27), Encouragements (vv. 28-31), and Warnings (vv. 32-33).

CONFLICTS IN THE MISSION (VV. 24-25)

Note the shift from *apostles* to *disciples,* referring to times after all the apostles had long been dead. True, there is some New Testament precedent for calling messengers of churches *apostles (apostoloi),* but they were apparently such in a sort of "church business" or ecclesiastical sense, not in any capacity as evangelists.[1] The Lord here supplied a way to explain the conflicts in which the disciples were sure to become involved. It is based upon a threefold relationship of the believers to the Savior.

In the first place, they are His disciples; He is their teacher. The disciple *(mathētēs)* is a learner. But the *mathētēs,* in the primary sense, is not the sort of learner who pays for a course down at the university, goes to the bookstore to buy text and workbook, and then attends lectures often enough to pass the examinations. Nor is he even so impersonal a learner as the one who joins a congregation and absorbs the folkways and doctrines of the group. He is, rather, one who undertakes the very personal relation of apprentice to the master of a craft or profession. He is one whose declared intention is to become the craftsman or professional that the master now is. This is the first meaning of *mathētēs,* disciple, and that is how Jesus employed it here. In this relation Jesus was their *didaskalos,* teacher. But it was not "teacher" in a broad sense but in the narrow one of master, i.e., the master of the craft who both tells and shows his disciples. Every *mathētēs* studies together with every other *mathētēs;* they recite together, share the same quarters and dining facilities, and work together. The arrangement builds on a sort of elitist principle: the learning process is not (at least in this case) as it is nowadays often considered, a democratic process. "One is your Teacher" (Matt. 23:8). The master is authority, source, and guide; not merely leader.

In the second place, they are Jesus' servants. The Greek word reflects the Hebrew bond-servant idea of Exodus 21:1-11 where, though obedience is paramount, it must be willing, committed obedience, freely given. A Hebrew did not have to become another Hebrew's bond-servant, but once the commitment was made it would be sin to refuse obedience. This is every believer's commitment to

---

1. Robert Duncan Culver, "Apostles and the Apostolate in the New Testament," *Bibliotheca Sacra,* 134 (April-June 1977):131-43.

Christ. He, on the other hand, is *kurios* (Lord). The Latin equivalent, *dominus,* includes, in the English language, dominion, domination, condominium. The central idea is control by virtue of ownership. When a man owns and controls some acres they are his *domin*ion. When two or more kings own and control a geographical area or when two or more parties own or control a house, it is rightly called a con*domin*ium. So Christians are the Lord's dominion; He is their *dominus,* Lord.

In the third place, Jesus spoke of Himself as "head of the house" (Matt. 10:25), *oikodespotēs,* literally "house-despot." The believers are "of this household" (v. 25). Christ gave the churches a continuing observance that is supposed to illustrate that for them—the Lord's Supper. Now, when one goes to a supper as a guest, or eats in his parents' home, it is the proper power of the host or other head of the house or his deputy to tell people where to sit and to choose the menu and the courses. So on that last fateful evening Jesus, the *oikodespotēs,* took charge. There were not simply thirteen men milling about a buffet. Jesus was the master of the house, "reclining at the table with the twelve disciples" (Matt. 26:20). Later it was He who directed the conversation and it was to Him that questions were addressed. He blessed the bread and broke it; He took "a cup and [gave] thanks, and gave it to them," directing them, "Drink from it, all of you" (see Matt. 26:26-27). Later it was the Lord who declared that their time in the upper room was over, saying, "Arise, let us go from here" (John 14:31).

The inescapable conclusions to be drawn minister powerfully to any faithful Christian witness. Jesus is our Master and Lord; believers are His apprentices and willing bond-servants; He is Master of the household; believers are the willing members of it. The Teacher is not taught nor is the Lord advised. Trials and persecutions will surely be "because of the word of God and the testimony of Jesus" (Rev. 1:9).

Jesus did not say that apprentices and bond-servants are more likely to be given verbal abuse by angry opponents than are teachers and masters, but He observed this: if the dignity of the teacher, master, or head of the house is no protection from slander by angry neighbors, then the lesser members will not be spared such abuse. Beelzebub was the "fly god" of ancient Ekron (2 Kings 1:1-8). The preferred text of Matthew 10:25 is Beelzebul (rather than the King James Beelzebub), which means "dung god"—a derisive change of the ancient name and a depreciating name for the devil. A bit later in the record it is seen (Matt. 12:22-37) that Jesus' own countrymen did indeed accuse Him of serving Beelzebul. It was, He responded, an unpardonable sin to slander the work of God as the work of Satan. "Woe to those who call evil good, and good evil" (Isa. 5:20; cf. 4:18-23). Paul once said, "Do not let what is for you a good thing be spoken of as evil" (Rom. 14:16), but sometimes it cannot be prevented.

Perhaps of all the unpleasant aspects of religious controversy there is nothing more utterly heartbreaking than to have one's good motives, good intentions, good works, or good deeds deliberately misinterpreted by perverse minds with unnecessary hurt to the faithful disciple. The statement of the Master of the house, "Father, forgive them; for they do not know what they are doing" (Luke

23:34), has been matched many times by the house member's cry, "Lord, do not hold this sin against them" (Acts 7:60), Stephen's way of saying what his Lord said. Peter later devoted his longest epistle mainly to discussion of this anguishing feature of the mission of world evangelism through the ages (see esp. 1 Pet. 4:13-19).

DUTIES ON THE MISSION (VV. 26-27)

It is a mistake to think that "therefore do not fear them" (v. 26) was intended by Jesus as a comfort. It is nothing of the sort. He is reminding believers, quite to the contrary, that it is their duty to speak out (due allowance being made for discretion in language and prudent choice of occasion) in spite of what men threaten. It is the same in sense as the Lord's words to Jeremiah: "Now gird up your loins, and arise, and speak to them all which I command you. Do not be dismayed before them, lest I dismay you before them" (Jer. 1:17). Christians are not to be surprised by opposition, but it is their duty to accept it and to get on with the work. Nothing else can explain the "confidence" of Peter and John (Acts 4:13) or such calm assertions as the one Peter himself later made: "Beloved, do not be surprised at the fiery ordeal among you, which comes upon you for your testing, as though some strange thing were happening to you. . . . If you are reviled for the name of Christ, you are blessed" (1 Pet. 4:12, 14).

It is an even more serious error to suppose (as unfortunately certain casual students do) that Jesus' references here to "covered" things is to sins and the "revealing" to the Judgment Day. On the contrary, the reference is explained specifically as having to do with the disciples' duty: "What I tell you in the darkness, speak in the light; and what you hear whispered in your ear, proclaim upon the housetops" (v. 27). The gospels tell of many occasions—even a period of several months—when Jesus drew his twelve apostles and others aside for private instruction. One of these was His explanation of the parable of the soils. It was precisely on that occasion that the duty of bold proclamation of the gospel to all men was laid upon them: "And He was saying to them, 'A lamp is not brought to be put under a peck-measure, is it, or under a bed? Is it not brought to be put on the lampstand? For nothing is hidden, except to be revealed; nor has anything been secret, but that it should come to light" (Mark 4:21-22). (See also Luke 8:16-18; 12:2-12; cf. vv. 35-40.) Then He spoke of how necessary it is that the disciple tell abroad what he knows. If he does not do so, the disciple will learn no more and lose what he already has. Salt, said Jesus, if it loses its savor, is fit no longer as a seasoning, but must be thrown out where men will walk on it. Thus moribund Christianity brings self-destruction upon itself. Thus Muslim northern Africa, once almost wholly Christian, is populated by the Muslim descendants of those moribund Christians. They are among the most resistant to evangelism of any people on earth today.

"Proclaim upon the housetops" (v. 27) is another ancient Jewish (or Mediterranean) feature of the chapter. In warm weather, life moves to the flat roofs of the houses. In towns and villages the houses are close together, the streets and alleys narrow. Houses built on hillsides thus exposed many of the scenes of family life to those on higher levels (see 2 Sam. 11:2 and 16:20-22; also Matt. 24:17). So, at the right time of day, an announcement loudly made from a housetop would soon be known to almost all of the village.

Everything in these two verses means this: take all I have told you—sermons, discourses, parables, explanations of parables, prayers, all private instruction— and regard it as designed for public knowledge. My kingdom is no mystery religion to be disclosed to initiates only. Digest it, summarize it, expound it, shout it, whisper it, use letters, pamphlets, books, newspapers, radio, telephone, phonograph records, television, and whatever is available. Give it the widest possible distribution. It is an interesting fact that many of the very finest technical advances in the arts and techniques of communication over the Christian centuries have been made by Christians interested in obeying this command of their Savior. For example, in ancient times Christians invented or at least first promoted bound books instead of scrolls, (some 30 or 40 feet long), so quick reference could be made to Scripture passages. The Hebrew Bible was on 22 scrolls. A codex (bound book) could all be under one cover, and any passage found in moments. Linguistics, the science of language, its translation, analysis, teaching, and learning, has been at various times almost the exclusive property of missionary scientists—from Ulfilas to Kenneth Pike. There is some need for alarm, however. Although proclamation in the name of Christ is today being made in unprecedented volume, two grievous flaws in the process have also developed. First, there is pressure to dilute the message. Elsewhere in this book, reference is made to the importance of pure, healthy seed. Paul spoke of a coming time when men's ears would itch for smooth-sounding words of supposed social or ethical improvement or other benefit and would no longer endure sound doctrine. Preachers are increasingly finding that they are either popular or dead! Much against their wishes many feel pressed into running a popularity contest. Lawlessness in the churches abounds while love waxes cold.

Jesus specifically admonished men to beware of the imminence of a second evil: the evil of hearing the sound of the message but not accepting its truth for one's self. "Therefore take care how you listen" (Luke 8:18); "He who has an ear, let him hear what the Spirit says to the churches" (Rev. 2:7, 11, 17; 3:6, 13, 22). Sadly, the gospel is "an aroma from death to death" at least as often as "an aroma from life to life" (2 Cor. 2:16).

ENCOURAGEMENT IN THE MISSION (vv. 28-31)

It is central to all ethical religion that men's souls "survive" the demise of the men at physical death. Even Emmanuel Kant found that necessary to a successful "Critique of Practical Reason." Jesus here clearly voices that doctrine. The resurrection doctrine is no competitor but a supplement to it. Paul's clear words (Acts 23:6-8; 26:5-8) say as much and he indicates that this had always been Israel's hope. How else can Hebrews 11:13, and 16 be interpreted, for the passage affirms that the ancient patriarchs, from Abel to Abraham (and Sarah), "died in faith . . . having confessed that they were strangers and exiles on the earth," desiring "a better country, that is a heavenly one. . . . [knowing] God . . . has prepared a city for them?"

For some years modern scholarship rejected the view that the older portions of the Bible taught of a resurrection. But recently a truly epoch-making work on the Psalms has about transformed all discussion of the doctrine of immortality and future life in the Old Testament. With evidences about Hebrew lexicography and poetry drawn from the Ras Shamra (Ugaritic) literature, Mitchell Dahood has shown that the Psalms teach a definite doctrine of the future life of believers with God—as older generations of exegetes and theologians have asserted.[2] This is true if only part of Dahood's data and arguments survive the fierce attack now in process. Gone are the days when any informed person could say the older portions of the Hebrew Bible have no doctrine of the future life. The author of Hebrews 11, who said the hope of the saints of old was always heavenly and that they sought a better country than any on earth, always knew better anyway—a much better guide to doctrine than any recent "biblical" theologian. No amount of so-called Old Testament theology can set aside (if it is faithful and believing) such statements as these in favor of a denial of this blessed hope to true believing saints in all ages.

Jesus meant for men to believe that men who kill the body only, threatening though they be, will not be allowed to divert the missionary of Christ. God has provided an answer. To die means to depart to be with Christ, later on to participate in a "better resurrection" (Heb. 11:35).

As near as can be determined, no one before fairly recent times interpreted Jesus' words about "Him who is able to destroy both soul and body in hell" (Matt. 10:28) as referring to Satan. Dr. Ewald Rudolf Stier[3] an excellent, highly regarded writer, gave the "Satan" view much currency. Though his view was generally rejected by leading English writers of the time, it is occasionally supported today. The plain sense has been modified as if Jesus meant, "Do not fear men, but fear evil and the spirit of evil in the Enemy of your souls. He will destroy you with remorse and hatred." But elsewhere Scripture says of God, "There is only one Lawgiver and Judge, the One who is able to save and to destroy" (James 4:12). Furthermore, there is no teaching to "fear" the devil, for that would inevitably lead to crude superstitions; rather, Christians are to defy and resist him: "Submit therefore to God. Resist the devil and he will flee from you" (James 4:7); "Put on the full armor of God, that you may be able to stand firm against the schemes of the devil" (Eph. 6:11). Those who are sensitive about the idea of God's destroying anyone (either in body or soul) in hell are right to remember that God does not wish to destroy any man (1 Tim. 2:4; 2 Pet. 3:9). But they should also remind themselves that if the world is to run on righteousness and truth, then, when all calls to righteousness and all offers of mercy through the gospel have been

2. Mitchell Dahood, *Psalms*, vols. 16-17a, *The Anchor Bible*. See particularly Dahood's introduction to the third volume, "Death, Resurrection, and Immortality," pp. xli-iii.
3. Ewald Rudolf Stier, *Die Redendes Herrn Jesu.*

exhausted, God is fully able to destroy men in hell and clearly says that He intends to do just that. Jesus is more emphatic to this effect than any other speaker or writer of Scripture (see Luke 12:13-21, 45-48).

Christianity began in a time when vast multitudes were in bondage to various irrational, superstitious fears of demon powers. The Jews, while not so bound as many others, were not fully free from unbiblical, harmful opinions in this regard. It was a boldness imparted by Christ, His Spirit, and His Truth that enabled the early missionaries to have no fear of the "dumb idols" of heathenism. Paul scoffed at idols (1 Cor. 8:4; 10:19-20; 12:1-2). He boldly marched into the capital centers of devilish idolatry (Acts 17:15-32) and consented to the destruction of the books about the stupid rituals of demon worship (Acts 19:11-20). He knew that, though the devil and demons indeed hated him, and though he must wrestle against their subtle attacks on his and other's minds, as far as his body was concerned, his foes were men—not men ten feet tall, but limited, vulnerable men like himself. The same holds true today. Like him, "knowing the fear of the Lord, we persuade men" (2 Cor. 5:11). This truth is a great encouragement to press on in the mission without enervating worry.

Furthermore, though God never promises immunity from persecution or martyrdom, *purposeless* suffering or martyrdom will never be the lot of the Lord's faithful missionaries. Not a hair of the believer's head will be purposelessly cut, singed, or lost! Nothing done for Jesus' sake will fail to be recorded in the annals of the mission, written in heaven.

WARNINGS ON THE MISSION (VV. 32-33)

It will help in applying these words about confessing or denying Christ if one notices that they are addressed to professed disciples. Jesus' statement should not be thought of in connection with an offer of salvation to those not yet believers; rather it should be seen as a glad promise coupled with a stern warning. "Christ Jesus," Scripture says, "testified the good confession before Pontius Pilate" (1 Tim. 6:13), without reference to consequences. Jesus gave a straightforward, candid statement of His own identity and claims (see John 18:33-37). Confessing Christ has always been unequivocally to acknowledge His personal claims as true and also to acknowledge Him as Lord. Confession is not to merely recite a creed in a church, nor to write a doctrinal statement correctly. Nor is it necessarily even to speak at all. It means to assume the risks of clear association of oneself with Him, without dissimulation or equivocation.

An Old Testament story will illustrate. Naaman, a Syrian army captain, came to Elisha, internationally famous prophet of Jehovah and worker of miracles. Naaman wanted to be healed and he was healed by Elisha—after dipping himself seven times in the River Jordan. So, "he returned to the man of God . . . [and] said, 'Behold now, I know that there is no God in all the earth, but in Israel; so please take a present from your servant'" (2 Kings 5:15). When it was declined he asked another favor: "Let your servant at least be given two mules' load of earth; for your servant will no more offer burnt offering nor will he sacrifice to other gods, but the LORD" (v. 17). On the assumptions of the time that all gods were national and local he felt he needed Israelite land on which to worship Israel's God—not good theology but hardly blameworthy considering his limited understanding. Perhaps Jehovah regarded it as a "good confession." But then Naaman added a request that the Lord pardon him when in his official relation to the pagan king he should be obliged to worship the god, Rimmon, in the national shrine (v. 18).

What the benighted captain failed to see was that consistent loyalty is the essence of biblical worship. For God to tolerate failure in this would be like a man accepting a marriage arrangement in which his bride would be allowed to sleep overnight with an old suitor once a month. It is not without great meaning that the Old Testament frequently compared the Israel-Jehovah relationship to the wife-husband relationship and that the church of the New Testament is called the "bride of Christ." Apostasy is a fatal sin when undertaken deliberately and without repentance (see Heb. 6:1-6; 10:26-31).

Perhaps the greatest problem ever encountered by the ancient church was not the Imperial persecutions but what to do with *the lapsed,* that is, the professed believers who, loving their lives more than their Lord, capitulated. Many saved their lives, not particularly by denying that they thought highly of Jesus, but by joining in public offering of minor sacrifices to the local god or by offering incense to the bust of the reigning Caesar. Thus they denied Jesus' lordship over all by, as it were, putting Him on a shelf with other gods. There were two important schisms over the issue of what to do with these people when, after the brief period of persecution passed (the authorities usually quickly lost interest in physical coercion of Caesar worship), the lapsed person applied for reinstatement to the church fellowship. The Novatian schism (third century) and the Donatist schism (fourth century) were both over this issue. Both the Novatians and the Donatists bitterly opposed any restoration at all and the defenders of "orthodoxy" were hard-pressed to prove them wrong.

There are many less drastic actions by which men deny Jesus before men. A personal illustration will serve to explain. In the late years of the Great Depression I was a very poor young preacher, years behind schedule in education, eking out a few hours' credit at a university in the state of Washington. One class in sociology was difficult because, after the ungodly professor and a professed communist student found out they had a genuine preacher in captivity, no opportunity for argument—sometimes scorn—came up without being gleefully employed. After a month I felt sure I must be the sole believer in the class of about thirty. In those days "Christian Endeavor" was the leading vehicle for good interchurch youth activity. During the second month of the course, "C.E." held a state convention in a church of the university town. Now to the point of the story: imagine my surprise and consternation when among the large youth choir I recognized several members of my sociology class, not one of whom had ever spoken a good word for their Lord in that class, though many opportunities had been given, and not one of whom had even dared to speak a word of encouragement to me or even to associate with me after the class! Singing in the choir at church did not in these circumstances seem to be confessing Christ, while their silence in the classroom certainly seemed to me like denying Him. In writing of one of the fiercest Imperial persecutions one of the church Fathers said, "The [whole controversy] is about a name."[4]

"Not everyone who says to Me, 'Lord, Lord,' will enter the kingdom of heaven; but he who does the will of My Father who is in heaven. Many will say to Me on that day, 'Lord, Lord, did we not prophesy by Your name, and in Your name cast out demons, and in Your name perform many miracles?' And then I will declare to them, 'I never knew you; DEPART FROM ME, YOU WHO PRACTICE LAWLESSNESS' " (Matt. 7:21-23).

The Lord, of course, does forgive sins—even that of denying Him. "The context shews plainly that it is a practical consistent confession which is meant, and also a practical and enduring denial. The Lord will not confess the confessing Judas, nor deny the denying Peter; the traitor who denied Him in act [actions speak louder than words!] is denied; the Apostles who confessed Him even to death will be confessed."[5]

The portion of Matthew 10 under discussion relates primarily to times long after the apostles were dead. The far corners of the Empire did not heat up with persecution of Christians for decades. But the apostles themselves experienced persecution. The martyrdom of four of them is either stated or implied in the New Testament: the aged John, restricted to the "island called Patmos, because of the word of God and the testimony of Jesus" (Rev. 1:9); Peter, knowing that Jesus had predicted his crucifixion in old age (John 21:18-19); Paul, in the Mamartine prison, calmly awaiting his beheading (2 Tim. 4:11-18); and James, the son of Zebedee, bravely maintaining the Christian witness at Jerusalem in the face of growing threats and eventual execution by the sword of Herod. These worthies typify the disciples' conflicts (Matt. 10:24-25), and duties (vv. 26-27), and show proper response to the encouragements (vv. 28-31) and warnings (vv. 32-33). Let Paul's noble expression stand for them all. He said he was

> in far more labors, in far more imprisonments, beaten times without number, often in danger of death. Five times I received from the Jews thirty-nine lashes. Three times I was beaten with rods, once I was stoned, three times I was shipwrecked, a night and a day I have spent in the deep. I have been on frequent journeys, in dangers from rivers, dangers from robbers, dangers from my countrymen, dangers from the Gentiles, dangers in the city, dangers in the wilderness, dangers on the sea, dangers among false brethren; I have been in labor and hardship, through many sleepless nights, in hunger and thirst, often without food, in cold and exposure. Apart from such external things, there is the daily pressure upon me of concern for all the churches. Who is weak without my being weak? Who is led into sin without my intense concern? If I have to boast, I will boast of what pertains to my weakness. (2 Cor. 11:23-30)

4. Tertullian *Apology* 2. 19.
5. Henry Alford, *The New Testament for English Readers*, p. 74.

This is the confession of a true Christian evangelist, caught up without any reserve whatsoever in the Christian mission of world evangelism. Is it likely that he mirrors so exactly the teachings of the Lord in Matthew 10:31-33 without any consciousness that Jesus had spoken them? It is extremely doubtful.

6

The Age-long Mission:
The Disciples' Relation to Others

(Matt. 10:34-42)

The phrase "Truly I say to you" has been shown effectively to set off Jesus' address to His disciples regarding the coming worldwide mission into three sections, the third and last being verses 24-42. Many commentators, theological writers, and editors (see ASV, RSV, NASB) further divide the third section into three parts. The first of the three (Matt. 10:24-33) has just been concluded. In his famous work on Jesus' life and times, Alfred Edersheim said that in those verses "the horizon is enlarged. The statements are still primarily applicable to the early disciples, and their preaching among the Jews and in Palestine. But their ultimate bearing is already wider, and includes predictions and principles true to all time."[1]

The second and third paragraphs of this final section furnish the material for this chapter. Of the second (vv. 34-39), it can be said that "our Lord's Discourse still further widens the horizon. It describes the condition of laws of His kingdom, until the final revelation of that which is now covered and hidden. So long as His claims were set before a hostile world, they could only provoke war. On the other hand, so long as such decision was necessary, in the choice of either those nearest and dearest, of ease, nay of life itself, or else of Christ, there could be no compromise."[2] The last paragraph (vv. 40-42), using very old Jewish figures and forms of thought, tells Christian believers and messengers of all ages what their rewards are going to be. Though the terms are as old as Moses, Samuel, and Elijah, the application is as recent as yesterday, today, and tomorrow.

NECESSITY FOR INITIAL CONFLICT BEFORE VICTORY (VV. 34-36)

There is a meaning of these verses that seems obvious: conflicts will come in the course of the great work of spreading the gospel and the Christian fellowship of believers to the ends of the earth. All are somewhat aware of some specific

---

1. Alfred Edersheim, *The Life and Times of Jesus the Messiah*, 1:648.
2. Ibid., p. 650.

past conflicts and of a few martyrdoms. The days of the so-called Christian calendar are full of days to memorialize ancient martyrs, though this is not as well-understood now as it once was. But all have heard of James and Stephen, biblical martyrs; Polycarp and Justin, martyrs of the first centuries; Savonarola and Hus, precursors of the Reformation; some may even have heard of Wishart and Cranmer, British Protestant martyrs. All their stories are interesting and inspiring.

There is, however, something deeper than the obvious in Jesus' meaning. There is a formulation of purpose here. Jesus is saying that He actually came *with purpose* to cause the tensions within both families and other social groups. Neighborhoods and families must be disturbed; people must become distraught if the gospel is to progress. Both "to bring" clauses in verse 34 are Greek purpose clauses. The nature of the disturbances is quarreling. When a single member of a close-knit social group steps out of the groove in which the social group has always moved, he seems disloyal. This inevitably produces hurt feelings, consternation, resentment, antagonism and even hate. Similarly, when a member of such a group advocates an idea contrary to accepted assumptions on which the group or society seems to rest, there is bound to be vocal disagreement. The very intensity of attachment within the family, extended family, tribe, clan, or community produces the intensity of resentment. But that social disturbance is a very means of making conversions. That is why Jesus came to cause family disturbances.

By *family*, Jesus referred to the extended family, today still a vital social structure in the orient. He mentioned five different persons: a man, his father, a sister of the man (or daughter of the family), the mother, the man's wife (or daughter-in-law of the family). All live under the same roof. A new religion wherein the one embracing the new faith is intransigent, as Christians must be, on moral matters and on the sole Lordship of Christ, inevitably introduces unwelcome change for everybody. The ties of love and filial piety are not enough to prevent quarrels, perhaps physical punishment, or even violent death.

The famous story of Saint Barbara will serve to illustrate. Her wealthy father was a pagan. As the story goes, when he was leaving for a long journey he left plans for a tower to be built as a protective retreat for his young daughter Barbara. It was to have the customary two windows. But she became a Christian and at her insistence the servants made it with three in recognition of the Holy Trinity. Sometimes the story includes a portion about her refusing to marry a pagan suitor whom her father favored. At any rate, upon his return, the father asked why three windows were in the tower. When his daughter told him, confessing the name of Jesus, he hauled her off to the magistrate and formally charged her with the crime of being a Christian. The enraged father executed his daughter by decapitation with his own sword. This dramatic story of the third century has resulted in widespread devotion (misplaced, of course) to "Santa Barbara" in all parts of Christendom, both Orthodox and Latin.

A great preacher of Reformation times wrote a famous commentary of the gospels. His comments on Matthew 10:34-36 follow:

What Christ just asked of His disciples [to confess Him before men, v. 32], each of us would for himself provide with no difficulty, if all the world were to subscribe with one accord to the teaching of the Gospel. But as the majority is not only opposed, but actually in bitter conflict, we are not able to profess Christ without strife and hatred of many. So Christ tells His people to be ready for battle, for there must needs be war over the testimony of the truth. This involves a double offence, which otherwise would have caused weak minds much perturbation. Since the Prophets always promise that under the reign of Christ there will be peace and tranquil times, what else would the disciples have hoped for, but that everything would be at once pacified, wherever they should travel? As Christ is called *our* peace, and the Gospel reconciles us with God, it follows that a state of brotherly concord is established amongst us. So for battles and strifes to be started in the world where the Gospel is preached does not seem to agree with what was announced in the oracles of the Prophets, and far less with the role of Christ and the nature of the Gospel. But that peace which the Prophets extol, being linked with faith, only flourishes amongst the pure worshippers of God, and in godly consciences. It does not penetrate to the unbelievers, although it is offered to them, and no more can they bear to return into a state of grace with God but are excited by the very message of peace into a higher degree of unrest. For as Satan, who has his throne with the wicked, goes mad at the very Name of Christ, so once the teaching of the Gospel is produced, the godless mood of these people, which before lay in a trance, comes sharply to life. Thus it is that Christ, who is truly the Author of peace, becomes, on account of the malice of men, an occasion for disturbance.[3]

Throughout Paul's missionary career he was plagued by religious people who deeply resented the sword driven into their group life by the gospel. In this he was in a measure anticipated by Jesus, who was attacked by the same people for similar reasons. At the end "they kept on insisting, saying, 'He stirs up the people, teaching all over Judea, starting from Galilee, even as far as this place' " (Luke 23:5). The trail of such controversy that surrounded Paul may be traced through the book of Acts (see especially Acts 13:49-51; 18:11-17; 19:10-41). Paul's ministry at Iconium almost caused him to lose his life to a mob. The short term of ministry at Philippi resulted in a beating and jail. He was driven from Thessalonica and Berea. The climax of the eighteen months at Corinth was a neighborhood row and court scene. Three years at Ephesus came to an end with a noisy, city-wide demonstration against the Christians and except for the friendly advice of a more reasonable pagan religionist (the town clerk), he might have lost his life in the arena. In each case the immediate social effect of acknowledging Christ was apparently the occasion for opposition; the theoretical (doctrinal) content of the Christian message, as such, seems to have played a lesser role.

Time has not changed this. Jesus, the Prince of Peace, comes initially with a sword, whether wrenching apart heathen family alliances, disturbing moribund orthodoxy, or rebuking ripened apostasy. There is much good in this as well as pain. He said "I came . . . to bring . . . a sword" (Matt. 10:34). This was a transitional purpose, for the turmoil of deep feeling is the very matrix from which feelings of guilt

3. John Calvin, *Calvin's Commentaries: A Harmony of Matthew, Mark and Luke*, 1:309-10.

and a desire for forgiveness, issuing in repentance and faith, are born. Peace with God, peace with man, and peace with self are the ultimate accomplishments. The conflicts take a thousand forms, but out of them may issue eternal life and peace.

NECESSITY FOR COMPLETE DEVOTION FOR FINAL VICTORY (vv. 37-39)

Verses 37 through 39 seem to be Jesus' first reference to the distinct manner in which wicked men would take His life—crucifixion. To take up a cross would be, in a figure, to do what they may have seen prisoners condemned by Roman magistrates do. For no doubt the sorrowful sight of condemned men carrying their own crosses to the place of execution, as Jesus later did, was familiar at least to some of the twelve.

Emphasis on this kind of devotion is not uncommon in Jesus' discourses and conversations. Several months later, immediately after the incident of Peter's great confession in the district of Caesarea Philippi, (Matt. 16:13-20), Jesus "began to show His disciples that He must . . . suffer. . . and be killed" (16:21). At that time of mystified sadness, they were no doubt shocked to hear Him say, "If anyone wishes to come after Me, let him deny himself, and take up his cross, and follow Me" (16:24). Much later, not many weeks before the end, He said it again, with great vivid elaboration: "If anyone comes to Me, and does not hate his own father and mother and wife and children and brothers and sisters, yes, and even his own life, he cannot be My disciple. Whosoever does not carry his own cross and come after Me cannot be My disciple" (Luke 14:26-27).

Jesus was saying, "Discipleship of the sort I require of you demands that I be put before every other interest." In the Hebraic manner, He spoke of perfect discipleship as hating other loyalties, though this is not an all or nothing situation as shown by how readily Jesus forgave and forgives the failures of genuine but weak disciples. And the idea of "hate" is certainly a Hebraic figure for something much less than that. It does not mean that true missionaries (as in some degree all disciples must be) must constantly be working up an emotional storm of "Oh, how I love Jesus!" Neither does it mean they are to abandon family or to separate themselves from men. The nub of the matter is simply: Christ and His kingdom must come first. Jesus had said that in His first long discourse (Matt. 6:33).

What are some ways in which men can put Jesus second or third and, as a result, become unworthy of Him? By excluding those in need of Christian friendship—whether believers or not—in favor of a clique—whether evangelical or not—believers are failing as disciples. By allowing the routines of civilized existence perpetually to fill their minds and hours to the exclusion of love of neighbor, believers have become the "priest and the Levite" rather than the good Samaritan who is the true witness. The whole world thus receives an utterly false view of who Jesus is, what His gospel means, and what His household of faith is like. Blood may be thicker than water, but those who put family traditions, clan loyalties, hoary but wrong-headed opinions, or unbiblical tradition and attitude ahead of clear Christian duty cannot be His disciples, or at least not good ones. This truth lies near the center of all fruitful execution of successful missionary evangelism. By deciding issues of moral importance or matters of simple justice, whether public or private, by looking first to see where family and friends stand rather than on the basis of truth, Christ is denied, His gospel is perverted, and efforts at evangelism are stalled.

How can true missionaries take up their own crosses and carry them? One way is by doing what is right simply and wholly because it is right! This must be regardless of financial, social, or physical consequences. A woman in Iowa nearly froze to death because she was turned away in a sub-zero blizzard from three roadside farmhouses. She was saved by a Greyhound bus driver. The farmers put theoretical consequences (fear of some unknown involvement) ahead of plain duty of man to man. There are many varieties of cross-bearing.

> Then to side with Truth is noble when we share her wretched crust,
> Ere her cause bring fame and profit, and 'tis prosperous to be just;
> Then it is, the brave man chooses, while the coward stands aside,
> Doubting in his abject spirit, till his Lord is crucified,
> And the multitude make virtue of the faith they had denied.
> Count me o'er earth's chosen heroes,—they were souls that stood alone,
> While the men they agonized for, hurled the contumelious stone,
> Stood serene, and down the future saw the golden beam incline
> To the side of perfect justice, mastered by their faith divine,
> By one man's plain truth to manhood and to God's supreme design.[4]
>
> (James Russell Lowell)

CERTAIN REWARD FOR THOSE WHO RECEIVE THE MESSENGERS (VV. 40-41)

This discourse ends where such an outline of challenges and duties ought to end—with a small paragraph of promises of reward. Hearing Jesus' words, the apostles must surely have thought of several incidents of Old Testment lore. Once the armies of Israel were poised to invade Canaan and two spies were sent from the camp at Shittim to explore Jericho across the Jordan to the west, for that was to be the point of first attack. The two strangers in town put up in the house of the harlot, Rahab. She not only "received" (see Matt. 10:40-41) them but hid them, fed them, and saw to their safe escape. She explained why: "I know that the LORD hath given you the land" (Josh. 2:9). Then she committed herself and her family (it was not considered so very bad in Canaanite religion and culture for a daughter to be a harlot) to the messengers and to Jehovah their God. Rahab and the two spies bound themselves by oath to stand together in this loyalty, and the woman put a "cord of scarlet thread in the window" (Josh. 2:18) to mark the house to which her family came for safety on the day of Jericho's destruction by the armies of Israel. Almost all of Joshua 2 is devoted to this story. Her faith, evinced simply by receiving the Lord's messengers, had saved her (Heb. 11:31; James 2:25). Just how wonderfully welcomed she was is seen in the fact that she was married to Salmon of Bethlehem, an important man in the tribe of Judah, and

---

4. James Russell Lowell, "The Present Crisis," lines 51-60.

became, through her son Boaz, an ancestress of the Savior (see Matt. 1:5).

To receive the messenger—in the full sense of that biblical word—is to receive the Savior who sent Him, as illustrated by Cornelius, Lydia, and the Philippian jailor. It is not historical to find a sending *group* of believers in Jesus' discourses on missionary evangelism—not even in the formal announcement of Matthew 28:19-20. That had to wait for later (see discussion of Romans 10 and 15). All other considerations aside, it is most important to remember that *Jesus is and always has been the true sender of missionaries.* By remembering this, it can be better understood why there is frequent conjunction of yieldedness of heart toward God and kind receptivity toward God's missionaries. Though spiritual need is no guarantee of spiritual thirst (Rev. 22:17), frequently, as in the case of Rahab, this receptivity is present among those in deep spiritual need. Another example is the needy woman at the well of Sychar whose openness to Jesus led to His hospitable reception by an entire community and possibly to the establishment of a strong church there (John 4; Acts 8). Thus, hospitality to messengers is a first sign that, as Paul at Corinth learned from the Lord, "I have many people in this city" (Acts 18:10; see also 16:14-15). It also helps one understand why earlier in this discourse Jesus said, "And whoever does not receive you, nor heed your words, as you go out of that house or that city, shake off the dust of your feet" (Matt. 10:14), and "whenever they persecute you in this city, flee to the next" (v. 23).

Unfortunately, because of the weakness of society, even Christian society under the condition of sin, evil influences sometimes enter a group of believers and turn the welcome into suspicion, ultimately even rejection. One may be sure John Calvin never forgot the men who set the good people of Geneva against him and sent him packing off to Strasbourg where he served for several years until the Genevans repented and invited him back. Nor did Paul forget the quarrelsome, proud, self-seeking fanatics of Galatia who turned the Christians of that region against him (see Gal. 4:12-20). The same would be true in large measure of the church at Corinth as most of his second epistle to them shows. Perhaps the people of Northampton, Massachusetts, had second thoughts, too. They dismissed from their pulpit the great Jonathan Edwards, who even then towered above all the saints and thinkers of America, being also the most effective of the native evangelists in the Great Awakening of the 1740s, mighty of word through his writings until the present day. History thoroughly substantiated the position of Pastor Edwards, but soon, of course, the evil seeds of worldliness had overcome the congregation and it never fully recovered.

In explaining why He resorted to parables in His teaching, Jesus equated the "prophet . . . and righteous man" (Matt. 13:17; cf. 10:41) with Old Testament prophets and godly people. In a later message, delivered in the very shadow of the cross (Matt. 23:29-36), He identified them with the gospel messengers of the Christian era. These statements about receiving the messengers of Christ highlight an answer to a frequent question about rewards in the world to come: How can "ordinary" Christians hope to inherit reward in heaven along with Enoch, Moses, Elijah, John, Bartholomew, Peter, and Paul? "He who receives a prophet in the name of a prophet shall receive a prophet's reward; and he who receives a righteous man in the name of a righteous man shall receive a righteous man's reward" (Matt. 10:41). Those verses also explain how every new cell of believers—every local church—begins: by giving Christ's messengers and their message a heartfelt welcome. "He who receives you receives Me, and he who receives Me receives Him who sent Me" (v. 40).

CERTAIN REWARD FOR HONEST LABOR IN THE MISSION (V. 42)

Who are the little ones of whom Jesus speaks in verse 42? The term is a common one for small children throughout the Septuagint (Greek Old Testament), those still usually in custody of women (e.g., Josh. 8:35). It is possible that in some of the occasions of its use in the synoptic gospels (used only there in the New Testament), it designates new adult believers (see Matt. 18:6). But an examination of all the passages does not seem convincing. Though some commentators assert that the term was "familiarly used of the scholars of a Rabbi,"[5] leading authorities reject this idea.[6] It seems more natural to understand "these little ones" [10:42] to be children in our Lord's audience.

So this leads to the understanding that ministry to needs of children and others (Matt. 25:40) has a place in evangelism. Jesus is not specific as to what needs and occasions. The important matter is rather that such kind acts be done in the name of Christ ("in the name of a disciple" [10:42]—that is, Jesus' disciple). Custom or purely human sympathy are not sufficient motives to qualify any act of charity as specifically Christian.

Sometimes only a little needed refreshment is all the occasion calls for. Sometimes large money collections or shipments of food speak volumes for the love of God. Several gospel miracles of Jesus were of healing the children of concerned parents, or even restoring them to life. Earlier in the discourse, the Lord authorized a ministry of physical healing to the apostles' audiences.

Does this not suggest the legitimacy of employment of missionary resources on these acknowledged secondary needs of mankind—in the course of missionary evangelism? Even though there has been a historical tendency, when evangelical doctrine is little understood by the community of disciples, to substitute medical, educational, or economic aid for the gospel of eternal salvation, that tendency does not obviate the need for physical ministry. However, observe from Matthew 10:7-8 that the physical ministry was only for accompaniment: "And as you go, preach, saying. . . ." The main task was preaching.

A respectable argument for the importance of such a ministry has usually been something like this: The "kingdom of God" is the reign of God in men's souls. For the present, it is the church's work to bring the gospel to mankind so that the reign of God will prevail there—that is, so that men will be saved. The gospel is

5. Charles John Ellicott, ed., *Ellicott's Commentary on the Whole Bible: A Verse by Verse Explanation*, 6:64.
6. Hermann L. Strack and Paul Billerbeck, *Kommentar zum Neuen Testamentum aus Talmud und Midrasch*, 1:591-92.

not designed merely to educate minds or to re-fashion society, though invariably immense improvements in learning and in social conditions follow the prevalence of Christianity among the people of any area.

Yet, even while attending to strictly gospel work, the argument goes, the material and social needs of men must not be disregarded. There are four basic reasons for this:

- The apostles were empowered to meet physical needs while on their evangelistic mission. They were not unmindful of the bodily and temporal needs of men.
- Furthermore, this principle finds enlargement in specific injunctions of several epistles. "Bear one another's burdens, and thus fulfill the law of Christ" said Paul (Gal. 6:2). James added, "Pure and undefiled religion in the sight of our God and Father [is this], to visit orphans and widows in their distress" (James 1:27). The same James spoke most disparagingly of professed Christianity that pays special honor to those with wealth (James 2:1-9), and, it is argued, James seemed to suggest that one who truly loves his neighbor ought even to rectify some of the material inequalities among men (James 2:8). In this connection John is often quoted: "But whoever has the world's goods, and beholds his brother in need and closes his heart against him, how does the love of God abide in him?" (1 John 3:17).
- It is further asserted that corporeal evils are obstructions to the reception of the truth, and hence must receive missionary attention if gospel promotion is to be successful. "Men suffering under disease, poverty, slavery, oppression, are certainly not in the best position to receive the Gospel. The natural tendency of corporeal evils is to strengthen depravity, close the heart against God and man, and nurse misanthropy and impiety into a chronic state."[7]
- "Earnest efforts to remove the corporeal evils of a people are among the most likely means to dispose them to listen to our doctrines. These evils are felt; and he who generously removes them is hailed as a benefactor, and the heart opens to his words."[8] Job is cited. When the ear heard him, it "blessed" him:

> Because I delivered the poor who cried for help,
> And the orphan who had no helper.
> The blessing of the one ready to perish came upon me,
> And I made the widow's heart sing for joy.
>
> (Job 29:12-13)

David Thomas used even stronger words:

Had the Church always acted upon this principle;—had it endeavored to give bread to the hungry as well as Bibles to the ignorant; had it sought to deliver man from social and political despotism of his fellows as well as from the despotism of Satan; had it struggled to redeem the body as well as the soul; had it appeared to men more as a secular benefactor, and less a theological belligerent, an ascetic devotee or a sectarian partisan; had the world seen it more in the acts of a genial messenger of a deep and genuine philanthropy, penetrating the darkest scenes of trial with a word to cheer and

---

7. David Thomas, *The Genius of the Gospel*, p. 152.
8. Ibid., p. 153.

a hand to bless, and less in pompous ceremonies, conflicting creeds, and affected pietisms; I say, had this been the past history of the Church, it would have been now the Sovereign of the world."[9]

The reader of the above will perhaps respond as this author did. Much of this is true, perhaps most of it. I have cited this argument precisely because it was written in Britain by a renowned preacher and advocate of foreign missions long before the current menage of somewhat secularized and politicized writers advocating a political-social-economic approach to the Christian mission had been born. David Thomas wrote as a genuine believer, though from the somewhat utopian standpoint of the latter half of the nineteenth century. The evaluation of his argument ought not be affected by similar sounding but truly contradictory contemporary arguments.

Thomas's comments convey a wholesome ring if not quite the certainty of eternal truth:

> The success of modern missions may be attributed in a great degree to the fact that missionaries have been recognized as secular benefactors. Though they have not been able to work miracles as the credentials of their mission, many have secured attention for their message by their skill in the treatment of bodily disease, by the introduction of domestic arts and manufactures as well as improved systems of agriculture. They have been the physicians, the legislators, the political economists, the promoters of trade, commerce, and industry, in addition to their especial function of religious teachers.[10]

The reader conversant with some of the bold, contemporary, revolutionary rhetoric about supposed missionary responsibility to bring social change by violence, if necessary, will readily acknowledge the greater balance in the older arguments.

For over fifty years now a "Comprehensive Approach" has been promoted among missions of liberal persuasion and is recently gaining popularity among some conservatives. The theory is that man exists only as a "whole" person in a particular geographical-social community. Thus is Christ's purpose to be Savior of the whole man in all of his relationships and the missionary's job to focus not on saving "souls" but on endeavoring to save the whole man and with him lift his community. Sometimes this idea is vividly, if crudely, put: "No man can believe the gospel on an empty stomach." The implication is that his stomach must be filled first.

Space does not allow extended discussion of this theory. The cup of cold water of Jesus' saying does not really turn the wheel of "comprehensive" approach as far as the above argument would try to lead Christians to believe. Harry R. Boer, after citing authors and missionary conferences in its favor, puts the matter in right perspective as follows:

9. Ibid.
10. Ibid., p. 154.

The premise underlying this conception of the missionary approach is a very basic one. It is that man's spiritual life "is indivisibly rooted in all his conditions—physical, mental and social." This statement will hardly bear close scrutiny. Had it been stated that man's spiritual life is affected by his conditions we would agree. But it is hardly true that his spiritual life is *rooted* in his conditions. It is rooted alone in his relationship to God. It is the glory of the life in the Spirit that it *transcends* and *overcomes* conditions.[11]

Boer goes on to say that Christian faith and life are often most powerful where conditions are terrible, "at a minimum—persecution, loneliness, poverty, sickness." He cites Hebrews 11. One of his best paragraphs begins: "The gospel . . . does not come to men in the form of a comprehensive approach, but in the form of a *comprehensive message.*" The message includes good news of renewal of man here and now, partaking here of the powers of a world to come. Christ, the *end* of the law and of the old age, the king of the new, has come. Man can live according to norms of the kingdom of God among the kingdoms of men. Boer concludes, "out of this fact alone the transformation of conditions arises which can properly be described as a manifestation of the kingdom of God. Social renewal is preceded by the renewal of individuals who understand the comprehensive significance of the gospel."[12]

Reformist, liberal church efforts at social betterment have sometimes been accompanied by bitter language and the appearance of great anger. But, says Scripture, "The anger of man does not achieve the righteousness of God" (James 1:20).

The case for social reform as part of the Christian mission in the world is being carried to the point of revolution today in what is called "liberation theology." The theologians of this movement being with Marxist social analysis, namely in terms of class conflict, and conclude by interpreting and trimming the Bible to support the programs of Marxist revolution.

Liberation theology has been until now mainly a movement among Roman Catholic scholars, clergy, and social-political activists in Latin America. Pope John Paul II has issued an eleven-thousand-word "Instruction on Certain Aspects of Liberation Theology," saying, among other things, that Christians truly must help eliminate evil social structures. But, says the document, Marxist influence on theology has led to "disastrous confusion between the poor of scripture and the proletariat of Marx" (the *Chicago Tribune*, September 4, 1984, section 1, page 5).

A helpful book *(Liberation Theology: An Evangelical View from the Third World*, Atlanta: John Knox, 1979) by J. Andrew Kirk, a British theologian who has served as a clergyman in South America, attempts to give an evangelical perspective. The book is flawed somewhat by omitting major attention to the radical

---

11. Harry R. Boer, *Pentecost and Missions,* pp. 239-40. Boer is quoting the *Statement* of the Jerusalem Meeting of the International Missionary Council of 1928.
12. Ibid., p. 241.

theories of Shaull and Boff, both of whom are aligned with liberation theology. The author also obscures his case and his own views by employing terms and a style familiar only to specialists in technical hermeneutics, advanced New Testament criticism, and Marxian theory.

The discussion will now move from consideration of Jesus' address on the practices of discipleship in missionary evangelism (Matt. 10) to His "seminar" on principles by which to interpret results of efforts at making disciples (Matt. 13:1-53 and Mark 4:21-29).

PART 2

PRINCIPLES FOR THE MISSION OF WORLD EVANGELISM:

(Matt. 13:1-53; Mark 4:21-29)

7

Jesus' Introduction of Parables

(Matt. 13:1-3a)

The world today is a world of statistics, measuring sticks, calipers, computers, and quantifiable data. Talk about such things is heard at school, at church, at business gatherings of all sorts, and especially in TV advertisements. Nothing must be left to surmises or imagination. At least the above is what many men today seem to think. "Tell it like it is" is a frequent way of stating the mood. "Get to the point" is a persistent demand.

Yet there is another, contrary mood present in the current culture. If advertisers employ statistics on the one hand, they also appeal to imagination on the other. And people are reading mountains of fiction of all kinds: science fiction, romantic, gothic, and historical fiction. TV is programmed heavily with fiction shows of all kinds. Social critics complain that some of the soap operas are closer to reality than the news shows.

Does this not suggest that man, on the deeper levels of his being, cries out for something to challenge his powers to think, imagine, and create? The type of literature that lives on in the affection of mankind always appeals to these aspects of man's nature. Such writing employs a great variety of symbolical, imaginative, and literary forms—allegory, fable, parable, romance. Figures of speech such as simile, metaphor, hyperbole, metonymy, and synecdoche likewise abound to excite interest, to amuse, to inspire, to entertain, and to instruct.

The Old Testament prophets and poets wrote just such literature as this and Jesus was fully informed in it from early childhood. It should not be surprising then, that at a certain point in His ministry Jesus adopted an almost completely symbolic method of presenting His ideas. An examination of the record leads to the discovery that He did so at the precise point where He began to unfold the missionary and evangelistic program His disciples were to carry out in the interim between His ascension and His second advent. That point is recorded in Matthew 13 although it took place in the midst of two events recorded in Matthew 10: the calling out of the twelve (10:1-4) and the instructing and sending out of the twelve in an initial apostolic circuit of Galilee (10:6—11:1). (The actual chronology is followed by Mark in 3:13-19; 4:1-34; and 6:7-13; and by Luke in 6:12-16;

8:4-18; and 9:1-6. The address of Matthew 10:5—11:1 came after the parables of chapter 13.)

Jesus' close followers noticed his shift to speaking in parables and asked about it: "And the disciples came and said to Him, 'Why do You speak to them in parables?' " (Matt. 13:10). Jesus' answer showed that He had more than one reason for doing so. At that particular moment (as will be studied in some detail in the next chapter) He was about to take steps to insure that the message of His work of worldwide redemption would be conveyed to the wide world that needed to hear of it. He was not about to raise the furor that would immediately be generated if He were to announce that plainly to the shallow-minded crowds. So He spoke of these plans in parables to the general public and explained their meaning to His immediate followers in private. The use of parables was for Jesus a

> new method whereby He might present as much truth to the crowds as they were able to hear while at the same time deepening His Apostles' and close disciples' understanding of the truth which they were shortly to [bear] . . . to the world. . . . The parable or similitude is essentially a laying side by side of earthly, material things and heavenly, spiritual things in order that upon sincere, sober reflection the earthly and material may contribute to understanding the spiritual and heavenly. Since the earthly side of the comparison is familiar to the hearer, there is danger that he may rest content that he knows what the speaker means simply because he knows about seeds or pearls or fishing or mustard or whatever and, not being willing to ponder or ask for explanation of the spiritual meaning, he may remain satisfied with the entertainment aspect of the story. Thus the parable is a form of judgment (Mt. 13:9-15) on his shallowness of heart. On the other hand, the spiritually minded will learn much spiritual truth by reflection and even more by asking the teacher to explain—which is exactly what the disciples did.[1]

He was in the latter part of the middle year of His three-year ministry and the shape of the future was now plain. He needed to prepare the disciples' minds for the disappointment of their immature expectations for His kingdom in order that they might be ready to be His apostles in the founding of a church within a kingdom of grace in the age to follow.

That He began to do on that notable day by means of a series of eight parables, seven of them reported by Matthew, one reported only by Mark. He may also have spoken other parables at this time that none of the gospels record. Brief note will now be taken of all of them; further background information will be given on Matthew 13. Extended attention will be given to the first parable in the next chapter of this book. He spoke, in order:

1. Of four kinds of soil for the seed of the Word of God (Matt. 13:3-9, 18-23); of how men will respond to the gospel in different ways.

1. Robert Duncan Culver, *The Life of Christ*, pp. 140-41.

2. Of a man who sowed seed in a field and patiently waited for a harvest (Mark 4:26-29). This is the only parable in the series not reported by Matthew. It explains the relative place of God's Spirit and of the human messenger in missionary evangelism.
3. Of the field sowed with wheat in which tares were also sown (Matt. 13:24-30, 36-43). The missionary sows the good seed in the field but the devil also sows seed in the same field. There are startingly mixed results.
4. Of a very small seed, the mustard seed, and its phenomenal growth (Matt. 31-32). This parable speaks of the unexpected worldwide extension of the church and some strange results of it.
5. Of leaven in a bowl of meal (Matt. 33). The gospel also works quietly and unseen by unspectacular methods. These two parables (mustard seed, leaven) teach us: *despise not the day of small things* (see Zech. 4:10).

The next two parables speak of two ways men come to awareness and acceptance of the Word of God. Jesus spoke:

6. Of a hidden treasure (Matt. 13:44). Men sometimes unexpectedly discover the good news.
7. Of a pearl of great price (Matt. 45-46). Christ and His Word are found after painful searching.
8. Of a drag-type fish net that gathered both good and bad fish, which had to be sorted (Matt. 47-50). Full recognition of hypocrites among true believers in the sphere of Christian profession and their separation from that sphere will not come until the judgment at the end of the present age.

There are two sections of the Bible, each comprised of a long chapter, that in symbolic language predict the course of the present age. Each begins with the time in which the speaker lived and each ends with the consummation of this age. The former, Daniel 2, predicts the course of national succession under the figure of a statue whose head is of gold, breast and arms of silver, belly and thighs of bronze, legs of iron, and feet of iron mixed with clay. The coming of judgment and establishment of the eternal reign of Messiah is represented by a stone that smashes the image. Jesus prophetically called this period of time "the times of the Gentiles" (Luke 21:24).

Matthew 13 (with some supplementing from Mark 4 and Luke 8) is the other long chapter. In it Jesus refers to "the kingdom of heaven" (Matt. 13:11 and through the chapter). That kingdom is plainly the sphere in which men would profess to be Christians, acknowledging Him at least with their lips as Lord and Christ. Parallel parts of Mark (4:11 onward) and Luke (8:10 onward) say "the kingdom of God." This is a matter of some controversy, but with some variation in emphasis most scholars agree that Jesus was speaking of the response men would make to the gospel after the disciples began to preach following His ascension and the Pentacostal outpouring of the Holy Spirit not many days after. There will be further discussion of this important point later in these pages.

It is instructive that prophecy concerning the present age in both Daniel and the gospels employs symbols as the chief vehicle. Without going extensively into the reasons why, suffice it to say that God never "tips His hand" ahead of time.[2] He tells some of what He is going to do, but prophecy does not chart the future exactly enough to allow men to bring the plans of God to pass through purely human means. Pilate and Annas and Caiaphas, for example, fulfilled prophecy by killing Jesus, but only the most informed and discerning knew that this was the case and they only after the fact (see Acts 4:27-28). Among the disciples, only Mary of Bethany, who anointed His still living body for burial a week later, seems fully to have understood. So "we see through a glass, darkly" (1 Cor. 13:12, KJV) in prophecy. But that does not mean that we see nothing at all. There is sufficient guidance for the believer to meet the future, even if not quite enough to draw a complete diagram of it.

Now, it is well known that Jesus' ministry was directed only to Israel. Gentiles received only "crumbs . . . from their master's table" (Matt. 15:27). To the very end this was the case. Why, then, did He choose the particular moment in His ministry that He did to disclose the future age when the gospel would be proclaimed by witnesses of every nation to every people, tongue, and nation under heaven? While no explicit answer is given, an examination of the immediately foregoing events may suggest one.

The first three gospels present the time that Jesus spoke this message as being one of the busiest periods of His career as teacher. Luke furnishes the framework of it (8:1-39) while Mark 3:20—5:20 and Matthew 12:22—13:53, 8:18 and 23-34 furnish details. He had already completed two tours of Galilee. The area had been essentially evangelized. Already the fickleness of the enthusiastic crowds was evident to Him.

Several incidents from the past several days clearly indicated the direction matters would take, leading to Messiah's rejection and execution at the demand of His own people. Shortly before, a man with a withered hand showed up at a Sabbath synagogue service when Jesus was present. Being challenged to say whether it was lawful or not to heal on the Sabbath Jesus promptly healed the man and delivered a stinging rebuke to the Pharisees, who were really behind the challenge. The reaction on all sides is important to this study: "But the Pharisees went out, and counseled together against Him, as to how they might destroy Him. But Jesus, aware of this, withdrew from there" (Matt. 12:14-15). Matthew, seeing the incident from the perspective of thirty or more years later, gave the significance of those events (Matt. 12:18-21; see Isa. 42:1-4):

In order that what was spoken through Isaiah the prophet, might be fulfilled, saying,
"BEHOLD, MY SERVANT WHOM I HAVE CHOSEN;
MY BELOVED IN WHOM MY SOUL IS WELL-PLEASED;
I WILL PUT MY SPIRIT UPON HIM,

2. See Robert Duncan Culver, "Were the Old Testament Prophecies Really Prophetic?" in Howard F. Vos, ed., *Can I Trust the Bible?*, pp. 91-116, esp. pp. 99-100, for further comment on the subject.

AND HE SHALL PROCLAIM JUSTICE TO THE GENTILES.
HE WILL NOT QUARREL, NOR CRY OUT;
NOR WILL ANYONE HEAR HIS VOICE IN THE STREETS.
A BATTERED REED HE WILL NOT BREAK OFF,
AND A SMOLDERING WICK HE WILL NOT PUT OUT,
UNTIL HE LEADS JUSTICE TO VICTORY.
AND IN HIS NAME THE GENTILES WILL HOPE."

The prophecy states that God's servant, the Messiah, would have a gentle, non-coercive program when He first came and that the goal of it would be to reach the Gentiles with the saving grace of His work among men.

The narrative of Matthew continues by telling how He healed "a demon-possessed man" and that even though "the multitudes were amazed . . . when the Pharisees heard it, they said, 'This man casts out demons only by Beelzebul the ruler of the demons' " (Matt. 12:22-24). At first Jesus patiently argued for the validity of the miracle as the work of the Spirit of God. Then, while the evil of the generation became more apparent by the minute He denounced His opponents. He pronounced the speech of the Pharisees blasphemy, saying, "Any sin and blasphemy shall be forgiven men; but blasphemy against the Holy Spirit shall not be forgiven . . . either in this age, or in the age to come" (Matt. 12:31-32). These representatives of the nation, as they later turned out to be, had already committed the unpardonable sin. Their reaction to Christ was an early sign of the official rejection that would come only a year and a few months later.

Later the same day several members of Jesus' family, including His mother, having walked over from Nazareth, appeared outside the building where He was speaking. Like all the rest, they seemed to have misunderstood Him, perhaps planning to take Him back to Nazareth to save Him from His lunacy. They asked to speak with Him, but "stretching out His hand toward His disciples, He said, 'Behold, My mother and My brothers! For whoever does the will of My Father who is in heaven, he is My brother and sister and mother' " (Matt. 12:46-50). Though many of Jesus' family became disciples after His resurrection, and though Jesus did not reject their persons nor the familial relationship with them, His kingdom had now to take precedence over any purely human, familial relationship. The time was at hand when the message of the reign of God the Son, demanding that men confess Jesus Christ as Lord (Rom. 10:9-10), would be going to all the nations of men.

So at that time Jesus took steps to begin to announce what later events would serve to clarify: The kingdom of divine power is to be manifest *after* a reign of grace. He assumed the throne of that reign at His ascension, being seated "at the right hand of the Majesty on high" (Heb. 1:3). Within that reign the new form of God's people was formally inaugurated at Pentecost and will be consummated at Jesus' second advent. How else can Peter's magnificent interpretation of the ascension and Pentecost be received? On the day of Pentecost Peter declared that, having fulfilled the prophecies of His death, burial, and resurrection (Acts 2:22-32), Jesus then ascended to heaven. There He was exalted to the position of

universal reign at the Father's right hand, being constituted both Lord and
Messiah. Considering the Jewish understanding of *Christ,* the Lord God's anointed king, and of *Lord,* Adonai-Jehovah of Old Testament history and prophecy,
nothing less than enthronement as universal king can be made of Peter's words in
Acts 2:33-36 (see Psalm 110):

> Therefore having been exalted to the right hand of God, and having received from the
> Father the promise of the Holy Spirit, He has poured forth this which you both see
> and hear. For it was not David who ascended into heaven, but he himself says:
>> THE LORD SAID TO MY LORD,
>> SIT AT MY RIGHT HAND,
>> UNTIL I MAKE THINE ENEMIES A FOOTSTOOL FOR THY FEET.
> Therefore let all the house of Israel know for certain that God has made Him both
> Lord and Christ—this Jesus whom you crucified.

During this age men will profess to acknowledge Jesus. A church was formed.
Christendom—a mixed condition wherein culture and Christ, true believers and
false professors, will seem scarcely distinguishable—came into being. In proceed-
ing through the Lord's address about the church it shall be found that He referred
to that as God's kingdom. Though there is some ambiguity about this, there
seems to be no way to avoid it. In the parables of the kingdom, the kingdom is the
sphere of the professing Christian church.

This can be better understood by examining another part of Matthew to see
how broad the meaning may be and yet how narrow. The section is Matthew
19:16—20:16. The section is treated as a unit in the common editions of the
Greek text and is so regarded also by several recent versions and many commentaries.

As the story goes, one morning, a rich, young ruler of the Jews, to whom Jesus
was immediately drawn in affection, respectfully addressed the Lord: "What good
thing shall I do that I may obtain eternal life?" It turned out that the young man,
while sincere, was still putting treasure on earth ahead of riches in glory. Attention to details of Jesus' conversation with the young man and, shortly after, with
the disciples, helps one to understand what Jesus and others of His time—quite
aside from any visible establishment of Messiah's reign on earth—thought the
kingdom of God to be. The young ruler first asked about "eternal life" (19:16).
Jesus then referred to the same as entering into "life" (v. 17). Later Jesus spoke of
the same, or some aspect of it, as having "treasure in heaven" (v. 21); and then to
the disciples, as entering into the "kingdom of heaven" (v. 23); and again to the
disciples, as entering into the "kingdom of God" (v. 24). The disciples understood
this as being "saved" (v. 25) and Jesus finally said this was to "inherit eternal life"
(v. 29). But in the same speech Jesus connected all of these with a future cosmic
"regeneration" (v. 28) when the Son of Man would "sit on His glorious throne" (v.
28) and His disciples would likewise judge (or reign) (see v. 28).

Those ideas have a common core: Jesus' royal rights to every man's worship in
a world that He owns, won by His redemptive career. This is manifest in many

related ideas. He who throws some of these ideas out so as to favor only one or two does not understand Jesus' message of the kingdom.

Significantly, Jesus on that same occasion went on to explain some of the young ruler's folly by introducing a parable. This He did in a manner reminiscent of the introductions to several of the parables of chapter 13: "But many who are first will be last; and the last, first. For the kingdom of heaven is like a landowner" (Matt. 19:30—20:1). There follows a famous parable about how a certain farmer paid off all his workers equally at the end of a day even though they had worked for greatly unequal numbers of hours, yet kept his agreement with all. Several features of the parable relate to the reign of God, just as the profession of Christ is an aspect of the reign of God in all the parables reported in Matthew 13, Mark 4, and Luke 8.

Of course, detailed information on the nature of the church cannot be expected this early in Jesus' career. True, chapter 16 of Matthew relates how Peter's confession of Jesus' deity and lordship caused Jesus such joy that, for the first time, He spoke of the great body of believers of the coming age of grace as "My church" (v. 18). Furthermore, shortly afterward He referred to the local group of believers as "the church" (18:17). Yet these references are understood today only in retrospect. The apostles did not have the New Testament. The parables under consideration do not specifically contemplate the church universal or local. Rather, Jesus was intimating by foresight some features of evangelism among the nations in the coming age.

At about this time Jesus addressed the apostles at length on the subject of their future ministry, giving a marvelous preview of the techniques the missionaries would employ in their future mission. He also told them of the persecutions they would receive. Only Matthew provides a very complete report of that address of instruction—all but four verses of chapter ten being devoted to it. This is the material studied in Part I of this book. But the much abbreviated reports of Mark and Luke help by making the chronology clear. As previously shown (pp. 53-54), the address of Matthew 10 really came after the parables of chapter 13.

Apparently, Matthew—as certain redaction critics of the last few years confirm—was particularly interested in the nature of the church and its mission, that is, a theology of the church. (For a brief discussion on critical interpretation—including redaction criticism—and how the interpretation relates to Jesus' parables, see Appendix A, "Notes on Recent Critical Interpretation of Jesus' Parables"—ED.) Furthermore, it is Matthew who most fully reported the post-resurrection setting of the final formal announcement of the church's mission of age-long world evangelism (Matt. 28:16-18) and furnishes the most detailed, standard form of it (Matt. 28:19-20). It may, therefore, be that in bypassing the gospels, especially Matthew, for all these years in pursuit of a biblical theology of the church and its mission, the only data in which that theology may truly be found has been neglected.

It is possible, then, to explore the Lord's parables of that day with a great measure of confidence, fully expecting to discover important information concerning the church's mission of world evangelism. Something of the very nature of evangelism can be learned: how it will be received, how it operates, what a Christian's responsibilities are toward it, who and what the enemies of the gospel are, what the earthly results will be, and what the eternal heavenly fruit will be. In fact, there is not a comparably complete deposit of such information in any other passage of Scripture.

If Christian men wish to understand their task in the mission of world evangelism they must begin with the only long discourses that Jesus directly addressed to that subject. These addresses are found in Matthew 10 and 13. They are supplemented only slightly by Mark and Luke. Matthew's accounts of these two "seminars" of Jesus, then, are the chief foundation for a biblical theology of the Christian mission of world evangelism.

8

Parable on Men's Response to the Word

(Matt. 13:36-9, 18-23)

The elements of this story are four: the sower, the seed, the soil, and the birds. Most attention is directed to seed and soils. It is plain to see that worldwide dissemination of "the word of God" is the subject of this parable. Nothing is made yet of the agencies that God may use. Inasmuch as almost immediately afterward the apostles were given specific instructions and sent out two by two to announce the presence of the kingdom (Matt. 9:35—11:1; Mark 6:6-13; Luke 9:1-6; see also chapter 7, pp. 53-54), Jesus must not have been referring to Himself alone as the sower of gospel seed. As the instructions just mentioned indicate, He was talking about gospel preaching in general and how men will respond to it. Any enlargement as to the human messengers, their behavior, human authority, and sponsorship must be found outside Matthew 13.

It will also occur to the careful reader that there is a silent presupposition underlying the whole parable: multitudes will produce no positive response whatsoever to the gospel. Such an inference seems to be rendered necessary by the fact that apparently all the seed sown in the parable is "sown in his heart" (v. 19). This is said specifically of the first, most unresponsive soil. Evidently even in the wayside soil the seed reaches the heart and makes some impact, even though only briefly and without any growth. Jesus did not here even contemplate the vast masses who do not hear or who hear so carelessly that the gospel never catches their attention, much less gets a brief lodging in their hearts. So there is some basis for saying the first class of hearers, unrepresented by any kind of soil at all, is comprised of those upon whom the gospel makes no impression at all. That is, so to speak, the first type of hearer, but since he is a "non-hearing" hearer, little more will be made of it here. The history of evangelism demonstrates the accuracy of Jesus' foresight of the coming age. To the present hour the gospel has penetrated the hearts of the masses in all lands no farther than water on the proverbial duck's back. Wishing it were not so will not change this, nor will work and prayer bring to pass the optimistic hopes of a millennium of world peace through missionary work of a few generations. This does not mean that the nations may not be affected for good when believers in number arise in them. In fact, the parable of the mustard seed suggests that many nations of men shall look to the enormously expanded church for shelter. Even that, however, is not necessarily an unmixed good. As is usual with all of Jesus' parables, this one has been made the vehicle for a great variety of exhortation and, it is to be feared, of not a little questionable doctrine. (For guidelines on the proper interpretation of parables, see Appendix B, "Reflections on Interpreting Parables.") The parable contains, however, at least these two main teachings about the mission of world evangelism: the seed of the kingdom is critical for any results; and the soil determines all else, granting the presence of otherwise normal growth requirements.

THE SEED OF THE KINGDOM OF GOD: CRITICAL ELEMENT FOR GROWTH

Though neither Matthew nor Mark mentioned seed as such in the opening sentence, they said, "Behold, a sower went forth to sow" (Matt. 13:3; Mark 4:3). Seeds are presupposed. But Luke was graphic in his emphasis on seed, to the point of awkwardness: *Exēlthen ho speirōn tou speirai ton sporon autou,* which might literally be translated, "The seeder went out to seed his seed" (Luke 8:5). If anything is emphatic about that sentence it is seed. It is a most un-Greek sentence but utterly like the type of Semitic idiom that Jesus may have employed when He first spoke the parable. (The Semitic idiom that characterizes the sentences provides an insight as to why Jesus' words are so variously reported in the gospels, though the essential meaning is preserved. Luke 8:5 is a literal rendering of the Aramaic original into awkward Greek while Matthew and Mark strive for more idiomatic Greek.) Four times the parable speaks of how the sower scattered seed. In the interpretation, Jesus spoke of the parable as "the parable of the sower" (*tou speirantos,* Matt. 13:18).

What the seed is is known exactly: "The seed is the word of God" (Luke 8:11); "the sower sows the word" (Mark 4:14). It is further specified to be "the word of the kingdom" (Matt. 13:19). The same is twice called the "good seed" (Matt. 13:24, 27) in a later parable of the series.

At the time Jesus conducted this "seminar of parables" His redemptive work was not yet complete. The specific proclamation of that work could not yet be spoken to the unprepared minds of apostles and disciples. "Nothing but the blood of Jesus" would have been rejected out of hand by our Lord's closest friends. "Being justified as a gift by His grace through the redemption which is in Christ Jesus" (Rom. 3:24) could be articulated only after the "precious blood" had been shed and redemption actually finished. Yet the message was to be a transforming gospel leading to heaven and to eternal life. It causes men to be saved. Looking back at the story of the rich young ruler (Matt. 19:16-29), a most enlightening incident, a question about how to have eternal life is seen also to be about life, treasure in heaven, the kingdom of heaven, the kingdom of God, and how to be saved.

Thirty-five years later Paul's understanding of the Word that was to be preached was no different as to essential content, even though articulated more fully on the basis of completed redemption. Near the end of his third journey in an address of great pathos to the elders of the church of Ephesus assembled at nearby Miletus he declared: "I went about preaching the kingdom" (Acts 20:25), testifying "solemnly of the gospel of the grace of God" (v. 27). It consisted of "testifying to both Jews and Greeks [i.e., Gentiles] of repentance toward God and faith in our Lord Jesus Christ" (v. 21). What Jesus spoke of in general terms, Paul spoke of in specifics.

There can be no mistake: the seed of the kingdom of God is the Christian gospel. It is the word of God. In largest frame of reference it is "the whole purpose of God"—the entire Christian revelation inerrant in every part. It leads to eternal life, to heaven and to God, to treasure in heaven and to being saved. What gospel preachers announce in their sermons, despite all their personal failures and rhetorical mistakes, is the word of God. They must be treated as divine messengers.

It has been seen that the seed, i.e., the message of Christ, is called the word of the kingdom and the word of God in the parables and their interpretation. Earlier in His ministry, Jesus spoke of His own message as "good tidings" (Luke 4:18, usually rendered "gospel"). It has also been noted how Paul spoke of His gospel as the kingdom message.

Many distinctions can be drawn, for although the word of the kingdom may indeed be the word of God, the gospel of grace, good tidings to the poor and may include both repentance and faith, these things are not precise equivalents. Jesus never preached anything except the word of God; but it was not all good tidings by any means, for not infrequently He pronounced the damnation of hell upon His unbelieving audience (see Matt. 23:13-36; esp. v. 33). In His conversations with Nicodemus (John 3) and the woman at the well of Sychar (John 4) it is evident that He sought to make both perfectly miserable in their sins before He gave clear announcement of the good news of salvation. Likewise Paul, who announced the gospel of Christ as the theme of Romans (1:16-17), devoted the first large section of his epistle to announcing the wrath of God—a preachment of law—before he got around to the details of the gracious gospel. Hence a true presentation of the word of the kingdom must always clearly make known man's sinful condition and God's holy wrath. The word of God must always be a "whole counsel," all of biblical revelation in balance, if the gospel is to be understood truly. It will inevitably be emasculated or sentimentalized if sinful men are not made to understand why they need the good news of forgiveness.

Furthermore, though the good news may be presented in many different ways and the emphases may vary, it must always declare what God has already done in redemption, rather than to suggest what the hearer or even Christ can do for those who will repent and believe. More of this will become apparent in the discussion of Matthew 13:10-17, between Jesus' giving of the first parable and His own interpretation of it (see chapter 9).

At this juncture, it will be helpful to refine the meaning of Paul's phrase, "the whole purpose of God" (Acts 20:27) and to reflect further on his insistence on it. It will also be helpful to look a bit further at the context: "Therefore I testify to you this day, that I am innocent of the blood of all men. For I did not shrink from declaring to you the whole purpose of God. Be on guard. . . . I know that after my departure savage wolves will come in among you, not sparing the flock; and from among your own selves men will arise, speaking perverse things, to draw away the disciples after them" (Acts 20:26-30).

Innocent of the blood of all men . . . declaring . . . the whole purpose of God"— what does that mean? One can hardly escape seeing a reference to one of God's messages to His servant Ezekiel. God had appointed Ezekiel "a watchman to the house of Israel" and instructed him: "Whenever you hear a word from My mouth, warn them from Me. When I say to the wicked, 'You shall surely die'; and you do not warn him or speak out to warn the wicked from his wicked way that he may live, that wicked man shall die in his iniquity, but his blood I will require at your hand (Ezek. 3:17-18).

Again, what does God mean, "his blood will I require"? And Paul, "innocent from the blood of all men"? A recent writer has said in relation to this question and this passage:

> Now Paul explained the basis upon which he felt totally confident that he was "innocent from the blood of all men" in the province of Asia where he had lived for three years. It was not his emotional involvement . . . nor was it his contribution to the partial and temporary relief of their deep social, economic, political and physical needs, obvious as those probably were. He states it with unmistakable clarity: "I am innocent from the blood of all men, for I did not shrink from declaring to you the whole purpose (counsel) of God."[1]

So Paul dared not mute the message or leave any of it out. God's purposes must be declared "whole" or the messenger will have blood guilt. This was the man who, viewing the idolatry of the Acropolis of Athens and a spot named for Mars, the god of war, gave a speech on the stupidity and blasphemy of idolatry. In doing so he announced that "God . . . now [declares] to men that all everywhere should repent" (Acts 17:30). He went on to speak of the coming judgment of all men by God. He also declared that in the resurrection of Christ, the Christian faith has a sure historical foundation, secure from attack by any man.

Paul's strategy was good. It was as good as the seed of the kingdom he planted in the soil of the province of Asia about Ephesus over the three years of his mission there. Not only did "all who lived in Asia [hear] the word of the Lord, both Jews and Greeks" (Acts 19:10) but great demonstrations of conversion took place in public. A huge pile of pagan books on magic, worth 50,000 pieces of silver, was burned at one time (v. 19). Even the makers of idols registered claim that their business was being destroyed (vv. 24-28). Ephesus and Asia were never the same again. No soft-sell tracts or booklets announcing only God's love and His humanitarian interest would have produced such thorough changes in men and communi-

---

1. John C. Whitcomb, *An Analysis of Evangelical Missions and Evangelism in the Light of the Great Commission*, p. 10.

ty. That God loves men must be preached, but it is hardly the doctrine with which to begin to declare the whole counsel of God. Paul no doubt said something of God's love, and surely he preached grace and faith, for these are the heart of the gospel, but his testimony shortly afterward was that "from the first day that I set foot in Asia [the Roman province], . . . I was with you the whole time, . . . I did not shrink from declaring to you anything that was profitable, and teaching you publicly and from house to house, solemnly testifying to both Jews and Greeks of repentance toward God and faith in our Lord Jesus Christ. . . . I do not consider my life of any account as dear to myself, in order that I may finish my course, and the ministry which I received from the Lord Jesus, to testify solemnly of the gospel of the grace of God. . . . I did not shrink from declaring to you the whole purpose of God" (Acts 20:18-27).

It is clear therefore that good seed is critical not only to a large harvest but to a genuine one. The city of Ephesus became one of the greatest centers of strength in all of Christian antiquity. If Paul had omitted to emphasize the doctrine of original sin, including innate depravity and inability to turn to God apart from the special grace of enlightenment by the Holy Spirit; if he had said little or nothing of the price to the Godhead of redemption; if Paul had demanded little by way of holy life in the new believers; then no such strong church as that described in Revelation 2:1-7 would ever have developed there.

In so far as men have been faithful to the whole purpose of God they have been successful in eternity's view. It must be acknowledged, however, that with the advent of scientific persuasion techniques joined to modern advertising, there has been a clear tendency on all levels of evangelism to trim away any aspects of the whole scriptural message that offend either some segment of the public or some segment of the cooperating evangelistic forces. Sometimes "Evangelism in Depth" has seemed to be shallow evangelism by shallow doctrine and shortened line of attack. Efforts are made to unite every group in a community or nation bearing the name Christian in a campaign of mass evangelism. This has sometimes obscured the whole purpose of God at the very points where the gospel must be utterly plain.

Legitimate efforts at distinctly evangelical, cooperative strategy in world evangelism have produced mixed results. This has been owing to the difficulty, on such a grand scale, of preserving the whole of the Word of God in the platform of proclamation. With every good intention and at considerable personal cost, Christians have convened assemblies on the mission of world evangelism—Berlin (1966), then Singapore, Minneapolis, and Lausanne (1974). Much good came from those meetings. Yet the best statement of doctrine from any of them (as of this writing), the widely published Lausanne Covenant, has been faulted for serious omissions. Anyone who has helped to form a common doctrinal platform for the various evangelical efforts knows something of the dimensions of the problem. Nevertheless, it must be admitted, even though very reluctantly and regretfully, that the result has been a semi-Pelagian de-emphasis on the total effects of Adamic sin on the ability of men to respond to the gospel. A leader in cooperative evangelism recently let himself be quoted to the effect that the Christ men reject is their caricature of the real Christ, that anyone would accept a presentation of the genuine. One wonders in such a case why Jesus' own generation crucified Him. Why do these cooperative statements always seem to omit any mention of the dangers from unbiblical teachings about divine healing, about tongues speaking as a necessary proof of baptism in the Holy Spirit, and especially about the mere application of water in baptism, apart from repentance, whether of adults or infants, conveying regeneration? Not long ago Francis Schaeffer, in defense of the purity of the seed of the kingdom, quoted Martin Luther as follows: "If I profess with the loudest voice and clearest exposition every portion of the truth of God except precisely that little point which the world and the devil are at that moment attacking, I am not confessing Christ, however boldly I may be professing Christ. Where the battle rages, there the loyalty of the soldier is proved, and to be steady on all the battlefield besides, is mere flight and disgrace if he flinches at that point."[2]

God's insistence that if evangelism is to produce results in the kingdom of God then the seed of the kingdom must be—to borrow from horticulture—certified seed cannot be escaped. Nothing more and nothing less fully merits the time and effort of God's people in planting. This is not to say that God has not overruled the doctrinal errors of some missionaries. There is a valid distinction between primary and secondary truths. Yet the fact remains that the Christian may be guilty of his "neighbor's blood" (to use the language of Ezekiel 3 and Acts 20) if less than the whole purpose of God is delivered. On the other hand faithfulness can hope that it will happen again as in Ephesus long ago: "So the word of the Lord was growing mightily and prevailing" (Acts 19:20).

An illustration may help to fix the point. Recently my wife asked me to assist her in preparing a garden. Among other things, I brought home five pounds of certified seed potatoes. When she had planted these there remained about six feet of a row for which there were no potatoes. So she cut and planted three or four potatoes from the grocery supplies she already had. Long after the good seed had produced tall plants, nothing had appeared in the last six feet of the row. Finally a plant or two appeared. Come autumn, there was a fine crop except that the "bad seed" had produced no fruit at all, only some dwarfed stems and leaves. They were not worth the effort. The lesson is plain for anyone to see. Good crops grow only from good seed.

THE SOIL: CRITICAL ELEMENT FOR FRUIT

Four kinds of hearers are specifically indicated in the Lord's great seminar on evangelism (Matt. 13). But as noted earlier a fifth is indicated even though indirectly. In each of the four the seed of the Word of God lodges in the heart of the hearer. As already seen, even the least responsive of the four, represented by the wayside ground, is positive to some degree. The hearer does not understand it, but the seed was "sown in his heart" (Matt. 13:19). The Bible presents the

2. Francis Schaeffer, *The God Who Is There*, p. 18.

heart of man as being the center of his being, not just emotion, mind, or will, but all of those together. The record of Jesus' ministry and of missionary evangelism of all ages since demonstrates that the large majority of listeners has made no response at all. They were simply too hardened in their sinful ways and the Spirit of God did not soften their hearts. The Lord referred to this multitude in the interlude between the first part of the seminar and the parable of Mark 4:26-29. The missionary evangelist must accept as fact that men rejected the Savior outright in His own time without giving Him any consideration at all. Evangelists can be no more persuasive than He, and they must not be discouraged by the general indifference of men.

There are more ways than one of applying the message about the four kinds of soil. No one responds the same way to the Word all the time—not even believers. Sometimes Christians are petulant and rebellious, sometimes overwhelmed by troubles, sometimes preoccupied with worldly cares or worldly ambitions. Sometimes, thankfully, they are in a frame of mind to listen to God and to do as He says. These four states in which true believers can be found do correspond with the parable. A case might also be made for referring the message of four soils to different whole audiences. Every minister becomes aware of how a whole audience may be uncomprehending (wayside), troubled (shallow ground), preoccupied and inattentive (thorny ground). He struggles with the sermon and leaves the pulpit greatly discouraged. At other times the whole audience is responsive and appears willing to obey God: "So the word of the Lord was growing mightily and prevailing" (Acts 19:20).

Yet the *original* intent of the parable is clearly related to the response that previously unevangelized and unbelieving men make to the gospel of God's gracious salvation.

THE HARD SOIL

"And as he sowed, some seeds fell beside the road, and the birds came and ate them up" (Matt. 13:4). "When anyone hears the word of the kingdom, and does not understand it, the evil one [Satan, (Mark 4:15)] comes [immediately, (Mark 4:15)] and snatches away what has been sown in his heart" (Matt. 13:19).

The fields of biblical Palestine were of many sorts but they tended to be small enclosed areas of a few acres at most. The footpaths from the village, where the peasant farmers lived, out to those patches of growing crops, wind in and out along the stone walls and sometimes lead directly across a larger field. Those paths, hardened by foot traffic, are referred to by Jesus in His mention of "the wayside."

"The evil one comes and snatches away what has been sown in his heart." Thus the Lord indicated that even while the gospel messenger is speaking and the lost man is trying to listen, Satan is busy, too. "If our gospel is veiled, it is veiled to those who are perishing, in whose case the god of this world has blinded the minds of the unbelieving, that they might not see the light of the gospel of the glory of Christ" (2 Cor. 4:3-4). Perhaps those words apply equally well to those in whose hearts the Word finds no lodging at all.

Satan employs various means for hardening hearers and "we are not ignorant of his schemes" (2 Cor. 2:11). Anything that deflects the hearers' attention away from the message—any prejudice, habit of thinking, or resentment—will do. Pastors often observe that they are (quite helplessly) the means Satan uses. The pastor's duty is to inform, to exhort, to warn, and to reprove; publicly, for the most part. More often than not some resent what is said. When people let resentment rise in their hearts against the messenger, because he has done his duty, then nothing that minister says in the future seems to be received into those hearts. Satan is indeed very full of wiles and devices.

A supernatural work of grace is always necessary to prepare men's hearts to actually accept the gospel. If hearts are not plowed by the Spirit, the well-springs of thought, emotion, and action are never tapped. Repeated exposures to the message will not make any change. As the story of how Jesus lost all His enormous Galilee following in a single hour (see John 6:22-71; especially v. 66) demonstrates, mass movements of apparent faith are usually just that: apparent. People respond favorably precisely because they do not understand. Upon being compelled to glimpse something of the offense of the cross by an outreach that truly evangelizes in depth they may quickly draw away. They never do really understand either their lost condition or the redemption in Christ that might save them from it.

Any missionary evangelism must come to terms with the fact of hardpacked, wayside soil, where any response at all will be very brief.

THE SHALLOW SOIL

"And others fell upon the rocky places, where they did not have much soil; and immediately they sprang up, because they had no depth of soil. But when the sun had risen, they were scorched; and because they had no root, they withered away" (Matt. 13:5-6). "And the one on whom seed was sown on the rocky places, this is the man who hears the word, and immediately receives it with joy; yet he has no firm root in himself, but is only temporary, and when affliction or persecution arises because of the word, immediately he falls away" (Matt. 13:20-21).

The feature of nature in Palestine giving point to this part of Jesus' lesson is the limestone bedrock that lies fairly close to the surface of all the highlands. The farmer contends with stones from the size of his teacup to the size of his head in plowing, but the rock that fools him is the bedrock just below the point of his plow. After the grain is up a few inches and the spring rains have slacked off, the plants turn yellow. The plant roots cannot penetrate the rock and the soil is too shallow to retain moisture, so the plant dies for lack of water. Because the soil is shallow, and thus warms early, it is common for the seed to sprout there earlier than on the deep soil. So the soil that shows the quickest response may be the first to fail.

Some types of persons who do not think or feel deeply may respond favorably and quickly to any sort of attractive propaganda. As buyers, they wind up with all sorts of useless junk and gadgets in the house. "Impulse buyers" they are called. They try (briefly, of course) every new idea or offered pleasure but quickly turn to another and another. They respond not only quickly but with initial enthusiasm.

As a personality type this is also discernable among genuine Christians. Among His apostles, Jesus must surely have seen Peter as being from that mold. He spoke with enthusiasm first and regretfully did his thinking later. He rushed into the open, empty tomb while the more contemplative John waited a moment. He jumped overboard at sight of the risen Christ on the shore while steadier hands than his brought in the bountiful catch of fish. As a personality trait in believers, it is not all bad, and among a congregation of stony-faced hearers the preacher sometimes searches his audience for the faces of a few of these people.

But as Jesus presented things here, something more decisive than a personality trait, such as a severe and willful act, must be in view. The hearer is more likely a searcher for entertainment than for truth. He has more resemblance to the bored-with-life Don Juan seeking new thrills than to the sincere shepherd David whose heart panted for the living God as the deer pants after the water brooks (see Psalm 42:1). The real thing *interests* these hearers but it does not *awaken* them. They remain dead—utterly inactive and insensitive—regarding eternal life and other spiritual things. Their hearing is of sounds and apparent meaning, not of the truth that sets the heart, the will, and the conscience free. "Such an one *is without root in his own inner being,* i.e., he is destitute of that faith (Eph. 3:16 f.) which, as a power in the heart, is fitted to maintain and foster the life that has momentarily awakened by means of the word" (ital. in orig.).[3] Those short-term disciples never awake to the kingdom of heaven and eternal life. They remain in the torporous sleep of eternal death.

THE SOIL CHOKED WITH THORNS

"And others fell among the thorns, and the thorns came up ["the thorns grew up with it," (Luke 8:7)] and choked them out" (Matt. 13:7). "And the one on whom seed was sown among the thorns, this is the man who hears the word, and the worry of the world, and the deceitfulness of riches [and "pleasures of this life," (Luke 8:14)] choke the word, and he becomes unfruitful" (Matt. 13:22).

Do not think of the seed as falling among thorn bushes but among the thorn-like thistles that in Palestine grow annually from seeds and can be waist-high as early as April. Think of the thistle seeds as being already in the soil or else as sprung up and unremoved. What happens is plain enough. The evil seed is initially stronger than the good seed and has a head start. So, although there is good deep soil, the evil seed takes greater advantage of it than does the good seed. The result is that the good seed does not mature to the point of fruit.

It would be pressing the details too far to insist on a special meaning for lack of fruit from the good seed planted in this soil rather than destruction of the seed and death of the plant as in the first two kinds of soil. It seems doubtful that Jesus

3. H. A. W. Meyer, *Critical and Exegetical Commentary on the New Testament,* 1:256.

meant to say some soil produces believers who endure but never bear fruit. Without being doctrinaire about it, it seems best to regard Jesus as saying that there is too much competition for interest in some peoples' lives for the gospel seed ever to lodge in their hearts long enough for genuine faith to come.

What are the things that preoccupy the minds of lost men or distract them to the extent that faith is never generated in them, with the result that they never enter the kingdom of God? The worry of the world, the deceitfulness of riches, and the pleasures of this life are some of them. None of these things is itself evil. Each of them is rooted in the good things of life from the God above who gives men "richly all things to enjoy" (1 Tim. 6:17, KJV). The worries of the world come from overconcern about such things as job, home, and family—things that God meant for blessings. The man so preoccupied with providing food, clothing, and shelter for his household that he never thinks long or deeply of eternal things is letting thorns choke the growth of the good seed. The deceitfulness of riches speaks of the wrong response of fallen man's heart in putting his faith in the bounty of earth's mountains, plains, fields, streams, and oceans. And what are the pleasures of life but the many good things of God's creation that may be evilly spoken of or employed?

The great lost multitudes of the nations are not lost primarily because they are debauched by drink, drugs, violence, and illicit sexual indulgence. They are too busy for that. The common grace of God restrains them from complete self-indulgence or the race would die out. Their sin is mainly that God is not in their thinking. It was so in Noah's time: "They were eating, they were drinking, they were marrying, they were being given in marriage" (Luke 17:27), and it was so in Lot's time: "They were eating, they were drinking, they were buying, they were selling, they were planting, they were building" (Luke 17:28). Yet the judgment of God did not wait. They were judged not merely because they were corrupt, but because their hearts were so full of the world's cares, riches, and pleasures that there was no room for God.

Jesus thus warned all missionaries who aspire to bring the seed of the kingdom to the nations that there are three responsive but unfruitful types of human-heart soil among those who pause long enough to listen. Each of the three will receive the word into "the heart." Yet they will be too hard of heart to yield to God; too shallow to stand up to trial; too distracted and preoccupied to follow very far as would-be disciples.

THE GOOD SOIL

"And others fell on the good soil, and yielded a crop, some a hundredfold, some sixty, and some thirty" (Matt. 13:8). "And the one on whom seed was sown on the good soil, this is the man who hears the word [and "accepts it," see Mark 4:20], and understands it; who indeed bears fruit, and brings forth, some a hundredfold, some sixty, some thirty" (Matt. 13:23). Luke is helpful in giving a more precise report of Jesus' words: "These are the ones who have heard the word in an honest and good heart, and hold it fast, and bear fruit with perseverance" (Luke 8:15).

It is well at this point not to draw too many conclusions from the parable as Jesus spoke it and interpreted it, as to why only certain ones among the multitudes respond fruitfully to the word of eternal life, although the explanation for the result of the sowing will be discussed later (see Matt. 13:11-17). For now, it is important to look at the characteristics of faith as seen in the Apostles and in Lydia and the Philippian Jailor.

1. *The true children of the kingdom truly hear the gospel message.* "And the one on whom seed was sown on the good soil, this is the man who hears the word . . ." (Matt. 13:23). But did they not all hear? The text seems to say they did (vv. 19-20, 22). Even the masses who never turned an eye toward the Lord also frequently heard. What is distinctive about hearing the gospel in the case of the good ground? The answer lies in the special meanings all men put on the words they use. As with many words, *akouō,* "to hear," in the Greek language of the New Testament, has a first, literal meaning; a second, refined meaning; and a third, extended, metaphorical meaning. In the case of the word *to hear* Luke said that when Paul had his transforming experience on the road to Damascus both he and his traveling companions "heard" the Lord's voice (Acts 9:4, 7). Yet later Luke reported Paul as saying he, himself, heard it with understanding while his companions did not (Acts 22:9, NASB; the KJV has the expression "heard not," but the meaning is the same as "did not understand" in the NASB). In the former case Luke was referring to the sound, which the travelers all heard in that they sensed certain sounds. In the latter Paul conveyed the thought that only he understood the message. Later, in reporting the incident again Paul made no mention of whether his companions heard or not. A third sense appears (together with the first) in Jesus' words about hearing the voice of God. He said that in the last great day "all who are in the tombs shall hear His voice" (John 5:28). They will comprehend and comply, for they must appear before God for judgment (v. 29). But earlier, referring to the dead in sin (but physically living) Jesus declared, "An hour is coming and now is, when the dead shall hear the voice of the Son of God" (John 5:25). He seems to have been thinking of all who stood before Him. They all heard the sounds and understood the linguistic sense of the words. But of those who heard in the sense of understanding (contrast Matt. 13:19) and of believing compliance Jesus added, "And those who hear shall live" (John 5:25). So what Matthew reported as "hear," Mark qualified by adding "and accept" (Mark 4:20). *To hear,* then, sometimes is equivalent to *to believe.*

2. *The children of the kingdom have "an honest and good heart" (Luke 8:15).* The soil is good because the heart is sound and true. Caution is needed in interpreting these words of the Lord. With admirable wisdom Henry Alford said:

> The fourth class must not be understood as . . . well-marked company, excluding all the rest. For the soil is *not good by nature:* the natural man receiveth not the things of the Spirit of God; but every predisposition to receive them is of God:—even the

shallow soil covering the rock, even the thorny soil, received the power to take in and vivify the seed, from God. So that divine grace is the enabling, vivifying, cleansing power throughout: and these sown on the good land are no naturally good, amiable, or pure class, but those prepared by divine grace—receptive, by granted receptive power.[4]

3. The believing hearers understand the message. Matthew said this plainly. The three hearers deficient in saving faith did not have a lack of knowledge of the meaning of the gospel seed, for the seed had some temporary lodging in the hearts of each. But their understanding was not adequate. In the case of the wayside hearers, deep, intellectual perception was prevented by hardness. Their hearing was inexact and dull by reason of the hardness of undisturbed carnality. The problem with the hearing and understanding of the second type of hearer was shallowness. They accepted initial impressions, drew unfounded conclusions, and took action too soon. The third group had an understanding clouded by lack of the single eye; their attention was divided.

True faith involving clear understanding lays great weight on the intellectual side of the Christian gospel. It must penetrate the mind and appeal to the rational faculties. The gospel is not a rationalization, but it cannot be and is not irrational. That explains why, wherever Christianity has long endured, it has developed a decent apologetic. Why would Paul otherwise have spent three months "reasoning and persuading them about the kingdom of God" (Acts 19:8) or two years thereafter "reasoning daily in the school of Tyrannus" (Acts 19:9) during his evangelistic mission at Ephesus (see Acts 19:8-18)? The same may be asked about his two years at Rome. Though he was under house arrest, he continued expounding and testifying so as "to persuade them concerning Jesus, from both the Law of Moses and from the Prophets. . . . preaching the kingdom of God" (Acts 28:23, 31). A sound evangelism will appeal to the emotions but dare not do so directly. It is easy to overdo the aesthetic, the sentimental, and the titillating in evangelism. Some sincere men have overdone the appeal for decision by means of "hidden persuaders" directed at men's emotions and intended expressly to bypass the will. Ultimately the one whose will is not reached decisively via the intellect will fall away. He "is only temporary" (Matt. 13:21) and when persecution or the appeals of this life press in, he "falls away" (v. 21) and "becomes unfruitful" (v. 22).

It has been noticed that the first type of hearer has more the faults of careless, inattentive childhood; the second, of ardent, shallow youth; the third, of worldly, self-seeking age. These divisions are general and approximate. The borders of each merge into the next. They do not exclude one another and one may move forward to good ground condition or backward to thorny, shallow, or hard soil, or even to no soil at all. The gospel usually is preached more than once to the same persons. The Spirit, on the one hand, continues to work in men's hearts while, on the other hand, men can and do harden their hearts.

Jesus' own words compel people to be careful how they hear. Only those who

---

4. Henry Alford, *The New Testament for English Readers,* p. 98.

hear with sufficient attention for their minds to be captured by the message and are thus led to understand it will ever call upon God to be saved. "He who has ears, let him hear" (Matt. 13:9). Let them then call upon God, for "WHOEVER WILL CALL UPON THE NAME OF THE LORD WILL BE SAVED" (Rom. 10:13).

> Seek the LORD while He may be found;
> Call upon Him while He is near.
> Let the wicked forsake his way,
> And the unrighteous man his thoughts;
> And let him return to the LORD,
> And He will have compassion on him;
> And to our God,
> For He will abundantly pardon.
>
> (Isaiah 55:6-7)

Finally, Jesus' interpretation of the four soils suggests an answer to a question that an anonymous person asked of Jesus during the last months of His ministry: "Lord, are there just a few who are being saved?" (Luke 13:23). While the question—which Jesus did not answer directly—must be left to God for some time yet, the redeemed featured in the Revelation promise that even a relatively "small" number of true believers will one day equal innumerable multitudes.

9

Jesus' Reason for Speaking Parables

(Matt. 13:10-17)

This section must be regarded as being a delayed introduction to
Jesus' new use of parables. It is incidental that Jesus spoke the words after stating
the first parable (the four soils) but before explaining it. One might think of Him
as speaking loudly from the boat (Matt. 13:2) when giving the parable but in
subdued tones to the disciples about Him in the boat (Luke 8:9) when He spoke
the words of interpretation. On the other hand, one gains the impression from
Mark 4:10-20 and Matthew 13:10 that the interpretation was set forth at a later
time.

Those interpretive sayings of Jesus answered some of the disciples' questions,
yet, at the same time they introduced new truths and raised more questions.
Those verses relate to the Christian mission of world evangelism as it was then
laid before the scarcely comprehending minds of Jesus' immediate disciples, as
will be noted.

First, observe that Jesus was carrying on a two-fold program of communication. On the one hand, He was presenting to the multitudes the word of God, the
message of the kingdom, and Himself as the fulfillment of the Law and the
Prophets. That would, as He already knew, lead to His rejection and death. On the
other hand, He was communicating truth of a higher sort to the understanding of
the men who were to be founding apostles of His church, teaching them the form
of the kingdom on earth between His ascension and second advent. The parable
in a unique way served as a means of doing both. Those interesting stories were
proclaimed in public. When necessary, He gave further explanation to His close
disciples in private. In doing this Jesus set an example for Christian proclamation
and instruction through the ages. There must always be two levels, one addressed to the "natural man" in language to capture his attention and to impart to
him what little he can catch of eternal truth as the Spirit moves. Meanwhile, on a
much deeper level, the wise Christian teacher will be instructing disciples in
whatever the biblical revelation has to tell them.

This is the thrust of Jesus' answer to the disciples' question, "Why do You
speak to them [the multitudes] in parables?" (Matt. 13:10). The question seems to

imply that a Jewish rabbi would normally speak parables to his disciples rather than to the general public. This seems to have been normal among the Jews in later antiquity though little is known of the situation in Jesus' time. Strack and Billerbeck say, "The parable became one of the favorite means of representing [truth] in the Palestinian schools [of the rabbis]; it was very rare however among the [schools of] Babylon. As employed by the learned—from the pre-Christian time we meet only a parable of Hillel (about 20 B.C.). . . . In the Mishnaic period there was one, Rabbi Meir (about A.D. 150), who gave the parable-sayings fame."[1]

Further, the New Testament concept of mystery is first introduced here. The English word, derived from the Greek *mustērion,* usually refers to something of itself essentially unknown. Sometimes it can be thought of as unknowable also. The biblical sense is similar, but in an important way dissimilar. Biblical mysteries are truths of a religious and spiritual sort, known to God from eternity, but known by men simply and exclusively because God has revealed them. Paul used the word in that sense in Romans 16:25-26 and Ephesians 3:3. Since a supernatural opening of the mind is necessary to understand some of these things, the New Testament mystery often takes on the added sense of a truth explained only to initiates. Pagan Greece was familiar with this sense also. The idea without the word appears in Paul's remarks about inner workings of the Corinthian assembly (1 Cor. 5:12-13).

That only God can explain spiritual realities to men and then only to the spiritually ready is a truth proclaimed by biblical poets, prophets, and apostles everywhere. Those parables can be understood as occasions when Jesus, in private, would explain to intimate, initiated followers the truth that had to be announced to the multitudes but that they could not fully understand, with or without explanation.

As verses 12 and 13 of Matthew 13 make certain, Jesus' special use of parables had a double force. Both revealing and concealing were innate in the parable. The one who had the Spirit of God in his heart ("whoever has") heard with the ear and with the heart understood as well. More was given to him. That was the main purpose of the parable. Thereby the church became possessor of the Lord's own insights as to the work of evangelism, insights that would otherwise never have been had. But those divine matters are only for the prepared heart. The one who does not have the Spirit of God is not necessarily harmed by these revelations. True, if he turns away such crumbs of truth as he does catch, his heart will be further hardened. It is also a fact, though, that repeated exposures to the Word of God have been required for many before the seed penetrated the heart deeply enough to produce a saving response. The fearful fact that the truth of God becomes a form of judgment for the persistently impenitent and unbelieving may not be avoided. Paul spoke vividly of these antipodean effects of divine truth. Speaking of how he had manifested something of the knowledge of God "in every

---

1. Hermann L. Strack and Paul Billerbeck, *Kommentar zum Neuen Testamentum aus Talmud und Midrasch,* 1:654-55.

place," he wrote: "For we are a fragrance of Christ to God among those who are being saved and among those who are perishing; to the one an aroma from death to death, to the other an aroma from life to life" (2 Cor. 2:14-16).

The truth held in unrighteousness too long becomes the instrument of judgment by which God gives men up. The Lord's words were echoed again when on the last day of His public ministry He spoke, in another parable, of the "servant" who produced no fruit: " 'Therefore take away the talents from him, and give it to the one who has ten talents.' For to everyone who has [knowledge with faith and obedience] shall more be given, and he shall have an abundance; but from the one who does not have [faith, obedience, or fruit], even what he does have shall be taken away. And cast out the worthless slave into the outer darkness; in that place there shall be weeping and gnashing of teeth" (Matt. 25:28-30).

Isaiah's prophecy quoted by Jesus (Matt. 13:14-15; cf. Isa. 6:9-10) introduces the Christian missionary to the most dreadful obstacle to the fruitfulness of the seed, even while it helps explain why Jesus resorted to instruction by parables at all. It is the dread fact of inborn sin. That doctrine, so clearly announced by several of the Old Testament prophets and applied in a thorough way by Paul (Rom. 1:18—3:23; Rom. 5; 1 Cor. 2:14; Eph. 2:1-3; 4:17-20), was never fully appreciated by ancient Judaism, nor has it been so appreciated by modern Judaism. It should be clear to all readers of the New Testament that even during the time of Christ Judaism was not the biblical faith of the Hebrew Scriptures. It was actually a Pharisaic corruption of the Scriptures. Modern Judaism is even less the religion of the Hebrew Bible. Jewish religion today finds scarcely any defect in human personality and behavior traceable to Adamic sin. Its views are essentially identical with the Christian heresy known as Pelagianism.

Many failures of evangelistic effort—especially the quick decline from evangelistic zeal, through mere social activism, to dead, formal religion—are traceable to concessions to this erroneous denial of the effects of original sin. Charles G. Finney, for example, made it plain enough in his *Revival Lectures* that evangelistic success is as much a sure-fire thing as producing a crop of wheat under favorable conditions of soil, seed, temperature, and moisture. Though Finney believed in prayer and awakening grace he failed to discern as clearly as he should the utter deadness of human mind, heart, and will regarding things of the Spirit of God apart from awakening grace. The Oberlin theology he advocated maintained its spiritual force therefore scarcely beyond the lifetime of its godly founder. It is to be hoped that if Christ's person and claims are presented clearly enough men will certainly respond favorably. Yet, quite to the contrary, the people of Palestine rejected the Lord when He was the preacher. So this hope is not based on Scripture. John, in commenting on the wretched unbelief of Jesus' contemporary countrymen, quoted those same words of Isaiah to explain it. At the very end of His public efforts John said, "These things Jesus spoke, and He departed and hid Himself from them. But though He had performed so many signs before them, yet they were not believing in Him; that the word of Isaiah the prophet might be fulfilled" (John 12:36-38). Then John quoted Isaiah 53:1 followed by the same Isaiah 6:10 Jesus employed in explaining His use of parables.

The curse of death that fell on the race through Adam was indeed a curse and is removed only when the Word enters into the heart by supernatural, Holy Spirit power to remove the veil that has universally settled over the hearts of men. Nothing can remove that curse except the grace of God. Let Paul tell it and again quote Isaiah's dictum (Rom. 11:6-8; cf. vv. 9-10):

> There has also come to be at the present time a remnant according to God's gracious choice. But if it is by grace, it is no longer on the basis of works, otherwise grace is no longer grace. What then? That which Israel is seeking for, it has not obtained, but those who were chosen obtained it, and the rest were hardened; just as it is written [Deut. 29:4; Isa. 29:10; see also Isa. 6:10],
>> GOD GAVE THEM A SPIRIT OF STUPOR,
>> EYES TO SEE NOT AND EARS TO HEAR NOT,
>> DOWN TO THIS VERY DAY.

Near the close of his third journey, Paul found occasion to quote Isaiah 6:9-10 again to explain why after carefully "explaining to them . . . the kingdom of God, and trying to persuade them [Jews at Rome] concerning Jesus, from both the Law of Moses and from the Prophets. . . . some were being persuaded, . . . but others would not believe" (Acts 28:23-24, cf. 25-27).

Jesus then pronounced the disciples' eyes and ears blessed, being privileged by grace to see and hear and understand from Him the very words and deeds that Old Testament prophets and saints had understood only by way of promise (Matt. 13:16-17; cf. 18-23).

Peter was among those who heard Jesus that day and he must have been much impressed, for the thought of Matthew 13:16-17 appears thirty or so years later in Peter's first epistle (1 Pet. 1:9-12). Also, in his second epistle, Peter's theologically oriented "exordium" at the opening (1:1-4) declared that his readers "have received [from God, of course] a faith of the same kind as ours," that their need was for more "grace" from God, that what they had by way of equipment for "life and godliness" had been by divine power "granted to us" and that the now fulfilled promises [God's Son and His Spirit] had also been "granted" (2 Pet. 1:1-4).

The missionary evangelist therefore must keep steadily before his mind that there is not sufficient rhetorical power on earth to persuade men to enter God's kingdom of grace and love. Even with the aid of marvelous miracles of power and meaning (referred to in the New Testament by the words "work" [ergon], "power" [dunamis], "wonder" [thaumazō], and "sign" [semeion]), the Son of God Himself did not persuade the Jews of old to be His loyal disciples. Faced with the enormous popularity that the miracle of feeding the five thousand had generated, He lost His entire audience (except the apostolic circle, and Judas should have left) in one address at Capernaum (see John 6:1-71; esp. vv. 66-67). It can all be traced to human objections to the doctrine of divine election and calling that were brought to a peak of clarity and emphasis that day. The multitudes who had been fed the miraculous bread and fishes on the east of Lake Genessaret frantically searched for Him and found Him at Capernaum back on the west side. Then He plied their ears and consciences on the subject of salvation by grace alone. "Do not work for the food which perishes, but for the food which endures to eternal life, which the Son of Man shall give to you" (John 6:27), He said. God the Father gives the true bread (John 6:33). Then Jesus made Himself plain: "But I said to you, that you have seen Me, and yet do not believe. All that the Father gives Me shall come to Me" (John 6:36-37), and "of all that He has given Me I lose nothing" (John 6:39), for "no one can come to Me, unless the Father who sent Me draws him. . . . It is written in the prophets, 'AND THEY SHALL ALL BE TAUGHT OF GOD' (John 6:44-45; see Isa. 54:13). Even many of the disciples thought these words "a difficult statement" (John 6:60) and Jesus knew that His hearers had been offended by them—just as men still are today. So, still driving hard on His theme that human words and deeds cannot accomplish spiritual conversion, Jesus added, "It is the Spirit who gives life; the flesh [human words and deeds, even miracles] profits nothing" (John 6:36). It is fitting that He should close with the statement: "For this reason I have said to you, that no one can come to Me, unless it has been granted him from the Father" (6:65); at that the few remaining disciples, except the twelve, simply walked out and did not come back (6:66-71).

Those verses from chapter 6 form part of the background for John's summary of the close of Jesus' public ministry found in John 12.

10

The Christian's Duty of Propagating the Good News

(Mark 4:21-25)

From the time of the first prophet of God, men have always disliked hearing that they lack natural spiritual capacity (not intellectual capacity) to understand the Word and to believe it for salvation. This was evident even in Jesus' time, as has just been seen. The chief objections may be stated as follows: 1) It doesn't seem fair (Rom. 9:14); and 2) God can't find fault with us then (Rom. 9:19). Paul wiped the objections all away as unworthy of rational answer because of essential unbelief toward God (Rom. 9:14-18).

In the section of Jesus' discourse under discussion, the Lord employed a different approach. He anticipated men's objections to His doctrine of divine grace by asserting what their duties are. He used a kind of argument from analogy, but in the final analysis He simply commanded. These anticipations of men's objection come at precisely the same place in both Mark and Luke. These proverbs and sayings appear in Matthew as well, though at another point in the narrative, probably because Jesus, like any good preacher, used the same striking anecdotes, proverbs, and sayings in many sermons. This should not be surprising (see Matthew 5:15; 7:2; 10:26; 11:15; 13:12).

The situation contemplated in the aphorisms of Mark 4:21 was that of a home of the common people. It was a single large room in which the furnishings were few. There was a bed—perhaps consisting of blankets or quilts, pillows, and mats—that was rolled against a wall during the day. There were one or more wooden bins containing somewhat less than an English peck. There was a lamp or two, each with a simple lampstand of wood or pottery. The lamps were simple, tiny pots for oil with a notch or spout for the wick. There might also be a low stool (2 Kings 4:10).

The sense of what He said was pretty plain—as proverbial sayings usually are. In essence He said: "I have been speaking parables to you. Though they may be obscure to the multitudes, they have been explained to you. You will hear more of them and you are going to gain greater proficiency in interpreting them [cf. Matt. 13:51-52]. You are to regard yourselves not merely as depositories of truths but as dispensaries of them also. You are not to be grudging or lazy about this. This seed of the kingdom is intended for worldwide distribution. It is to shine to all in the room—the whole world. 'Let your light shine before men' [Matt. 5:16]. Let them see your good works too, for men dull toward divine truth will nevertheless be able to judge correctly the character of the messengers of truth and some, at least, will be drawn to hear more."

For a more modern paraphrase: "The things told you in the shelter of the believer's assembly—including those parables—were intended to be public truth. It has been given you by those who taught it to you so that you in turn may pass it on. It must be given away! And like the cruse of oil in Elijah's case, your source will never run dry. You cannot 'share your faith' but you can share the truth that your faith embraces and do so indefinitely. That is why I gave it to you!"

Jesus presumed His disciples would do what He said and thus Mark 4:23 ("if any man has ears to hear, let him hear") can be interpreted as addressed to their hearers, not His: "If you have the natural capacity to hear these servants of mine (ears in working order) then hear with attention and interest for, 'faith comes from hearing, and hearing by the word of Christ' " (Rom. 10:17). If, on the other hand, Jesus was thinking of the disciples, then He was admonishing them to attend carefully to what He was presently saying so that in due season they could make known the gospel of God's grace in a competent way.

The words of Mark 4:24 (about measuring out to others and receiving proportional measure back) provide a new and striking application of what He had uttered previously (Matt. 6:33; 7:2; Luke 6:38; cf. 12:31; 19:26). The disciple must look attentively at what is set before him by the Word, not only as to what it says and means but as to the duties imposed by it. If he assesses it accurately and disseminates its message freely he will receive a corresponding reward; indeed, much more than that shall be given. He who, for the sake of the Lord and the gospel, gives up kindred and friends shall reap a hundredfold and, in the age to come, everlasting life.

11
Parable on the Need for Missionary Patience

(Mark 4:26-29)

The parable found in Mark 4:26-29 teaches about successful missionary evangelism and presents a spiritual lesson. It seems to be intended both to encourage the messengers of the kingdom and to raise a hand of warning. The "man" scattering seed indicates any human agency—not Jesus personally nor the apostles, even though they were the first of Jesus' messengers—any sowing of the seed of the Word of God. "Upon the soil" implies prepared ground. Thus the interest of this section is only in the good soil of the previous parable, for there will be harvest of fruit. Something more of the operative process can be learned when evangelism is truly successful. There is nothing for the farmer to do for a good while after he has planted seed grain in his field. Soil, moisture, sunshine, and seed act and react upon one another. They must be left alone to act and react normally. The farmer must be patient at this stage. Almost anything he does out of anxiety or curiosity to disturb the soil or move the seed will do great harm to the plant. He may be as busy as he likes—about other things, perhaps other parts of the farm. The earth will produce fruit of herself. The Greek word is *automatē*, from which comes *automatic*. In doing evangelism the soil preparation comes before sowing, not afterward. The next parable indicates that after the true plant of God is growing, one must be careful even in pulling weeds.

An agency entirely invisible and inexplicable causes seed to germinate, shoot up a blade, grow to maturity, and produce fruit. The Author of this process is quite as much the quickening agent in evangelism as He is in nature. The power is no less mysterious in the one case than in the other.

Nothing in nature is more interesting to men than this annual process—the worship and festival year of ancient Israel was built around it—nor is anything more important. When unfavorable weather interrupts the process of sowing seed, maturing grain, and joyful harvest, everyone is deprived and saddened. But it is all up to God! God gives the increase, though a Paul may plant and occasionally some Apollos may artificially supply water!

The main spiritual lesson is patience. The preparation of the soil, care to sow not only good seed but at the right time and in proper amount, appropriate methods of harvesting, and like matters are important in farming, but not to the lesson of this parable.

The discouraged or impatient missionary needs to pick up the hands that hang down and confirm the feeble knees. The work he is in takes lots of time—as long as he lives. Copious amounts of seed must be rightly distributed. The work must be done and then there is waiting. That is a favorite theme in the book of James, whose words are peculiarly applicable: "Be patient, therefore, brethren, until the coming of the Lord. Behold, the farmer waits for the precious produce of the soil, being patient about it, until it gets the early and late rains. You too be patient; strengthen your hearts, for the coming of the Lord is at hand" (James 5:7-8).

That truth is a great benefit to any faithful pastor, teacher, or parent who is inclined toward undue anxiety. After the seed of the Word has been planted, one may pray, but then he should relax. He should do something else. The farmer may mend fences or take some days off for fishing while the wheat grows, or maybe fix his wife's clothesline! The preacher (or other planter of seed) may need to catch up on reading. His wife and children may need some long neglected attention. Perhaps the busy man has neglected to visit his mother or to write his brother a letter. God wants all of those things done, but they cannot be accomplished by impatient, overly conscientious assistants "helping God" vitalize and grow His own seed to maturity.

To summarize the lessons: There are only two things that can be done to gain a harvest of souls of men. They are to sow seed and be patient. The parable does not even mention soil preparation. Does this not suggest that preparation of men's hearts is also largely a matter of providence? What is sometimes thought to be the preparing of hearts (i.e., the soil), if done impatiently or anxiously, may turn out to be stirring the soil without really tilling it. Does violation of this truth account, in small part at least, for the abated force of some greatly successful missionary movements of the past? Two centuries ago Methodism was in first place among the evangelical missionary forces in the world and 125 years ago the force was already waning. Here is what a great evangelical preacher, pastor, and scholar said about the Methodism of his day in connection with this parable. Without intending to slander any man or movement, that man's words are worth pondering: "The seed sown in the heart is in its growth dependent on other causes then mere human anxiety and watchfulness:—on a mysterious power implanted by God in the seed and soil combined, the working of which is hidden from human eye. No trouble of ours can accelerate the growth, or shorten the stages through which each seed must pass. It is the mistake of modern Methodism, for instance [i.e., of 125 years ago], to be always working at the seed, *taking it up to see whether it is growing,* instead of leaving it to God's own good time, and meanwhile diligently doing God's work elsewhere."[1]

A painful experience illustrates the importance of leaving the seed of the Word for God to quicken the hearts of men who have given their ears to hear. I was asked to add a non-professional evening Bible course to my seminary teaching

1. Henry Alford, *The New Testament for English Readers,* p. 232.

schedule. Among the forty or so persons who attended each week was a handsome young lawyer from a nearby community. Recent disappointments in his life had driven him to seek help from God. He sometimes asked questions during class and after class stopped by my desk to discuss matters of Scripture teaching. The man was a seeker, not yet a believer but seemingly on the way to becoming one. There was also a very enthusiastic but naive regular seminary student in the course. He had been to a school of instant evangelism and thought he knew how to sow seed, germinate it, and reap all in one brief session. After one of the classes midway through the semester I saw him moving toward the specimen sinner, Bible and booklet of "laws" in hand. I saw the gleam in his unknowing eye and suspected what his intentions were even though I was powerless to interfere. I couldn't bear to witness the dangerous and almost certainly fruitless confrontation. Sadly, the lawyer did not return to the later sessions of the course and I never have heard from him again. It had been clearly wrong to scratch the soil and dig up the seed. "The soil produces crops by itself" (Mark 4:28). She does it *automatē* (automatically) or not at all. "God . . . giveth the increase" (1 Cor. 3:7, KJV).

Other valid lessons have been drawn from the parable of patience that have other emphases than missionary evangelism. It has been pointed out that the modern world does not lack zealots who want to do God's work for Him. Some are the youthful advocates of violence who wish to remake the world in the image of Marxian equality. Others are going to create Utopia by technical (modern farming in the "third world"), or social (education for everybody), or medical means. "What they all forget is that the creation of such a new order depends always on dealing with that intractable thing the Bible calls 'sin' and on changing men's natures. But, as God alone can create a seed and make it grow, only God can deal with 'the corruption of man's heart' and make new men."[2] The same author correctly thinks the parable speaks primarily to religious people with solicitude toward God, reassuring them that God's new order—the Kingdom—is operating in history—even if men cannot explain how it works.[3] They can safely trust in God's process and power even if they cannot trust any alleged inevitable "progress" or "evolution." Truth may be on the scaffold,

> Yet that scaffold sways the future, and, behind the dim unknown,
> Standeth God within the shadow, keeping watch above his own.[4]

James Russell Lowell's poem has encouraged and thrilled this author for more than forty years. Reassurance, however, does not seem to be the main thrust of the parable that emphasizes the intrinsic power of the Word itself, the right seed, planted in prepared soil. The parable primarily exalts the power of the gospel. This is how patience in evangelism is inculcated.

---

2. A. M. Hunter, *The Parables Then and Now,* p. 41.
3. Ibid.
4. James Russell Lowell, "The Present Crisis," lines 39-40.

12

Parable on Evil Within the Church

(Matt. 13:24-30, 36-43)

Though the scene of action in this parable is a wheat field, as in the first two of the eight, the theme is not the wheat *and* the tares, but the tares. The disciples so reacted to it and they were right: "Explain to us the parable of the tares of the field" (Matt. 13:36). Even before they received an answer from Jesus they must have known that the tares of "bastard wheat," as certain ancients called it, stood for evil in the kingdom. With their still unreformed and essentially carnal ideas, derived from Jewish teaching on that subject, they were puzzled. For reflective people of all places and ages the presence of evil in a God-ordered universe is an apparent inconsistency; especially in God's realm, the professing church, the subject of all the eight parables.

The Lord showed what He, Himself, is going to do with those who falsely profess His name and in that light shows believers what they are not to do. The force of the story, as will be seen, is essentially negative. Force is not to be used in exterminating false profession from the fellowship of professed believers. Readers of the gospels will recall that several months later two of His inner circle showed themselves still uncomprehending of the pacific manner of discipline in the present epoch of God's kingdom of grace. When a Samaritan village refused them hospitality, James and John were quite ready to call down fire from heaven to destroy the village, and Jesus had to rebuke them (Luke 9:51-56).

> The Parable of the Tares supplies an explanation of Christendom as it has existed all through these nineteen centuries, and as it is today; a mixed state of affairs; the true and the false side by side. . . . The "field" represents the religious world, in which the wheat and the tares "grow together." This mixed state of affairs has resulted from the work of the enemy at the beginning of this dispensation, the effects of which are with us till this day.[1]

Thus one author sees the interpretation in terms of the total history of the present age. He is essentially correct, even though some other elements of the

1. A. W. Pink, *The Prophetic Parables of Matthew 13*, p. 27.

future must be in the parable also. Another school of thought sees the parable as a reference to the whole history of the world from beginning to end. Since "the harvest" is said by Jesus to be the end of the world, the planting of wheat and tares must have been at the beginning of it, especially since Genesis 3 tells how the enemy, that is, the devil, planted his seed immediately after God planted His. But "the harvest is the end of the age *[sunteleia aiōnos]*" (Matt. 13:39), presumably the present age inaugurated by the first advent of Christ, and to be consummated by His second advent.

The spiteful way the farmer's enemy sowed a noxious weed in his field under cover of darkness is a practice readily understood in the light of what is known of human nature, and there are many confirmed cases of such misdeeds. It is especially likely to happen where fields are small and where the farmers live close together in their villages. Every writer seems to have been impressed by Alford's anecdote: "The practice is not unknown even in England at present. Since the publication of my Greek Testament, a field belonging to myself, at Gaddesby in Leistershire, was maliciously sown with charlock [sinapis arvensis] over the wheat. An action at law was brought by the tenant and heavy damages obtained against the offender" (brackets in orig.).[2]

The impulse of the servants to "do something *now*" is entirely human and is the way people react to a dangerous situation. Yet the farmer's wisdom lay in what he knew both of the weeds and his servants. To allow them to attack the weeds in time of growing would have resulted in destruction of all the crop, the good being trampled or uprooted by the violence of the servants' undiscerning actions. As a personal example, as a child I was never able to recognize the harmful "wild oats" growing with the true oats with precision enough to remove the wild during growing season, even though I had many times seen my father cut or pull out a clump of the wild oats. To this day I cannot see the difference. The problem lay in the incompetence of the servants, not in the impossibility of the situation.

The farmer preferred to wait, knowing that his "reapers" (Matt. 13:30) were a different crew from the regular farm hands. They were specialists. That is not the usual case; normally it is not possible to gather out "first the tares" even in harvest time. A mixed crop of the sort described is usually a total loss. A good farmer might wisely cut it all down while still green to prevent the ruin of the field for future seasons. So, while the story is of a usual growing season at the beginning, the rest is not. It has a very unusual ending!

Jesus figuratively gathered the whole age into one annual season of seedtime, growth, and harvest. The age is the time that lies between the advents. It relates to the sphere of Christian profession during that time. After the Lord completed the provision of redemption and ascended to heaven He sent the Spirit. Through Him the church (universal) was inaugurated. Later, local churches grew all around the world. But the parable is not on the subject of church order, even though there may be some principles applicable from it. The kingdom of heaven arrived in the person of the King. Already during His life on earth there were "the

2. Henry Alford, *The New Testament for English Readers,* pp. 98-99.

violent" who would rush into it "by force" (Matt. 11:12), and there were many who would maintain it by brute force. It was with reference to the sphere of professed allegiance to Christ that Jesus spoke. The field is "the world" (13:38), to be sure, but only because the seed is there. The seed of the Word, as in the first and second parables, had produced true believing professors of Christ's name. They are "the sons of the kingdom" (v. 38), and it is they who, together with Satan's people, the tares, are the focal point of the parable.

The New Testament itself gives a rudimentary report of how the mixed planting of tares among the wheat got its start in this age. The twelve original apostles and later disciples were indeed sent out by Christ even during His lifetime, with instructions also applicable to missionaries throughout the rest of the age (Matt. 10:5-42). He said, "Behold I send you out as sheep in the midst of wolves; therefore be shrewd as serpents, and innocent as doves" (Matt. 10:16). The devil sent out into their world of profession and ministry his own sons (seed) also. Judas the traitor, for example, was partner to zealous Simon when the twelve first went out (Matt. 10:4). It would be interesting to hear Simon's report of how Judas operated as one of the devil's own seed. Jesus called Judas "a devil" (John 6:70) and used the same Greek word, *diabolos,* here in Matt. 13:39: "The enemy who sowed them is the devil." Early in apostolic history Satan's seed was noticed and identified. Ananias and Sapphira brought their perverted fruit to the same Christian assembly attended by apostles (Acts 4:32—5:4). Paul met one of them, Elymas by name, on his first reported missionary journey and even called him "you son of the devil" (Acts 13:10).

In the case of Judas, the offender soon eliminated himself by suicide. Peter's apostolic power took Ananias and Sapphira out of the way. Paul turned Elymas into an occasion for "church growth." But these are exceptional cases. The local congregation is commanded to judge and discipline members (1 Cor. 5) who would be "spots in [the] feasts of charity" (Jude 12, KJV) and to refuse fellowship with heretics (2 John 7-11). But in the field of "the world" (the sphere of Christian profession or the kingdom of God in the special sense of these parables) no coercive action is to be taken against unbelievers. As already noted, James and John once suggested that insults against them and their Master should be avenged. A Samaritan village had refused hospitality to their company, "And when His disciples James and John saw this, they said 'Lord, do you want us to command fire to come down from heaven and consume them?' But He turned and rebuked them" (Luke 9:54-55). Certain manuscripts add: "and said, You do not know what kind of spirit you are of; for the Son of Man did not come to destroy men's lives, but to save them" (Luke 9:55-56).

There is just such a mixed planting in every age and in every place where the message of the kingdom is announced. The conflict may always be assumed to be going on even when, perhaps especially when, the conflict is not yet sensed. The parable seems to see the two kinds of seeds (persons) as being dispersed throughout Christendom rather than throughout organized churches. There may be entire congregations of regenerate members here and there.

The time when the enemy did his surreptitious sowing appears to be part of the lesson, so obviously Jesus did not deem it necessary to comment on it. It was "while men were sleeping [that] his enemy came and sowed tares also among the wheat, and went away" (Matt. 13:25). Stealth coupled with dishonesty is part of Satan's regular procedure. Though the sons of the kingdom also sometimes operate in that way, they always do so out of character. No blame is implied for lack of watchfulness on the part of the farmer. The condition is inevitable. "The mystery of lawlessness [analogous to "the mystery of Christ"] is already at work" (2 Thess. 2:7) writes Paul, and John observed that "even now many antichrists have arisen" (1 John 2:18). Jude indicates very specifically, "For certain persons have crept in unnoticed, those who were long beforehand marked out for this condemnation, ungodly persons who turn the grace of our God into licentiousness and deny our only Master and Lord, Jesus Christ" (Jude 4). Even the Pergamum church, declared by Jesus to be faithful to the point of martyrdom, had among them those who implicitly advocated idolatry, immorality, and other fatal errors (Rev. 2:14-15).

Another important part of the lesson in missionary evangelism concerns what Scripture calls the devil's "schemes" (2 Cor. 2:11; Eph. 6:11). It has already been observed that he is nocturnal, a night operator. Basic to all is deceit. Tares are so similar to wheat that except for the expert they deceive everyone until the fruit is fully developed. Peter and Paul, as seen earlier in this discussion, had no trouble detecting the false wheat, but, then, they were apostles and had special, divine, spiritual insight. Satan is a deceitful being. Jesus spoke of him as the "father of lies" (John 8:44). The way he employs spurious Christians to cause trouble in the company of professed believers is rather fully set forth in 2 Corinthians 11:

> But I am afraid, lest as the serpent deceived Eve by his craftiness, your minds should be led astray from the simplicity and purity of devotion to Christ. For if one comes and preaches another Jesus whom we have not preached, or you receive a different spirit which you have not received, or a different gospel which you have not accepted, you bear this beautifully. (vv. 3-4)

> For such men are false apostles, deceitful workers, disguising themselves as apostles of Christ. And no wonder, for even Satan disguises himself as an angel of light. Therefore it is not surprising if his servants also disguise themselves as servants of righteousness; whose end shall be according to their deeds. (vv. 13-15)

So the devil not only has his own false gospel, but false believers and false apostles as well. There is no hint here that his "clergy" shall exceed the church's true ministers in numbers but occasionally it seems to be so, for they love to take over the theological seminaries and supporting organizations as well as the reins of local churches. They frequently excel in academic respectability and world renown. Their gospel (usually of works-righteousness), being deadly, calls forth some of Scripture's most severe denunciations (Gal. 1:7-9). Some of them zealously reject the idea of good news in the gospel and employ law-works as the way to salvation rather than preaching the righteous requirement of the law as the reason why only by grace through faith alone can God justify the sinner (Rom.

10:1-3). Some forms of the devil's "gospel" go to the other extreme of advocating licentious behavior in the name of godliness. The New Testament has extensive sections on both forms of the "doctrines of demons" (1 Tim. 4:1).

In the final days of this age, just before the harvest, Satan shall furnish the world with a false church and a personal false Christ also (2 Thess. 2:6-12; Rev. 13).

It should be noted that the wheat field remains throughout a *wheat* field. Jesus does not even hint that somewhere along the line the problem becomes one of the wheat among the tares—even though sometimes it might seem to be that sort of situation. It is always God's kingdom and the tares do not belong there.

It is tempting to try to identify tendencies of this advancing age in the parable. Is there a current fulfillment of the prophecy of binding the tares into bundles? One fine author,[3] noticing that binding in bundles precedes the tares' removal, points out that society is separating out its various functioning elements into collective associations (the German word *bund,* cognate to *bind* and *bundle,* familiar in days of *der Bund* of Hitler, comes to the mind of older people) preliminary to the judgment of the end. In the commercial world there are trusts, cartels, and syndicates; in labor, unions and combines of unions (AFL-CIO, for example); in the social scene, cliques, guilds, fraternities; on the international level, alliances—holy, grand, and otherwise. Even in religion there is a new "ecumenism"—a variety for Romanist, another for liberal Protestants and the Orthodox, and both are getting together. There are even several fundamentalist-evangelical "ecumenical" associations. Applying the parable to contemporary organizations does seem to be carrying the symbolism in Matthew 13 to the limit, but perhaps not past it. A number of texts of prophecy elsewhere in Scripture (most notably Daniel and Revelation passages) suggest these things.

The parable has been searched, hotly discussed, and variously applied at different times. It seems to rebuke the Christian principle of separation from the world. But does it? The Novatians (3rd century) thought not. Numbers of Christians had capitulated to civil oppression in the very severe Decian persecution. The Novatians felt it would be disloyal to Christ to receive back into the church the short-term apostates after the storm of persecution was over. They wanted a pure church, they said. The Christians of that time could not conceive of any association of congregations other than under the territorial (diocesan) bishop, by that time a well-established system. A Christendom including all professed believers everywhere was thus already in existence long before Constantine and his successors established the church as religion of the Roman Empire. The doctrine of salvation only through sacraments administered by a clergy was growing in acceptance also. The rigorists wanted none of the repentant apostates back in the church. Arguments against this stand were marshalled by the orthodox, relying strongly on the parable of the tares. Cyprian was leader of the party of moderation while Novatian, another Roman churchman, was the chief rigorist. A century later the same issues and arguments arose in connection with the persecutions of Diocletian. Only by that time the church was about to become the favored state

---

3. Pink, pp. 33-34.

religion. Even before the general adoption of the geographical, episcopal organization that is now associated with Roman Catholicism, the "orthodox" everywhere tempted the church to employ state police power to compel conformity to orthodox, catholic edicts. The last Roman persecutions produced fanaticism, multitudes morbidly seeking the martyr's death as a sure ticket to heaven. Afterward many of the finest Christians felt that the ones who had lapsed during the persecution should, upon repentance, evidence of contrition, and a period of probation, be received back into fellowship. Augustine, then bishop of Hippo, was a leader of this transparently correct policy that set mercy and forgiveness high on the list of virtues and values. Again the parable of tares was employed against the rigorists. Unfortunately both sides appealed to the state power (Emperor Constantine, still a heathen) to enforce their policy by seating their bishop. Augustine somewhat reservedly applied the parable against the rigorism of the separatists, called Donatists (after their leader Donatus), holding that the severe church judgment of permanent excommunication was an unbiblical anticipation of the judgment of God. Almost every one of those arguments was marshalled again by the rigorists (Anabaptists) on the one hand and the Calvinists and Lutherans on the other.[4] All of those discussions and arguments have been quite unconsciously replayed in controversies over church discipline and separationism in modern conservative Christian denominations.

But none of the ancient parties, on account of their notions of territorial, state religion and of the necessity of sacraments administered by ordained clergy for salvation, saw the true application of the parable. The orthodox violated it by employing a state-backed police force to compel compliance of the Donatists, and the Donatists in turn violated it by seeking the emperor's authority to turn the orthodox bishops out. All seemed ready to call in Caesar's legions to root out the tares—and this bears on the main points of the parable, of incalculable importance to the propagation of the church and its governance in all ages and in all lands.

Some of the main points of the parable, stated as propositions, are:

1. Both good and evil, in the sphere of Christendom as elsewhere, are capable of growth. All the good in the world has developed from God's planting: specifically, Christian care of orphans and the chronically insane, and the promotion of many aspects of what has come to be called *welfare* (however presently misconceived in secular socialism). All the political, social, and religious blights of human society are but the development of ideas and principles planted by the devil. In many cases the names of the devil's children who started them are known. All these have a fertile soil ready in the fallen human heart.
2. Evil grows more readily in this world (of which Christendom is a part) than good. (Weeds of some sort grow anywhere and everywhere, but wheat requires careful cultivation.) The biblical Proverbs have much to say about this, for example:

---

4. John Calvin *Institutes of the Christian Religion* 4.1. 12-16; and Willem Balke, *Calvin and the Anabaptist Radicals*, pp. 223-35.

> Foolishness is bound up in the heart of a child;
> The rod of discipline will remove it far from him.
>
> (Proverbs 22:15)

3. The difference between evil and good is seen in their growth: "Then the tares became evident also" (Matt. 13:26). That is true of associations of men under evil principles. Studying the development of the atheism of the French Encyclopedists, the National Socialist party (Nazi), or the Unitarian church—now a wholly anti-Christian moral influence—will dispel doubts. The same is true of individual men and women. By the time, however, the tares are recognizable, short of divine grace, it is too late to remove them. At first little children, like wheat and tares, look and act pretty much alike:

> But let them grow into the forms of acts, habits and institutions and the dissimilarity becomes obvious. You will have great difficulty in convincing the foolishly indulgent parent, who ministers more to the bodily appetites and fantastic wishes of his child than to the conscience, who instills the principles of pleasure rather than duty, that he is wrong; but let the boy or girl reach maturity, and he shall have heartbreaking proof of his error. You may have difficulty in convincing an atheist that his principles are bad, but let them grow and become embodied in the life of a nation, and, as in France, the enormity shall be written in blood and proclaimed in thunder. The difference between good and evil principles appears more and more as they are left to grow.[5]

4. Separation from evil men cannot be effected in the world. Evil men will not only be in the community but in the assemblies, too. The Lord does not allow the use of any external force to remove evil men from Christian associations. But the history of application of this principle compels the observance of two important cautions.

   a. Believers must not shrink from seeking to root out evil thoughts, desires, and deeds from themselves. Jesus most solemnly explained why (Matt. 5:27-32).

   b. The parable has nothing at all to say about the exercise or nonexercise of discipline within the congregation of the Lord's gathered people. The assembly is where purity must be guarded—though this too may be mindlessly carried to extremes. Nevertheless, hypocrites and rebellious persons must be formally excluded as both Jesus (Matt. 18:15-17) and Paul distinctly taught (1 Cor. 6:1-20).

To observe those parallel principles (a and b) will not adversely affect the next proposition.

5. The parable of the tares does not encourage any slackening of efforts to sow the good seed, so strongly encouraged in the parable of the soils. What restraint this poor world has on its mad rush to sin comes from God's grace,

5. David Thomas, *The Genius of the Gospel*, p. 232.

including most prominently His gracious gospel. God has placed restraints on the more violent expressions of evil by ordaining civil government, but the church has no business calling in the coercive power of government to regulate its own members and to purge its rolls of hypocrites or heretics. When the church does so, often the wrong people are purged. In times of a false, enforced, religious conformity such as in medieval Europe, this force was invariably turned against the best people. The wheat—true evangelicals such as the Waldensians and Savonarola in Italy, Huss and the Hussites in Bohemia, Wycliffe and his supporters in Britain—was rooted out. They became the martyrs and exiles while the tares remained at peace in the field, unmolested until the Judgment Day.

The servants wanted to clear the field of tares, tear them out root and branch, leaving nothing but pure wheat. That would be to make a martyr of every pseudo-Christian. It must not be forgotten that the procedure has been tried more than once in the history of Christendom. The first nation (Armenia) to adopt Christianity as the national religion was made "Christian" by force of arms. More than one tribe has been driven to the water of baptism by the sword of "Christian" soldiery.

> To the wish of these over-zealous "servants" Christ utters an emphatic "lest while ye gather up the tares, ye root up also the wheat with them." As the roots of the tares and the wheat are so intertwined in the soil that the pulling of the one would involve injury of the other: so men of this world are so interblended by their relationships of country, family, and friendship, that the martyrdom of the bad would injure the good. It is of service to the bad—it keeps them in a position of [possible] improvement; and it is service to the good. Holy character is strengthened and perfected by contact [conflict] with palable evil.[6]

The striking consummation of the story furnishes ample motive for active obedience by all Christians in the mission of world evangelism. The sons of the devil shall be cast into that final Gehenna with great terror and pain, if the Lord is to be believed. The children of the kingdom shall be received into the blessed granary of heaven (see Rev. 14:14-16).

The parable has much more to say about eschatology, that is, good and evil at maturity, the time when angels assist the Son of Man in judgment. But, lest these lines become too long, the next stage of the Lord's seminar on a theology of world evangelism will now be reviewed.

6. Ibid., p. 233.

13

Parable on Quiet Workings
of the Church

(Matt. 13:31-33)

Before attending to the three verses under consideration, comment must be made on some important features of the Lord's teaching at this point in His career. This will be by way of review and further investigation.

Earlier in this book it was observed that there appears to be some causal, as well as sequential, relation between Jesus' parabolic approach to teaching in chapter 13 and two distressing events of chapter 12. Those two events were His total rejection by the Jewish leaders (Pharisees), who in rejecting Jesus charged that He was an agent of the devil; and the misguided efforts of His family to deter Him from His intended mission. "And it was in this connection that, first to the multitude, then to His disciples, the first series of Parables was spoken, which exhibits the elementary truths concerning the planting of the Kingdom of God, its development, reality, value, and final vindication."[1] "All these Parables refer, as is expressly stated, to the Kingdom of God; that is, not to any special phase or characteristic of it, but to the Kingdom itself, or, in other words, to its history."[2]

Matthew told how Jesus "withdrew from there" (12:15) and saw in that withdrawal a sign pointing to the coming world mission to the nations (Gentiles) (vv. 18-21). Much earlier in the narrative, Matthew had reported a prophecy of Jesus that foreigners would replace the natural descendants of the Hebrew patriarchs in that kingdom (8:11-12). Matthew noted that Jesus had been prompted to make this amazing declaration upon observing the strong faith of a Gentile (vv. 5-10). Near the end of His career Jesus announced to the rebellious, murderous stewards (Jewish leaders) of His Father's vineyard (nation of Israel) that they were to be passed by, adding, "Therefore I say to you, the kingdom of God will be taken away from you, and be given to a nation producing the fruit of it. . . . And when the chief priests and the Pharisees heard His parables, they understood that He was speaking about them" (21:43-45; see vv. 33-42). Thus, when in chapter 12 Jesus held up the faith of the Gentile men of Nineveh (vv. 38-41) and of the

1. Alfred Edersheim, *The Life and Times of Jesus the Messiah*, 1:579.
2. Ibid., p. 586.

heathen queen of the south (v. 42) as a shame to the obdurately blind Pharisees (vv. 22-24, 28), those words became more straw in the wind blowing toward our Lord's soon-to-be-announced worldwide evangelistic mission.

One can therefore better understand why the Jewish crowds were both baffled and hardened, why the "mystery" of the kingdom was deepened by the parables, especially of the four soils and of the tares.

Throughout His life, and nowhere more so than in chapter 13, Jesus was the biblical Hebrew. His hearers were Jews also. Learning how the Jews of the time understood His references to the mysteries of the kingdom of heaven will be helpful. The Old Testament Hebrew words that might be translated "mysteries" do not help much, for they turn out to signify what the New Testament calls parables (see Matt. 13:35; cf. Psalm 78:2).

The leading authorities on the contribution of Jewish learning, ancient and medieval, are the writers of a German work of several volumes, not translated into English. The title can be translated *Commentary on the New Testament out of the Talmud and Midrash,* by Hermann L. Strack and Paul Billerbeck. Those reliable scholars reported that in general the rabbis understood the idea of "mystery" as referring to the things revealed by God to Israel but not to Gentiles. They cited Psalm 147:19,

> He declares His words to Jacob,
> His statutes and His ordinances to Israel.

They understood God to mean that "no other nation should be mixed with Israel, nor be able to learn their mysteries, but they should be for you alone in this world."[3]

In particular Strack and Billerbeck also observed five distinct varieties of mystery in Jewish thought about the subject:

1. The traditional teaching of the rabbis. This is the Mishna or traditional comments of the ancient rabbis, the primary part of the Talmud. Whoever possesses the "mystery" is "My son" (i.e., God's). God put Israel under oath that the mystery should not be revealed to the peoples of the world.
2. Circumcision. Circumcision was held to be the "secret" of Psalm 25:14,
   > The secret of the LORD is for those who fear Him,
   > And He will make them know His covenant.
3. The time of the beginning of the Day of the Lord. Genesis 27:1-2 is cited to show that Isaac desired to make this day known to Esau, but God hid it from him. Genesis 49:1 perhaps more clearly relates this to Jacob and his sons.
4. The reckoning of the Jewish lunar year. Ezekiel 13:9 was cited to show that no one but learned Jews could calculate the calendar properly. Other calculations—the annual solar calendars of other nations—were regarded as "lies."
5. Certain materials of the Torah (the five Books of Moses). Among those were the regulation of the ritual system and its meaning, laws regarding many things.

3. Hermann L. Strack and Paul Billerbeck, *Kommentar zum Neuen Testamentum aus Talmud und Midrasch,* 1:659-60.

The Jews did have a "mystery" to handle, viz., how to make the myriad regulations of the Torah operate, all presupposing the existence and operation of a central sanctuary in the land of Israel, when the sanctuary went out of existence and the Jewish people were scattered throughout the world.

Jesus bypassed all this clannish chauvinism and gave His disciples "a mystery" that was to be declared to every nation under heaven. Thus while presupposing Jewish modes of living and employing Jewish patterns of thought, Jesus taught something totally foreign to the thought of the reigning Judaism of His day. Knowing this helps one understand the exceeding reluctance of the first Christians to depart the land of Israel, and the tardiness of Peter and others in accepting that Gentiles could become Christians without first becoming Jews (see Acts 10). It also explains the presence of "the concision" (Phil. 3:2, KJV) the Judaizers who plagued the mission of Paul and necessitated Paul's epistle to the Galatians.

Alfred Edersheim, a Jew himself by national origin, wrote of the extremely un-Jewish character of Jesus' teaching in the parable of the leaven.[4] Two later series of parables—found in Luke 10-16, 18 and Matthew 18, 20-22, 24-25—demonstrate much of this same "un-Jewishness."

Many writers have pointed out the exceedingly un-Jewish character of Jesus' teaching throughout this initial seminar of parables. The Jews thought Israel would not be hard, stony, or thorn-choked soil, but fertile and fruitful; this being in direct contrast to parable number 1. It is in the Jewish apocryphal literature that one meets the exaggerated Jewish expectation, current in Jesus' time, of a physically prosperous and opulent golden era of Messiah, without holiness and without mission of salvation to the Gentiles. The Old Testament prophets spoke of world restoration (see Isa. 35, 65-66), but the same prophets spoke of the need for Israel's repentance (Isa. 55), of Israel's blindness, and of Messiah's suffering and death (Isa. 50; 52:12—53:12). If even the disciples did not comprehend the full meaning of the first parable and had to ask Jesus for an exposition, how un-Jewish and unacceptable it must have seemed to the crowd as a representation of anything they expected to come with Messiah's reign!

It is important, therefore, to do what His contemporaries could not do because of their blindness, and that is to see in these parables an outline of truth regarding the propagation of the gospel to the very ends of the earth.

The parables had a distinctive place in the scheme of gospel history and progressive revelation. But what were they like apart from their place in the larger record? All the parables put action, power, life, and movement on parade. The ones studied so far have described the vital action of good, strong seed in four kinds of soil. The second showed how seed, soil, and environment supply all the dynamic elements for the vital explosion that is the growth of a fruitful plant from a small seed. The third is initially disconcerting with information about two vigorous types of seeds and their resulting plants, the one (wheat) representing sound, normal growth and the other (tares) representing the strong, but perverse and powerful, growth of evil.

4. Edersheim, 1:594.

The two studied now still speak of seeds of sorts and of growth, but very differently! Because they are short, the parables will be quoted in their entirety:

> He presented another parable to them, saying, "The kingdom of heaven is like a mustard seed, which a man took and sowed in his field; and this is smaller than all other seeds; but when it is full grown, it is larger than the garden plants, and becomes a tree, so that THE BIRDS OF THE AIR come and NEST IN ITS BRANCHES." He spoke another parable to them, "The kingdom of heaven is like leaven, which a woman took, and hid in three pecks of meal, until it was all leavened." (Matt. 13:31-33)

The parables of the kingdom all relate to Christian history in the world—both yesterday and today, as well as tomorrow if the Lord delays His return. It is always important therefore to be reminded that Scripture imparts a special understanding of everything that goes on in the world. The world was made by God and blessed by Him, yet also cursed. It is evil, yet redeemed. Christ's peace is with men in all ways, yet in the world there is tribulation. The kingdom of God and the kingdom of this world are both present on earth today.

Before investigating those two parables in detail, the background ideas should be pursued a bit further. In the fine words of a contemporary New Testament scholar:

> The world will yet behold the coming of God's kingdom with power. But the mystery, the new revelation, is that this very Kingdom of God has now come to work among men but in an utterly unexpected way. It is not now destroying human rule; it is not now abolishing sin from the earth; it is not now bringing the baptism of fire that John had announced. It has come quietly, unobtrusively, secretly. It can work among men and never be recognized by the crowds. In the spiritual realm, the Kingdom now offers to men the blessings of God's rule, delivering them from the power of Satan and sin. The Kingdom of God is an offer, a gift which may be accepted or rejected. The Kingdom is now here with persuasion rather than with power.[5]

Each parable of the series relates to the history and character of the present mystery form of the kingdom of the Father. Prominent among the teachings are that though that kingdom shall yet come with power and glory it is already present among men in and through the disciples of Jesus. His Spirit, Word, and testimony are now bringing the blessings of the age to come to men in this sin-cursed realm of the prince of this world. In the two parables about an almost invisible vital kernel (mustard seed) and a totally invisible (before microscopes) vital force (yeast), both performing immense wonders, Jesus set in bold relief those truths of the present and coming power and glory of His kingdom.

Even nature reminds that being small and unobtrusive has its advantages, as the Scripture says:

> Four things are small on the earth,
> But they are exceedingly wise:

5. George Eldon Ladd, *The Gospel of the Kingdom*, p. 55.

The ants are not a strong folk,
But they prepare their food in the summer;
The badgers are not mighty folk,
Yet they make their houses in the rocks;
The locusts have no king,
Yet all of them go out in ranks;
The lizard you may grasp with the hands,
Yet it is in kings' palaces.

(Proverbs 30:24-28)

THE PARABLE OF THE MUSTARD SEED

Several often-asked questions of tangential importance might delay study: What is the plant referred to as mustard? Is it really the smallest of all seeds? Is the growth described normal to the plant or abnormal? The first two questions are irrelevant and the answer to the third, contrary to a certain school of interpretation, is stated clearly enough in the text as normal growth. As in all the other parables of this discourse, Jesus employed wholly natural phenomena as His illustrations. As can be seen elsewhere in this gospel (Matt. 17:20), the mustard seed of Palestine was regarded as a symbol of anything very small. Numerous citations from the ancient Jewish Rabbis demonstrate this. For example, the beginning of a woman's menstrual "uncleanness" was said to be when a drop of blood the size of a "mustard seed" appeared. Furthermore, mustard was, as in the parable, regarded as a field plant rather than a garden herb by the Jews.[6] A distinction is still made between field and garden plants, not on the basis of size of seeds but on the kind of plant produced. It is certain that the *sinapi* or mustard seed was simply the smallest seed a Palestinian farmer would put in a field and that it grew to be the largest of the annually sown crops.

The kingdom of heaven, specifically the growth of Christian profession, is in some important respect like that smallest-to-greatest sequence. This parable (unlike the four soils, the seed in the field, and the tares, which have aroused a fair consensus of interpretation) has called forth apparently diametrically opposed interpretations. One interpretation sees a prediction of the universally successful extension of the gospel. That is said to be verified in the history of the early church, which from small and humble beginnings increased and spread to such extent that already in apostolic times the whole civilized world felt its power.[7] There is nothing out of harmony with revealed truth in that view. The other views include it.

Another interpretation takes an optimistic view of the present age: "The little seed which Jesus and His disciples sowed shall one day grow to proportions . . . vast. All the other productions of the world shall be small in comparison with it. Or, to change the figure, 'the little stone cut out of the mountain without hands' [Dan. 2:34, 45] will roll on and grow in every revolution until it becomes a great

6. Strack and Billerbeck, 1:669.
7. J. J. Owen, *A Commentary . . . on Matthew and Mark,* p. 167.

mountain to fill the whole earth."[8] The view holds that the final victory of the Christian mission will be when all men become Christian. Such interpretation seems to be, at least in part, in direct contradiction to the teaching of the parable of the four soils and of the tares in the field of wheat. It is the view of postmillennialism.

A common premillennial interpretation sees the growth of the tiny seed to large proportion as a monstrous, abnormal development. The parable predicts the total course of the age. The birds nesting and resting in the mustard plant represent evil. The "tree" speaks of earthly greatness, worldly notoriety. The parable predicts how the devil changed from tactics of persecution to subversion very early in the age.

> In the first parable the assault was from without—the fowls of the air catching away the Seed. In the second parable his activities were from within—he sowed his tares among the wheat. In the third parable we are shown the effects of this. Satan now moved worldly men to seek membership in the churches of God. These cause the Truth to be watered down, discipline to be relaxed. . . . Soon Christianity ceased to be hated by the unregenerate: the gulf between them and the "Church" was bridged. . . .
>
> In the days of Constantine the so-called Church and the State united, and became a vast political-religious system.
>
> . . . There we may discern in the first three parables of Matt. 13 a striking and sad forecast of the development of evil. In the first, the devil caught away part of the good Seed. In the second, he is seen engaged in the work of imitation. Here, in the third, we are shown a corrupted Christianity affording him shelter.[9]

This approach sees specific historical (or dispensational) meaning to many elements of the parables that other approaches do not. Mr. Pink sees, for example, in the "hundred . . . sixty . . . thirty-fold" amounts of harvest in the first parable distinct historical references.

"These words are too plain to be misunderstood. We believe that the 'hundred-fold' had reference to the yield borne in the days of the apostles; the 'sixty' at the time of the Reformation; the 'thirty' the days in which we are now living."[10] It seems to make too much of the details to discover a schedule of the present age in this and other parables. Even though Mr. Pink's scheme of things may be right in larger part, this parable, at least, is too small a horse for so large a saddle.

The disciples were puzzled enough to ask what the story of the tares meant (Matt. 13:36) but they thought they understood the mustard seed lesson. Since, however, Jesus explained the tares but not the mustard seed modern man must be more puzzled about the parable of the mustard seed than the disciples were.

8. David Thomas, *The Genius of the Gospel*, p. 236.
9. A. W. Pink, *The Prophetic Parables of Matthew 13*, pp. 41-43.
10. Ibid., p. 21.

The essential idea of great growth of Christendom from tiny beginnings is not missed by any thoughtful reader and all those cited above catch this. That may be about all Jesus had in mind. There is great encouragement for the evangelist in this.

There really is one more important truth set forth here. As in other parables, the kingdom of God continues to be the subject. This kingdom, which at the second advent of the Son of Man shall fill the earth, is now here among men; yet in a manner the sons of the kingdom (the Jews) did not expect. It is like a tiny seed, but its power may not be despised.

Let that single great truth be embodied in a scriptural aphorism: "Who has despised the day of small things?" (Zech. 4:10). The times of Zechariah's prophecy in fifth century B.C. Israel were bad; the people were only moderately well-off materially and they were, though orthodox enough religiously, remarkably back-slidden spiritually. Years had passed and they had not finished the modest temple they had started upon their return from Babylon. Their civil leader, Zerubbabel, was not highly respected and Joshua, their high priest, was being neglected. Being small in number among hostile neighbors, they even despised themselves. But though Satan opposed (Zech. 3:2) and men ignored the community, God's word by the prophet came saying, "Not by might ["army," ASV marg.] nor by power [money, numbers, secular influence], but by My Spirit says the LORD" (Zech. 4:6). The motto, so to speak, was to be "Grace, grace" atop the temple (Zech. 4:7). "The hands of Zerubbabel have laid the foundation of this house, and his hands will finish it. . . . For who has despised the day of small things?" (Zech. 4:9-10).

There is hope for the tiniest group of believers that they may gain not only inner strength by God's appointed means, but growth in numbers also. First there was John the Baptist, whom a king beheaded. But in dying John cleared the way for the One greater than himself. Then there were Jesus and six disciples for a year, then twelve, then only eleven, then 120, then 3,000, then 5,000 more and at the end there will be an innumerable multitude of every kindred and tongue.

"For consider your calling, brethren, that there were not many wise, . . . not many mighty, not many noble; . . . and God has chosen the weak things of the world to shame the things which are strong" (1 Cor. 1:26-27; see also vv. 28-31).

So also it is with the beginnings of faith. Not many are attracted to Christ initially through the powerful discourses of persuasive giants of the pulpit. It is more likely the smile of a friend, the comforting word of a neighbor, the appeal of a child, the striking cover of a tract, or even a snatch of tune from an old hymn heard in childhood or a half-remembered verse of Scripture. Within the last generation, dozens of small foreign mission enterprises, which began in the hearts of one or two or three concerned men, have grown into mighty enterprises through which multitudes have been saved. Some have been in small denominations (Evangelical Free Church, Christian and Missionary Alliance, and Grace Brethren are examples); some came into existence as faith missions (Wycliffe Translators, Far Eastern Gospel Crusade, Greater Europe Mission).

The Parable of the Leaven

As in the case of the mustard seed the Lord gave no interpretation of the parable of the leaven. It needs hardly to be explained that the two are similar. They are the first to depart from seed wheat as one of the central items (four soils, seed cast into a field, tares in the field). Mustard seed and leaven are each seeds also, but of new and different kinds. In keeping with the theme of all five parables, however, seeds and their future growth are the illustrations employed.

The interpretation that sees the mustard seed story as illustrating abnormal growth—the alleged change of God's field into Satan's, God's planting into the devil's—has already been rejected. Prophecy is clear enough that this age shall see development of apostasy among the churches, and that false religion shall raise its ugly head viciously at the end. But the notion is rejected that the kingdom of heaven on earth in its present form is now or ever shall be an essentially evil thing. However the message of the parables of the kingdom be interpreted, each one relates to that marvelous blessing, the kingdom of the Father in and through His Son. The scene of action is that marvelous good. Jesus brought it and God acknowledges it as His kingdom, whatever flaws may develop in it among men. After all, what good gift of God have men not misused?

In all epochs there have been those who, holding a defective view of man's fallen nature, have insisted that the gospel will some day prevail over all the world, changing all society and bringing in the millennium. The nineteenth century was its heyday. The misguided liberal theologians and churchmen of the day hailed the present century when it arrived as "the Christian Century." Tennyson, poet laureate of this school, sang of how in the Parliament of man, the Federation of the world[11] would wrap a happy earth in endless peace. The parable of the leaven was their great proof text. To them, the woman of the parable was the church; the leaven was the good news of salvation (plus a generous supplement of human self-sufficiency). The three measures of meal were all mankind: perhaps Shem, Ham, and Japheth; or Greeks, barbarians, and Jews; or even mankind itself: body, soul, and spirit.

Another, rather widely held approach turned the interpretation just described upside-down. In this other view the leaven stood for evil, for the growth of apostasy; the woman for the false church; and the three measures of meal for either the whole visible church or for the human race—often interpreted as Jews, Gentiles, and the church. A variation of such a view held the meal to be Christ the true bread, the woman chiefly the papacy and perhaps certain other corrupters of divine truth, and the leaven false doctrine. The leaven in each of the three measures was thought to be the leaven of Pharisees, Sadducees, and Herodians.

There is also a form of dispensational doctrine that asserts that while the Holy Spirit remains on earth amongst the saints, God's truth will be proclaimed. While He is here, there is a hindering cause, preventing the "whole" from being "lea-

11. Alfred, Lord Tennyson, "Locksley Hall," line 128.

vened." But at the Rapture the Hinderer will be "taken out of the way" (2 Thess. 2:7), and then the "whole" will be leavened. The "salt" (Church) will be removed, and nothing will be left to stay universal corruption.[12]

A sound eschatology cannot be erected specifically upon the basis of this or any other parable. Of course it is not wrong to bring a particular understanding of last things to the parables of Jesus for such aid as it may give in interpretation. But it seems clear that the program of doctrine just cited (and it has been widely held) is again putting too large a load on the parable, more than it was meant to carry. This view does not seem to be as widely advocated now as earlier in this century and those who do hold to it do not seem to be quite so certain of it as formerly.

Several recent authors, including the editors of the *NEB*, put much symbolism in the "three measures." It is said to equal enough to feed 150 men. A. M. Hunter affirms: "No ordinary housewife in her senses would bake such an enormous quantity of bread. Its very vastness shows that we are dealing with no ordinary human situation but with an extraordinary divine reality—with what the sovereign power of God in action can really do. Finally note the last words of the parable—'till all was leavened.' Is not this the very nature of leaven? It leavens the whole lump—no part of the flour can remain unaffected by it." This interpretation goes on to hold that "when the reign of God invades history, nothing can be unaffected by it." God's kingdom is here affecting all humanity, disturbing it, reforming it, changing it. The Christian is therefore to take heart and trust the living God.[13]

Some attention will now be given to details and then a summary will be attempted. There are two decisive issues: the general subject of all the eight parables and the specific symbolism of the leaven. The former has been noted previously, so only the leaven will be discussed here.

It is frequently asserted that leaven always stands for evil in the Bible. It was excluded from all sacrifices, it is said. First Corinthians 5:6-7 and Galatians 5:7-9 are cited in further proof that it must signify evil. That leaven frequently stands for evil must be acknowledged as correct, but it does not symbolize evil in every case. Sometimes it is falsely assumed that in a given passage leaven stands for evil. A parallel unproved assumption is that exclusion of leaven always signifies the removal of evil. Leaven was, indeed, excluded from the Passover festival bread. The reason, however, was that in the first instance (the Passover of Ex. 12-13) there was such haste that there was no time for bread to rise (12:37-39). The first reference to the omission of leaven in later times was historical, to remind Israel of the haste of the departure from Egypt, a very abrupt event, taking place in a single night. The text is very specific about this historical significance. Haste was also the apparent, necessary reason for lack of leaven in the bread set before angels who visited Lot (Gen. 19:3). Some Mosaic ceremonies required the ritual use of leavened bread. For example, the bread used in the festival of Pentecost had to be leavened bread, being a part of the offering

---

12. Pink, p. 51.
13. A. M. Hunter, *The Parables Then and Now*, pp. 44-45.

presented to God on the fiftieth day after Passover (Lev. 23:16-17, 20). It is an error to say that biblical precedent requires that the leaven always be interpreted as signifying evil.

The woman does not necessarily stand for anyone or anything in particular. The bakers of bread in Scripture would normally be women. A parallel is the man who sows seed in the second parable of the series (Matt. 13:24). Sowers of seed were usually male as bakers of bread were usually female in the world of the Bible. Nor do the three measures of flour stand specifically for three of anything in particular, A. M. Hunter to the contrary (see note 13, above). Three measures of a certain size made a standard batch of dough. Abraham's words to Sarah from an earlier time illustrate that well enough: "Quickly, prepare three measures of fine flour, knead it, and make bread cakes" (Gen. 18:6). Incidentally in this case also, though the text does not specifically say so, the bread had to be unleavened, by reason of haste. There were no instant-acting baking powders available in those days. The fact that angels were to eat this bread had nothing to do with it—as advocates of the "principle of evil" view insist.

Both common interpretations miss the Lord's point, both by claiming too much. The parables are not allegories. In an allegory each detail stands symbolically for something else. *The Pilgrim's Progress* by John Bunyan is an example. The symbolism is indicated by the names the author gives to the persons, things, and actions in the book. The names are self-interpreting. The allegory may or may not represent things as they are in the real world. Jesus' parables, on the other hand, have no such complicated meanings. Usually only one main idea is being illustrated in each parable. The parables may or may not be self-interpreting. Of the eight parables under consideration here, Jesus interpreted only two for His disciples. The others were evidently to be self-interpreting, or at least were easy for the disciples to understand (Matt. 13:51-52).

Furthermore, the parables fit the scene of nature, men, and things as they really are; even though real, historical persons need not be introduced. This can be seen inescapably in the three parables of Luke 15. Each takes up a situation common to real life: a lost sheep, a lost coin, and a lost son are the leading items in the three parables.

There is a single main point taught in each of the three. Not only so, the main lesson is the same for all three: the recovery of lost men to God will occasion joy among all true disciples. The details of each parable are only clothing for this one, single lesson. It is illustrated three times. There may be, of course, as repeatedly seen in this study, truths supplemental to the main truth.

Serious errors arise when these parables are used as basis for doctrine. A whole spate of liberal writers nowadays are drawing their doctrine of forgiveness (as a basis for rejecting vicarious atonement) from the way the father of the prodigal forgave that bad son without amends or punishment of any kind. But the story of the prodigal is relevant only as a means to get the main point across. It is mischievous to employ it in the way those subverters of biblical atonement do. It is obviously contrary to the Lord's intention and frequent statements (Matt. 20:28).

The parables of the mustard seed and of the leaven are not quite identical in purport. William Hendriksen is surely correct in observing that "the two parables . . . are a pair, the first referring to the outward, the second to the inward growth of the kingdom of heaven. These two cannot be separated: one might say that it is because of the invisible principle of eternal life by the Holy Spirit planted in the hearts of the citizens of the kingdom and increasingly exerting its influence there, that this kingdom also expands visibly and outwardly, conquering territory upon territory."[14]

The main point of the parable of the leaven is similar to that of the mustard seed. Anyone new to the action of yeast (leaven) is surprised by the results of mixing it thoroughly into a batch of warm, moist flour. Two or three cups of the flour will expand in volume until a bowl of several quarts' capacity is filled. And it keeps on working and enlarging the volume unless worked down by repeated kneadings and finally killed by the heat of baking.

There is no noise to the process, no commotion at all, only a pleasant odor. Yeast does its good work quietly.

The point of the parable, as in the previous parable, is "Who has despised the day of small things?" The kingdom of God in the person of Messiah stood among those conniving, hardened Pharisees. Jesus said, "Behold, the kingdom of God is in your midst" (Luke 17:21). His authentic personal claims were as striking as His own words and deeds. But they could not see the Messiah in Him, for they missed the "boast of heraldry, the pomp of power, all that beauty, all that wealth ere gave."[15]

> Who has believed our message?
> And to whom has the arm of the LORD been revealed? . . .
> He has no stately form or majesty
> That we should look upon Him.
>
> (Isaiah 53:1-2)

In that way Jesus again illustrated the truth that the kingdom of the Father may appear to be a small, insignificant thing. The world may therefore despise it. What could a Nazarene carpenter, some unlettered fishermen, a tax collector, and a rustic farmer or two do in the world? But the parable says, "Do not be discouraged or misled. The day is coming when God's kingdom will fill all the earth just as leaven, almost undetectable, fills a whole large bowl with pungent, nourishing bread dough."

> He will not fail nor be discouraged,
> till he have set justice in the earth;
> and the isles shall wait for his law.
>
> (Isaiah 42:4, ASV)

14. William Hendricksen, *Matthew: New Testament Commentary Series,* p. 556.
15. Thomas Gray, "Elegy Written in a Country Churchyard," lines 33-34.

In a general sense the parable is both history and prophecy with a thousand fulfillments: an obscure virgin, teen-age girl of Nazareth, peasant parents [of John] at Ain Kerim, a baby in a manger, a man of sorrows, some itinerant evangelists, a crucified donkey (as one of the graffiti of early Christian times represented the event), only twelve apostles, only 120 believers in Jerusalem and 500 in Galilee. In pre-Reformation times there were harried mountaineers in Italy and oppressed farmers in Bohemia; in later times a conscience-stricken German monk in a monastery, lonely British scholars translating Scripture in attics, penniless students and, throughout Britain, dismissed evangelical pastors. It has been so until the present times: the small and weak overcoming the great and strong to enlarge the kingdom of God.

Similarly, in the narrow personal sense, the small beginnings of faith have had correspondingly gentle stimulation, insignificant and feeble by worldly standards, but with effective results: taking a neighbor's child to Sunday School, helping an overworked neighbor with a sick child, befriending a lonely student far from home. There were many young men who risked their lives, and some who lost their lives, in the wars of 1941-46, 1950, and that long one in the '60s and '70s, who went off to face death in battle with some peace and hope because of the simple words of loving teachers, parents, and pastors, words—only words (Acts 11:14-15)—spoken about Jesus and in His holy name. The entire propagation of the kingdom of God among men, in its historical beginnings long ago, and in its beginnings whenever men are led from sin to faith has been in this way. "Despise not the day of small things" (see Zech. 4:10).

There may have been other doctrines that Jesus meant to teach by these two parables. It seems best, however, to place these suggestions in the category of applications of the parable rather than specific teachings. These belong in the categories of homiletics and exhortation rather than doctrine.

As an aspect of the central truth of this and the previous parable it seems probable that Jesus also intended to teach that the power of the seed—as in the first three parables: the Word of God—is inherent. The Word has the divine power. It has been said on this point that

> if the progress of the Kingdom of Heaven be *towards corruption, till the whole is corrupted,* surely there is an end of all the blessings and healing influence of the Gospel on the world. It will be seen that such an interpretation cannot for a moment stand, on its *own* ground; but much less when we connect it with the parable preceding. The two are intimately related. *That* [mustard] was the *inherent self-developing* power of the Kingdom of Heaven, as a seed, containing in itself the principle of expansion; *this* [leaven], of the *power which it possesses of penetrating and assimilating a foreign mass,* till all be taken up into it. And the comparison is not only to the *power,* but to the *effect* of leaven also, which has its *good* as well as its bad side, and for that good is used: viz. to make wholesome and fit for use that which would otherwise be heavy and insalubrious.[16]

16. Henry Alford, *The New Testament for English Readers,* p. 100.

14

Parables for Disciples Only

(Matt. 13:44-50)

Before considering these three parables it is important to review both the main points Jesus had made through the first five parables concerning the Christian mission of world evangelism, and actions Jesus took in several stages of delivery of those parables. In that connection also, note the truth spoken to the disciples but not as a part of the parables.

In the first parable the Lord taught that among those who respond at all to the Word of God, there are four sorts of hearers. Among those, only one ever produces fruit to eternal life and that with greatly differing degrees of fruitfulness. Presumably multitudes upon whose ears the Word falls have no heart response at all. The purity of the seed, the Word of God, is presupposed as is its wide dissemination (Matt. 13:1-9, 18-23).

Then came a break during which the Lord spoke to the close disciples only. He explained how the Spirit is sovereign in creating a believing response to the preached Word. The shallow-minded multitude was being taught a little by parables, perhaps being entertained by the stories as well, but not learning the true mysteries of God's kingdom. Those mysteries must be taught to the heart by the Spirit of God (Matt. 13:10-17).

After that in some exhortations and another parable Jesus explained the importance both of vigorous activity and of patient waiting. Like a lamp, the witness's testimony must be on prominent display; he must to some degree "go public." Yet—changing His figure from lamp to seed again—once the seed has been planted the development of the seed to precious fruit of harvest must be left to God (Mark 4:21-29). That is the parable of patience.

Next, the story of the tares growing in the wheat field that was planted by God's servants is a parable of forbearance. It teaches that the kingdom must, for now, remain a mixed situation. The vindication of the true believers and the judgment of hypocrites must await the Judgment Day (Matt. 13:24-30, 36-43).

The fourth parable (mustard seed) and the fifth (leaven) say to the missionary: Do not despise the day of small things. Both in externals (mustard tree) and internals (leaven in dough) God's means are tiny in the view of men (Matt. 13:31-

33), yet possibility of spectacular success, both inwardly and outwardly, is inherent in the seed of the Word. Both of those parables were spoken to His close disciples after Jesus "left the multitudes, and went into the house" (Matt. 13:36). There they asked Him to explain the parable of the "tares of the field." This He did (Matt. 13:36-43) and spoke of the mustard and the leaven.

While still in the house, away from the carnal gaze of the thrill-hungry crowds, the Lord continued the session in the three parables now under consideration. He spoke of the future growth of the kingdom of God among men by two stories, illustrating two different ways by which men come to receive Christ. In the one case the result comes without seeking—the gospel discovers the sinner. In the other, the sinner discovers the gospel. Then Jesus closed the session with the parable of the great catch of fish showing more about what a Christian's attitude must be toward the presence of hypocrites and hypocrisy while awaiting the consummation.

HIDDEN TREASURE: BEING DISCOVERED BY THE GOSPEL (Matt. 13:44)

Probably none of the eight parables did more to fire the imagination of the disciples than this one: "The kingdom of heaven is like a treasure hidden in the field, which a man found and hid; and from joy over it he goes and sells all that he has, and buys that field" (Matt. 13:44). Every village of Palestine had its story of someone who had become instantly wealthy through finding long forgotten treasure on his own property. Even to the present time the village people are sometimes hard to convince that professional archaeologists poking about the mounds (tells) and other ancient ruins, which frequently lie at the village border, are truly hunting for material remains in pottery shards, stone foundations, walls, and inscriptions, and not specifically for buried treasure of precious stones and metals. And people still find treasure-troves where modern people have built their own civilization over older ones.

There is a special reason for this. There is evidence in the gospels that ancient communities had banks for deposit of money and gaining of interest. But, then as now, many folk, especially unlettered people of toil, did not trust banks. In China, for example, the goldsmiths, and silversmiths, and gem cutters to the present day do brisk business as the community bankers, in a manner of speaking. The people put their money for long-term savings in portable wealth—gold, silver, gems—that can be hidden away and carried on the person in times of civil disorder. Some of this is not reconverted to money in a person's lifetime, and heirs of the deceased may not know where the wealth is hidden. "Lucky" people of later generations then unexpectedly find it.

But what is in the ground belongs to the owner of the ground not to the renter or the trespasser! And that is the rub of the story. Customary law dictates that the owner of the ground owns the untitled treasure, if any, hidden away there. So a man unexpectedly discovering wealth in land owned by someone else has a problem if he wishes to claim the wealth. Should he surreptitiously carry it off there would not only be the crime of theft involved but perhaps insurmountable problems in trying to explain where he got the wealth when he tries to dispose of it for money. On the other hand, if he were to apply to the landowner for permission to remove the wealth, the owner would naturally claim it as his own—with every legal and moral right.

So the only honest and safe thing to do is to remain silent about the discovery, buy the land, and then claim the hidden treasure. Sell all—and borrow, too, if the value of land and treasure justify it—to buy that property! Jesus was saying that likewise many people who are saved by faith in the gospel come to faith very unexpectedly. They come to Christ without prolonged, earnest seeking. One exposure is enough. They have been prepared by God's Spirit to hear with faith. They are more discovered by the gospel than discovering it.

Perhaps no gospel personage better exemplifies this than Levi (Matthew), the author of the chapter now being studied. Only a very little earlier, says Luke, Jesus "went out, and noticed a tax-gatherer named Levi, sitting in the tax office, and He said to him, 'Follow Me.' And he left everything behind, rose and began to follow Him" (Luke 5:27-28). When Levi saw the treasure, he "sold" all that he had and "bought" the whole field.

Many competent expositors have been at pains to point out that there seems to be meaning in the fact that the man bought not the treasure only, but the field in which it was found. He "buys" in the slang of our time, the local church association in which he hears the Word. The new people, obligations, duties, and privileges he willingly adopts as his own, for though each man must do his own repenting and believing, he normally does so in the company of and with the aid of other believers. If he grows in grace, knowledge, and other virtues there will be brotherly love (2 Pet. 1:5-7)—a bit hard to come by in a hermitage! If believers are ever to be monks, then, let it be in communities, not in solitude!

Another matter calls for comment. The man of the parable who found the treasure did then what he did with "joy." So this type of conversion is usually a joyous one. All the freshness of new discovery surrounds the event and for a while, at least, he cannot cease, in his own way, to praise God and to tell any audience he can find all about it. As every missionary discovers, these sudden conversions often produce the most zealous new believers. They become the cutting edge of almost every fresh advance in evangelism.

PEARL OF GREAT PRICE: DISCOVERING THE GOSPEL (Matt. 13:45-46)

About the only explanation needed to update this story is to note that in Jesus' time pearls were preferred over rubies, emeralds, and other stones by discerning handlers of gems. Then as now gems were esteemed not only as ornaments but as media for storing value. It is known that pearls were already being sought in most of the places on earth where they are today found in nature. Divers in the Arabian Gulf, the East Indies, and other exotic and distant spots as well as in the Mediterranean Sea, had a busy trade in pearls among the luxury-minded of the Roman Empire. Even fishermen of Galilee would have their imaginations stirred by thoughts of a rare pearl. Cleopatra is known to have had a special fancy for pearls. It is alleged that pearls supplied the motive for the invasion of Britain by the Emperor Claudius. Paul picked out pearls along with gold and expensive clothing as peculiar temptations away from modest living for women (1 Tim. 2:9; see also Matt. 7:6).

In this parable, as in the preceding one, Jesus taught that the immense value of the kingdom of God must be received through faith in the gospel. That was a central motif in all Jesus' teaching, but in this case the new truth taught was that some people discover and appropriate this great value only after long and tiresome search. The man who trades in jewels will travel far and wide; he will endure danger and separation from home and family to locate and buy pearls. Some people seek the kingdom of God, find it, and receive it for themselves like that.

There are many people whose desire to know eternal truth and to experience fellowship with the living God has set them off on similar searches. The Psalms speak of how their authors cried out to know God and sought Him. The great evangelistic prophet, Isaiah, seemed to imply that man can never comprehend God (Isa. 40:12-17), much less find Him. Job complained that God always escapes discovery (Job 11:7-9). But, the Scriptures assert elsewhere that God's thoughts toward men are "plans for welfare and not for calamity. . . . [therefore] you will seek Me and find Me, when you search for Me with all your heart" (Jer. 29:11-13). There is a Scripture portion treated earlier in this book (chapter 9) in which Jesus several times affirmed the sovereignty of God in election and calling (John 6:44-45, 64-65). It is therefore impressive that in a single sentence of that chapter in John Jesus brought together the importance both of human seeking (of course in response to God the Spirit's seeking man) and of divine choice: "All that the Father gives Me shall come to Me, and the one who comes to Me I will certainly not cast out" (v. 37).

What more can be said about such conversions? How do they fit into the work of evangelism? Some have said, "This case corresponds to only such Christians as have been trained up in the way they should go from youth." The settled habits necessary for such self-direction and such focus of effort are indicated by the parable. Yet, even here there is discovery that happens at a certain time. The seeker has found many valuable and lovely things in life but finally he discovers the supreme value of Christ, Himself. Vital Christianity at all cost ("all that he had") must now be his. There is no field in this parable; it is the pearl alone that is worth the price.

Paul is without doubt the supreme biblical example of this kind of seeking, finding, and selling all. He told his story in Philippians 3:4-9. He did not know it was Christ and grace and faith that he sought, but it was. He was a diligent seeker, nevertheless. The lonely, but ebullient, youthful Luther, sought in religious exercises and in scholastic learning, and finally, with some aid from his ecclesiastical superior, all at once found Christ by faith—at least so it seemed. Still more striking, and in his own way even more the seeking, humanistic, religious analyst was the preconversion Calvin. He tells his story in the *Epistle to Sadolet*. Augustine tells the story of his discovery and of how he sold all to follow

Christ in *The Confessions* as Francis Thompson does in "The Hound of Heaven" and Dorothy Sayer in her "Letters." The reflective Nathaniel and the less reflective but nevertheless thoughtful woman at the well are biblical examples of still other seekers who found and told. It is significant that the stories of Nathaniel's enlistment and of the woman's conviction are told as part of John's program of persuading his readers to believe. The examples of enlistment and of conversion given by John—and there are a good many in his gospel—have been highly persuasive in and of themselves.

People of that type become the leaders of Christian thought. Observe that the biblical and historical examples just cited were all in one way or another teachers of the church. Some are reflective, insightful, and orderly in thinking before they "find the Messiah" and tend to become teachers and preachers. Others are likewise reflective and insightful but more imaginative and expressive. These often become the church's hymnists, musicians, painters, and architects.

PARABLE OF THE DRAGNET: INCLUSIVENESS OF THE KINGDOM OF HEAVEN (Matt. 13:47-50)

Of all the eight parables this last stands out, to use Chrysostom's phrase, as "the fearful parable"—to be feared rather than explained. It is both amazing and frightening that the last words of this, the last parable of the Lord's seminar on the future mission of preaching the good news, should end with a warning of hellfire for hypocrites.

Even those who have never seen a dragnet in operation will have little trouble visualizing what one is and how it works. It is a long fish net with generous width. Weights are fixed along the length of one edge and floats to the other. It is let down at some distance from a ship or (in this case) shore and may reach clear to the bottom. Every fish of every kind large enough to be kept by the net is drawn in. Once drawn in, the edible and legal fish are sorted to one side; the out-of-season, or inedible fish are discarded. One thinks of how saving the porpoises drawn in with such catches of tuna is a problem for fishermen today.

Jesus did not need to explain this parable. The disciples' minds had been prepared by the similar parable of the tares among wheat. The disciples thought they knew what it meant and said so (see 13:51).

Holding in mind the things learned in the study of the previous parables, the meaning for evangelism should be fairly clear. Diverse kinds of peoples may be expected to be brought into the sphere of Christian profession. The fish are of "every kind" (v. 47). If they are to come from all nations and all classes and conditions, what else can be expected? Each will alter in some way the complexion of the visible church. A congregation ought to reflect the human characteristics of the community about it, where, if it is a faithful church, it is casting the gospel net.

The parable does not tell of malicious efforts by the devil to get his followers into church here as in the case of the parable of the tares. Rather, the normal process of "gospelizing" will bring in some who (the figure fails here) by grace are transformed into sound believers as well as others who will remain what they have always been: bad fish—in this context, false believers. The net is cast many times a day in small-scale fishing, as in evangelizing. Converts to Christ, like fish, thus tend to come in waves—to mix the figure. Awakenings, revivals, renewals, and special, concerted, evangelistic efforts from time to time—when joined truly with the awakening grace of the Holy Spirit—bring large numbers in. By no means have all genuinely repented of their sins and turned in faith to Christ, as did the new group at old Thessalonica (1 Thess. 1:9-10). Some come to be part of a new "in group." Others have hope of material gain (see Acts 8:14-23). The church that claims to be one hundred percent pure is failing God, for every strenuous effort at missionary evangelism must produce its share of undiscerned false confessors. Missionary evangelism, if it is successful at all in a large way, will draw into the professing church some who are not truly converted. Again, Paul's person and work illustrate the principles and practices of Matthew 10 and 13. He was always concerned about false disciples, grievous wolves, divisive members, deceitful workers, and false apostles.

One of the main points of the parable is that in due time, and only then, there will be a separation made. When it is made God will make it by separating out the false and judging them eternally (Matt. 13:48-50 with Heb. 10:26-31). This is similar to the teaching of the parable of the tares, but the differences contribute considerably to an advance in understanding of the mission. For one thing, nothing much is made of the present mixture, as in the parable of the tares. Rather God tells us that there will indeed be a terrible future separation. In the story of the tares the man who sowed the seed wheat and the enemy who sowed the tares figured largely. Here no agents at all are mentioned. As just noted, there is not even a fisherman mentioned. The third person plural of verse 48, "they drew it up on the beach," is scarcely more pointed than the common idiom for the passive voice "it was drawn to shore" (cf. "cast," v. 47). If the human preachers were in the mind of Jesus He would likely have had them sort the fish. But the angels are going to do it, He said, with results almost too dreadful to talk about. "So it will be at the end of the age; the angels shall come forth, and take out the wicked from among [notice the emphasis on their presence in the sphere of Christian profession] the righteous" (Matt. 13:49). The Greek is even more graphic, *ek mesou tōn dikaiōn* (out of the midst of the righteous). Even now the wicked in his death is separated from the righteous, for there is between them a "great chasm fixed" (Luke 16:26).

This parable is both instruction and warning to disciples on their mission—the instruction is, "Do not shrink from bringing men of every kind of nation, personality, class, and condition into the professing church. There will be problems and some will be false believers, but continued teaching coupled with careful church discipline will bring many of them later all the way to eternal life and ultimately to entire sanctification." There is implicit reliance here on everything found in Paul's letters about private and public church discipline and pastoral preaching, teaching, and exhortation, warning, and rebuke. The warning is: "Be prepared for difficulties in the professing church as one of the results of faithful missionary evangelism; difficulties with immature and even false believers." Even the true saints will be only sinners on the way to perfection and some of the professed believers will be hypocrites. That will have to be left to God, except as they show themselves certainly to be false believers.

There is also a note of encouragement: the presence of hypocrites in the church, though painful to know, is God's business. The gates of hell will not prevail against the church of apostles and prophets (see Matt. 16:18). Ultimately God will separate the false professors out. Then they "who have insight will shine brightly like the brightness of the expanse of heaven, and those who lead the many to righteousness, like the stars forever and ever" (Dan. 12:3).

15

Parable on Preparedness

(Matt. 13:51-53)

Of course, Jesus' manner or tone of voice as He asked His inner circle of disciples if they understood the prior parables cannot be known (Matt. 13:51). Some suppose a tone of reproach, but any word of reproach for dullness or resistance is absent. On the contrary, there seems to be only the most tender willingness to enlighten the disciples on any point of the eight parables that might remain hidden. It is proper to assume that though He only explained two of the parables to them, the four soils and the tares among the wheat, it was clear to them that those two were the key to the other six. This principle has been used throughout this book in interpreting those other six. The subject of Jesus' "seminar of parables" must be treated as the same throughout. On that basis Matthew 13 becomes comprehensible. The parables speak only of the progress of the gospel and of the sphere of Christian profession—the kingdom of heaven.

It seems safe to assume that there was no direct explanation given of any except for the two and that those explanations were intended to be sufficient for the twelve—and for people today—to interpret the other six. Joachim Jeremias raised the question of whether Jesus actually presented any interpretation of the parable of the seed and four soils.[1] He said the early church produced that part of the tradition reported by Mark and then taken over by Matthew. A. M. Hunter, who usually takes a mediating position, asserted that even if so, it makes no difference, for "any good sermon on the parables today would include both elements, both the Lord's teaching and the church's exposition."[2] This sort of reasoning, however reassuring it seems to be, is remarkably like assigning the same authority to a Sunday School quarterly or pastor's sermon as to the Scripture text on which they are based. If Mark and Matthew are really presenting the interpretation of mere hearers of the Word then it seems justifiable to set their ideas aside for better contemporary ones. And that is precisely what the modern liberal-critical interpreters quite freely proceed to do. On the other hand, the

---

1. Joachim Jeremias, *The Parables of Jesus*, pp. 77-79.
2. A. M. Hunter, *The Parables Then and Now*, p. 39.

interpretations presented thus far have very deliberately paralleled the main interpretations and applications of saints and godly scholars ancient, modern, and contemporary. Striving for novelty would be utterly out of place (see 2 Pet. 1:20), and unfaithful to the clear purposes of Jesus, though perhaps the Spirit of God may use this book to open some new avenues of thought for the reader.

The disciples' answer does not imply that the twelve understood the mysteries of the kingdom as well then as they would later, when the promised Spirit aided their understanding and brought to "remembrance all that I said to you" (John 14:26; see also 16:12-14). They understood as much as was then possible, gaining fuller understanding as time went on; much as long after her marriage the good daughter of a wise mother better understands her mother's premarital advice on marriage relationships. A mother's words before the wedding mean *something*. Truth is perceived to a *degree*. But years later, now a married woman and mother herself, the daughter *really understands* what her mother meant years before.

Mark's summary (4:33-34) says Jesus spoke "the word to them as they were able to hear it; and He did not speak to them [the crowds] without a parable; but He was explaining everything privately to His own disciples." It is not necessary to suppose that this meant Jesus spoke directly to the twelve on the meaning of every parable, but only as need prevailed. In the case of these eight parables, Jesus intended that the two were to explain the other six.

Later on the Spirit of Truth revealed new truths to the twelve. Also, old truths acquired new and larger meanings in expanded perspective. What is the relation of the old and the new? Jesus answered that question with a comparison: "And He said to them, 'Therefore every scribe who has become a disciple of the kingdom of heaven is like a head of a household, who brings forth out of his treasure things new and old' " (Matt. 13:52).

A good "head of a household"—father, head of a family with children, servants, and guests—has a closet or lumber room where garments, bedding, furniture, and appliances not in current use, are stored for the future. A wise householder does not just forget about them. Nor does he stop acquiring new equipment and goods. These too may perhaps not be put in immediate use, but stored away for awhile with the already acquired things. As need arises—children are born, sons and daughters establish homes of their own, charitable contributions are needed, guests are put up in the home—the wise householder consults his list of stored possessions and draws out of storage just the ones needed for those occasions. They are not emergencies, for the householder has anticipated them. When my wife and I, for example, visit the homes of our children we always take satisfaction in seeing good furniture in use in their homes that used to be in our home. There are a pair of solid maple, stepped lamp tables, our first bedroom suite, chairs for a kitchen, three sets of dishes, lamps, and a hand-woven rug.

Thus the disciples and those who walk after them, but in His steps, are to have in the storehouse of spiritual and practical Christian treasure, things old and new, not only for personal comfort, instruction, and blessing, but also for those who cross the Christian's path and for others to whom the Christian goes, as sent, in the mission of world evangelism.

There is a note of singular finality about verse 53: "He departed from there." Jesus finished something there on that day. Then He picked up His baggage and left. A revelation had been made in the eight parables. The principles would be employed later. Immediately and through the coming age recourse was and will be made to them. Some of those instructions were repeated in Jesus' discourses in a different region about a year later. But the matter was out! He made His announcement and let the matter rest, in the main, until with the completion of redemption, the promised Messiah died, rose again and ascended to heaven, after which the promised Spirit came. As the ages of the church roll along until the Lord returns, His faithful disciples must ever return to those instructions for guidance, for comfort, and for understanding as they pursue the Christian mission of world evangelism.

PART 3

PAUL'S MANDATE
FOR GOING AND SENDING

(Rom. 10 and 15)

How Paul conceived the mandate for some believers *to go* to the heathen world as "professional" missionaries of the gospel is of great importance. How he understood the mandate for other believers *to send* them (financial support, prayers, brotherly interest, correspondence; perhaps even local church ordination) is of equal importance. This is quite aside from Paul's own special apostolic commission, which has no direct application to other missionaries then or now. This section will first examine the portion of his writings (Rom. 10) in which he spelled out his reasons for the mission of world evangelism. Then, it will study how Paul further argued (Rom. 15) that the church at Rome should give him, not as an apostle but simply as a missionary, the kind of assistance necessary to get a missionary to a distant field and to keep him there. There is nothing in the Bible quite so much on target. Some Christians *must go*. Others *should send*. Not all must go, but some must do so. Others are challenged to send them.

When Paul wrote Romans he had been engaged as Christ's missionary to the Gentiles for a long time. From the moment of his conversion experience he had been aware of a special, personal commission from Christ to evangelize the Gentiles. The Lord stated as much (Acts 9:15-16) and Paul himself also said so (Acts 22:10-21; 26:16-20; Gal. 1:16; 2:9; Eph. 3:8). Many years later as he paused on his third missionary journey, he was able to write that as far as the eastern portion of the Roman Empire was concerned he had completely fulfilled his commission. That was according to his own standards and understanding of his special task assigned by Christ: "From Jerusalem and round about as far as Illyricum I have fully preached the gospel of Christ" (Rom. 15:19).

It would have been a good time to retire, assigning to younger people the arduous task of going to more distant places like the Roman West. Instead he paused at Corinth, midway in his third missionary journey, wrote a letter of missionary theology and of practical counsel to the church at Rome, and sent it off by the hand of Phoebe, deaconess of nearby Cenchrea. It was no desire for sightseeing that took Paul later to all those places mentioned in his last epistles, Titus and 2 Timothy. The portions of Romans about to be studied show how he began making practical tactical plans to evangelize the West personally, in the same manner that he had already evangelized the East.

As part of those plans the intrepid missionary took steps to gain a new base of operations, nearer to the new fields. It would be at Rome, center of the Latin West and springboard for commerce, government, and communication in the Occident in a way Rome never could have been for the older and more sophisticated Orient.

There is no evidence that Paul ever explained his situations to his "home church" at Antioch on the Orontes or sought their authorization. Paul was not really dependent on any congregation for missionary authority. The Holy Spirit had called him long before the Antiocheans laid the hands of ordination on him and Barnabas (Acts 13:1-4). Paul's mandate came from Christ. He was Christ's messenger before he became a church's messenger. If necessary he would doubtless have gone out without any human commission, just as many missionaries have done since that day. Many have gone out simply on the basis of the biblical mandate and an inward sense of call from God. Missionaries all too often must sense the imperative of their own mission long before their fellow believers do. Sometimes they go out with the burden of indifference on the part of all their brethren.

Paul also took a "comity of missions" approach. For he was determined, as a pioneer, not to infringe on the territory of other pioneers (Rom. 15:20-21). He also believed in human helps of many kinds and did not hesitate sometimes to ask for them. He even solicited financial help when his "own hands" were not quite equal to earning a living plus preaching. Perhaps tents were not in short supply in Spain, where he intended to go (cf. Acts 18:3-4 with Rom. 15:24).

Paul had never been to Rome and had no part in founding the church there. He claimed no personal authority over its members. His only authority was that of apostolic teacher. Yet he felt he could call for their help in the projected mission to Spain—and who can doubt that he intended to reach all the provinces out that way as he had already done in the eastern Mediterranean lands?

How did he appeal to them for their assistance? How did he try to convince the "weak" (see Rom. 14:1-12) Jewish Christians there that the gospel was not merely for Jews everywhere and such Gentiles as were willing to become Jews? How did he try to persuade the "strong" (see Rom. 14:13-23) Gentile believers that they had a Christian obligation to send gospel missionaries to pagans and Jews everywhere?

His arguments were based on the Old Testament Scriptures, or on rational inferences, or on his own special revelations and insights. For him the verbal expression of a great commission filled the whole Bible. This is plain in the opening verses of his epistle. He described himself as "Paul, bond-servant of Christ Jesus, called as an apostle, set apart for the gospel of God, which He promised beforehand through His prophets in the holy Scriptures" (1:1-2). For Paul, the Great Commission is Christ Himself, who He was and what He did. As Dr. Max Warren said in his book entitled, *I Believe in the Great Commission:*

> Jesus himself is the Great Commission. He is the Man who is sent. He himself is the Message. In his life and through his teachings and actions in his dying and his death and

by his resurrection, he is the proclamation of his Message. . . . This fundamental affirmation is the theme of the New Testament. As Christians we believe that this theme was foreshadowed in the Old Testament.[1]

The Great Commission that Dr. Warren believes in turns out not to be certain verses in the gospels and Acts at all, but the mighty theme of Christ, the Savior of the world throughout the Bible. Dr. Warren was right. This in a nutshell is what Paul said in all his writings. It comes to focus in Romans 10 and 15.

Especially significant to this inquiry into Paul's ideas about the missionary mandate is that he never quoted, cited, alluded to, or showed any awareness at all of some special moment in Jesus' career when He issued the marching orders of the church. There is in all Paul's epistles and recorded speeches nothing even remotely resembling that. The several reports of some of Jesus' last words to His disciples (Matt. 28:19-20; Luke 24:45-47; John 20:21-22; Acts 1:8) in which He does distinctly inform them about the coming missionary activity may be enlightening as to why this is true. They will be examined in the last chapter.

1. Max Warren, *I Believe in the Great Commission*, p. 13.

16

Argument for a Special Mission

(Rom. 10)

Paul wanted the "brethren" (the Jewish Christians at Rome) as well as the Gentile believers to become aware, first of his own prayerful passion to see men saved, especially Jews (Rom. 10:1); and second, that though unsaved Jewish people may have been both religious and zealous, they were in mortal danger, for they would not submit to Christ (vv. 2-3). Christ was the goal toward which true biblical Judaism had led. But now it was obsolete. Its service to the righteousness that comes by faith alone had been consummated. Its validity had been terminated. Its prophecies had been fulfilled. To persist in Judaism as a way of life without Christ was to reject the very righteousness that the deeper meaning of the law inculcated and to which it had led, in the coming of Christ the Savior.

The rest of Romans 10 shows why believers—especially Jewish believers who know the Hebrew Scriptures, but Gentile Christians also—must hold themselves responsible for bringing the news of Christ's redemption to the ends of the earth.

The climax is reached and the conclusion stated in the paragraph (indicated correctly in RSV) of verses 14-17:

> How then shall they call upon Him in whom they have not believed? And how shall they believe in Him whom they have not heard? And how shall they hear without a preacher? And how shall they preach unless they are sent? Just as it is written, "How BEAUTIFUL ARE THE FEET OF THOSE WHO BRING GLAD TIDINGS OF GOOD THINGS!" (vv. 14-15)

This classic text scarcely needs comment except to say that Paul evidently had in mind a human (not divine) sending in "unless they are sent," even though he did not expressly say so. Christ was sent by the Father and Christ sent out apostles. All believers are sent into the world by Christ. They are already in the world and are to be salt and light. But Paul was talking of human sending of other human missionaries by people who stay at home. "If the Gentiles could not believe in the Lord without hearing of him, unless he was declared to them, then it follows from the prophecy. . . . This quotation . . . was calculated to produce the strongest conviction of . . . the duty of preaching the gospel to the Gentiles."[1]

1. Robert Haldane, *Exposition of the Epistle to the Romans,* p. 524.

Paul cemented the point in the final verse of the paragraph: "So faith comes from hearing, and hearing by the word of Christ" (v. 17).

That is where Paul's argument leads. How did he get there?

He introduced his case by showing that the first part of the Jewish Bible, the Torah of Moses (Gen. to Deut.), actually teaches that righteousness is only by faith. When the Jews of the time employed the Torah to prevent the true faith of the gospel from breaking out of the ancestral stream, they did so wrongly. Paul's reasoning was plain to people who were as familiar with Moses' writings as people today are with the funny papers. His argument seems obscure today because there is less familiarity with Leviticus 18:5 and Deuteronomy 30:11-14, as well as less familiarity with the manner in which Jews of ancient times employed the Scriptures in discussions of religion.

Paul cited and quoted loosely, striving to free the passage from its ancient connection in order to apply it to the then present realities:

> For Moses writes that the man who practices the righteousness which is based on law shall live by that righteousness [Lev. 18:5]. But the righteousness based on faith speaks thus, "DO NOT SAY IN YOUR HEART, 'WHO WILL ASCEND INTO HEAVEN?' [Deut. 30:12] (that is, to bring Christ down) or 'WHO WILL DESCEND INTO THE ABYSS?' [Deut. 30:13] (that is, to bring Christ up from the dead)." But what does it say? "THE WORD IS NEAR YOU, IN YOUR MOUTH AND IN YOUR HEART" [Deut. 30:14]—that is, the word of faith which we are preaching, that if you confess with your mouth Jesus as Lord, and believe in your heart that God raised Him from the dead, you will be saved. (Rom. 10:5-9)

The author wanted his readers to understand that though there is an antithesis between the idea of a righteousness of works and the inward essence of faith, that does not mean that there is any contradiction between the Old Covenant (Testament) and the New one. The principles of Moses are as universally valid—in heaven above or in hell below—as Christ's principles. In fact they are, Paul claimed, the same principles. The Torah has two aspects in contrast with one another. One is external, a law of doing and working. The other is inward and spiritual, a law of faith and of righteousness by believing. The former was transient and temporary, the latter permanent.

The passage continues by showing that the universal offer of righteousness by faith implied by Moses was also announced by the prophet Isaiah and is now publicly experienced. "For with the heart man believes, resulting in righteousness, and with the mouth he confesses, resulting in salvation. For the Scripture says, 'WHOEVER BELIEVES IN HIM WILL NOT BE DISAPPOINTED' " (vv. 10-11; cf. Isa. 28:16; there is also an allusion to Dan. 12:2).

Mention of heart and mouth, the inner being of man and the medium of its verbal expression, take the reader back to the previous quotation of Deuteronomy 30:12 and 14. It also connects with Paul's previous words about "faith" present in the Torah. Eleven verses earlier (9:33) Paul had quoted Isaiah 28:16 to show that Gentiles have equal access with Jews to God in the gospel. Here in 10:11 he quoted the passage in Isaiah again and for the same purpose.

Paul fully stated the principle that all religious distinctions based on race (or any other human feature) are foreign to the gospel of Christ, "For there is no distinction between Jew and Greek; for the same Lord is Lord of all, abounding in riches for all who call upon Him. For, "WHOEVER WILL CALL UPON THE NAME OF THE LORD WILL BE SAVED" (Rom. 10:12-13; see Joel 2:32).

To make his point he scanned the whole Tanach (Jewish Bible). He employed two passages of the Torah (Lev. 18:5 and Deut. 30:11-14), one from the Prophets, the second division of the Hebrew Bible (Isa. 28:16), and alluded to one in the third, the Writings (Dan. 12:2). That would have had great weight with Jews, especially the Jewish Christians of the church at Rome.

That, then, is how Paul approached the now classical formulation of the mandate for the Christian mission of world evangelism. To resume the train of thought, here is Paul's version of the mandate for a world mission of evangelism:

> How then shall they call on him in whom they have not believed? and how shall they believe in him of whom they have not heard? and how shall they hear without a preacher? and how shall they preach, except they be sent? as it is written, How beautiful are the feet of them that preach the gospel of peace, and bring glad tidings [Gr., Those who evangelize] of good things! (Rom. 10:14-15, KJV)

There is no plainer statement of the mandate in all of literature, biblical or otherwise. Some must *go* with the gospel to the people who have not yet heard it and others must *send* them!

Technical scholars debate several questions raised by those two verses. Was Paul arguing for his own universal apostolate? That is, was he preparing to convince the Roman believers of his own mission to Spain? Perhaps. Were "they" who "call on him" both Jews and Gentiles? Certainly. Was Paul also arguing for an indefinite missionary personnel, referring to all missionaries then and ever since? Probably so. And finally, was the sending by God, congregations (churches), or private (parachurch) agencies? All the above.

The rest of chapter 10 (vv. 16-21) presents the contrasting responses of men to hearing the glad tidings. There is also another Jew versus Gentile contrast, glad faith on the part of many Gentiles as opposed to sullen rejection then increasingly the case with the Jewish people. The six verses were specially relevant for Paul's immediate concerns with the "weaker" (Jewish) "brethren" at Rome. They are also interesting both in that they show how Paul unfailingly relied on the Old Testament to support Christian doctrine, and because they serve as good examples of how a master theologian interpreted Old Testament Scripture in support of his doctrines. "Paul has done what we do or should do in every sermon: 1st. Disentangle from the temporary application, which is the strict sense of the text, the fundamental and universal principle which it contains; 2nd. Apply fully this general principle to the circumstances in which we are ourselves speaking."[2] These quotable words of Godet written a century ago, are

---

2. F. Godet, *A Commentary on the Epistle to the Romans*, p. 382.

not overthrown or much improved by the multitude of excellent contemporary monographs, articles, and commentaries on Paul's use of Scripture.

But Paul has now made the points persued in this book—mandate and instruction for going and sending in the Christian mission. He implicitly stated the mandate once more in verse 17: "So faith comes from hearing, and hearing by the word of Christ."

17

Argument for Some to Go and Others to Send

(Rom. 15)

In Romans 15:8-31 Paul made his "pitch"—a delicate appeal for spiritual, social, and financial help in his upcoming mission to Spain. He had been leading up to it through all the preceeding chapters. He led off with an expression of missionary purpose and passion (1:1-17). Then he explained the doctrinal basis of his mission in the body of the epistle (1:18—11:36) and principles of Christian faith and church order (12-14). In passing he formulated a rationale for sending missionaries (10). Then he came to what was perhaps the chief reason for writing the epistle. Romans 15:8 nevertheless seems to appear abruptly, for here Paul began in earnest to press the Roman believers for participation in his (and others') going to Spain to preach. He wanted them to do nothing less than to approve the mission in brotherly affection, to join him in it, and to support the mission with material gifts and with prayer.

Paul is not by any means as direct in his approach as the preceding paragraph might suggest. He had nothing directly to do with founding the church at Rome. They owed him respect and obedience due an apostle of Christ but not the affection due a father, upon which he based appeals in the two letters to Corinth and the one to Galatia. Whatever his rights and authority in a matter of practical action (the mission to Spain), Paul did not appeal to them. Neither, significantly, did he appeal to any command of Christ regarding worldwide evangelism. Specifically it may be confidently assumed that, in this as in many other such "practical" matters, he would have appealed to the dominical authority of the personal words of Jesus if he had known of any to which he might appeal (cf. 1 Cor. 7:10 with 7:25). Instead, he resorted fully to other kinds of argument. He based his argument on history (v. 8), the direct teachings of Old Testament Scripture (vv. 9-13), his own apostolic mission (vv. 14-21), and practical strategy and current need (vv. 22-33).

ARGUMENT BASED ON HISTORY (v. 8)

The history of Christ's earthly mission; "For I say that Christ has become a servant to the circumcision on behalf of the truth of God to confirm the promises given to the fathers" (v. 8), is the cornerstone from which Paul builds his whole argument.

There might have been some questions raised by Jews of the Roman church as to why Paul wanted to take his ministry to heathen nations when the Lord Jesus, Himself, never devoted any extensive ministry to Gentiles, even commanding his apostles on their first mission to avoid going to the Gentiles. Yet in the Olivet discourse Jesus gave a prophecy of such preaching: "And the gospel must first be preached to all the nations" (Mark 13:10); "and this gospel of the kingdom shall be preached in the whole world for a witness to all the nations, and then the end shall come" (Matt. 24:14). There were other historical reasons as well. For one, "the truth of God" was at stake. The promise of a Messiah was to the Jewish people. From the first promise to the fathers, the message of God to Abraham (Gen. 12:1-3), to the last promise in the last chapter of Malachi (Mal. 4:5-6) the Jews had a special place in God's plan. They were the chosen people, the only people of God at that time. To them belonged the covenants and promises. They were custodians of the oracles of God. Those covenants, promises, and oracles were theirs in the first place. Even the gospel, Paul said in Romans 1:16, is to the Jew first. Hence, Jesus lived out His days as a minister to the circumcision, authenticating thereby the promises made to Israel. The nativity accounts all bear this out, for there is nothing in the New Testament more intensely Hebraic than those early chapters of Matthew and Luke. When Jesus cried, "It is finished!" (John 19:30), among the items completed was His distinct function as "a minister of the circumcision" (Rom. 15:8, KJV). As a nation the Jews rejected Him and, for all they knew, did away with Him. As minister exclusively to the Jews, Jesus is no example for us. He was unique in that special responsibility to Israel. Yet, Paul said nothing to denigrate Israel, the special chosen people. Found nowhere else in Scripture, the expression, "servant of the circumcision" is likely used here to check the pride of "the strong," the Gentile believers at Rome, the so-called liberated Christians who lived without narrow-minded scruples (14—15:7), by elevating the people of the covenant (9:1-4) to their proper dignity. This also had to be said for the sake of "the truth of God" (15:8).

It is worthy of note that though Paul did not quote the first form of the promise made to the fathers, that promise did include a provision that strongly hinted at a worldwide mission of some sort, namely "in you [Abraham and his posterity] all the families of the earth shall be blessed" (Gen. 12:3).

The force of Romans 15:8 is to say that if Jesus' personal public ministry was solely to Jews, there was a historic reason that furnished no precedent for any other preacher. The exclusive Jewishness of Jesus' ministry should never be repeated.

ARGUMENT BASED ON OLD TESTAMENT TEACHINGS (vv. 9-13)

Many things impress the reader in these verses: in the first place, Paul, a former disciple of Rabbi Gamaliel, quoted from all three parts of the Tanach—the Torah (Law), the Neviim (Prophets), and the Kethuvim (Writings):

. . . and for the Gentiles to glorify God for His mercy; as it is written,
> "THEREFORE I WILL GIVE PRAISE TO THEE AMONG THE GENTILES,
> AND I WILL SING TO THY NAME." (Psalm 18:49)

And again he says,
> "REJOICE, O GENTILES, WITH HIS PEOPLE." (Deut. 32:43)

And again,
> "PRAISE THE LORD ALL YOU GENTILES,
> AND LET ALL THE PEOPLE PRAISE HIM." (Psalm 117:1)

And again Isaiah says,
> "THERE SHALL COME THE ROOT OF JESSE,
> AND HE WHO ARISES TO RULE OVER THE GENTILES,
> IN HIM SHALL THE GENTILES HOPE." (Isa. 11:10)

Now may the God of hope fill you with all joy and peace in believing, that you may abound in hope by the power of the Holy Spirit. (Rom. 15:9-13)

Paul found whole-Bible authority for a church's *sending* mission to the Gentiles. He followed Jesus in the then "new" understanding of what Christians have come to call the Old Testament for "He explained to them the things concerning Himself in all the Scriptures" (Luke 24:27).

In the second place, the praise of God from the majority section (Gentiles) of the human race rather than from a small tribe (Israelites) is an important thrust of the meaning of these select passages: "PRAISE . . . AMONG THE GENTILES. . . . LET ALL THE PEOPLES [note the plural] PRAISE HIM" (vv. 9, 11). No longer shall a remnant from the nations of earth, the Hebrews, alone have a saving covenant and receive salvation's praise-inducing benefits. All "the Gentiles" [i.e., nations *(ethnoi)*] shall "glorify God for His mercy" (v. 9). When explaining to Jews why he was turning from them and preaching to Gentiles, Paul sometimes quoted other texts, (e.g., Acts 13:46-47): "And Paul and Barnabas spoke out boldly and said, 'It was necessary that the Word of God should be spoken to you first; since you repudiate it, . . . we are turning to the Gentiles. For thus the Lord has commanded us.'" One might suppose he would have quoted the Great Commission or some primitive tradition of it (the gospels were not yet written). But he did not. He quoted Isaiah 49:6:

> I have placed You as a light for the Gentiles,
> That You should bring salvation to the end of the earth.
>
> (Acts 13:47)

It seems plain enough that Paul found this part of the missionary mandate in the Old Testament.

In the third place, Paul carefully distinguished *covenant* promise from *mercy*. God made a *covenant* with Israel (merciful to be sure, but, once made, a matter of fidelity on God's part) but He had and has *mercy* on the Gentiles. He confirms promises to Israel but extends mercy to Gentiles (Rom. 15:9). The covenant *with* Abraham and his seed mentions Gentiles. They shall benefit from the covenant, but it is never *with* the Gentiles in any primary sense. The Gentiles are never an

Israel—spiritual or otherwise. Of the Israelites, Paul said elsewhere in Romans that theirs is "the adoption [*huiothesia*, son-placement] as sons and the glory and the covenants and the giving of the Law and the temple service [*latreia*, public or reverential service] and the promises" (Rom. 9:4). What God has done in Christ for Israel (in Romans often referred to obliquely as "us" or "we") is, indeed, a matter of special arrangement in ancient covenant. For the Gentiles, (in Romans often "ye" or "you"), however, God's saving actions are a matter of "mercy" apart from covenant.

It is reassuring, if likewise disconcerting, to find that Paul was almost naïve about what are now considered obvious doctrinal distinctions. For example, when Romans is read today, part of the time it looks as though Paul favored one kind of modern evangelical theology concerning covenants and dispensations, while at another time it looks as though he espoused quite another position or as though he amalgamated the positions now held by differing evangelical groups.

ARGUMENT BASED ON APOSTOLIC MISSION (15:14-21)

The next eight-verse section again presents a hornet's nest of vexing textual problems—Septuagint renderings versus Hebrew, Pauline adaptation versus strict quotation. In no case, though, do these detract from Paul's plain thrust.

He completes his arguments based on Old Testament Scripture. He goes on to solicit help from the Roman Christians by telling them directly about his great project in the far West. Bold strategy coupled with courageous action has great power of persuasion, especially in the person of such an esteemed and highly regarded man as Paul. His own apostolic mission is his argument.

Verses 14-21 (as indeed all of chapter 15) try the pulpit expositor's patience and skill. Not many sermons are preached on them. The point of the chapter—an effort to solicit agreement, prayer, and support for the mission to Spain—is slow in coming. But, be patient with Paul. There were reasons for his circuitous approach. Remember, he was proposing something that had not, so far as is known, yet been done in any large way. Perhaps it was yet unheard of in Rome: Christians must do more than simply *take the gospel along* wherever they go. Jesus' message to the disciples in Matthew 10:7-42 was plain enough about that. Paul proposed that Christians should also mount campaigns of evangelism; they must dedicate life and treasure *to send* gospel messengers to foreign parts, and some Christians must *go*. They must also, from another perspective, be *sent*. There are personal reflections of the author to ponder and his personal history: "I myself also am convinced. . . . I have written very boldly . . . [I should] be a minister. . . . I have found reason for boasting. . . . I will not presume to speak . . . except what Christ has accomplished through me . . . I have fully preached. . . . thus I aspire to preach . . . that I might not build upon another man's foundation" (Rom. 15:14-20). Modern man tends to be impatient with that sort of rumination. It follows an intimate approach that seems odd today for one who was a stranger to most of his readers. The mixing of personal sentiment and emotion with the serious business being proposed should only heighten the awareness of the great delicacy of the matter of proposing a project on a grand scale to people who were strangers to Paul's person.

The author sought to build a bridge of mutual respect between writer and readers in verses 14 and 15: "My brethren, I myself also am convinced that you yourselves are full of goodness, filled with all knowledge, and able also to admonish one another. But I have written very boldly to you on some points."

They were, he said, well-taught, mature believers (v. 14). Perhaps these words of praise, expressing high esteem, were intended to overcome any antagonism produced by his rather sharp negative criticism in chapter 14. This served to put those rather sharp criticisms in the realm of loving reproof within family relationships. He also called them, "my brethren." Furthermore, he told them that though he had "written very boldly," it was only "on some points," *apo merous.* The very same expression elsewhere in Romans (11:25) means *in part, partly.* It seems best, and commentators agree, to take this as meaning only certain portions of his letter, as opposed to the whole. In addition to chapter 14 there were other rather severe statements, but generally Paul said very little by way of direct reference to the Roman congregation, either of praise or blame.

Next, Paul carefully explained the special character of his own work and its unique value to God. He explained that in Christ's own arrangement of affairs for mankind, he was "a minister of Christ Jesus to the Gentiles" (v. 16). He asserted that it was a special ministry, of a high value, and apparently generally recognized by Christians: ". . . So as to remind you again, because of the grace that was given me from God, to be a minister [servant, *leitourgos*] of Christ Jesus to the Gentiles, ministering [officiating as a sacrificing priest, *hierourgounta*] as a priest the gospel of God, that my offering [presenting a sacrificial victim, *prosforia*] of the Gentiles might become acceptable, sanctified by the Holy Spirit" (Rom. 15:15-16).

The figures drawn from the ritual, sacrifical rites of the ancient world, both pagan and Jewish, are transparent. They serve only to convey the religious-spiritual values, not to teach anything at all about any genuine Christian ritual sacrifice or ritual priesthood. Both Paul and the Romans knew that such have no place in biblical Christian religion. The device is not strange or unusual in Paul's writings, for even in the next chapter he said "Epaenetus . . . is the first fruits of [Asia] unto Christ" (16:5, KJV; cf. 11:16 and 1 Cor. 15:20, 23, in KJV). In this manner Paul put the projected mission of evangelists *going* to Spain and of others *sending* on the very highest possible level of human religious effort. It is difficult for the exegete even to discuss this passage without employing (albeit symbolically) ritual language that is ordinarily abhorrent to the post-Reformation age. Yet no other wording could more fully convey the holiness of the project.

Paul then deftly prepared to connect the "novel" missionary project with his own reasons for writing them a letter (Rom. 15:18-21). A few comments should serve to make the necessary connection between Paul's argument for support of his western mission and the argument of this chapter for authority in all Christian missions of evangelism. The Romans were informed that Paul's policy, under Christ's special assignment, was to do strictly pioneer work, preaching the gospel only in regions where others had not previously done so. That mission, amply authenticated by divine signs and power, had now been completed throughout the eastern Empire. Paul had evangelized from Jerusalem along the Mediterranean coast northwest through the regions of what are now called Syria and Asia Minor to Greece, and also to Macedonia and Illyricum (also called Dalmatia), a Roman province lying north of Macedonia and approximately the same as modern Yugo- slavia.

ARGUMENT BASED ON PRACTICALITY AND NEED (VV. 22-33)

Finally, Paul invited the church at Rome to join him in a particular missionary project and to share in the support of it. Some authors have pronounced all of Romans 15:14-33 an epilogue, his instructions and exhortations being complete. Others, certainly correct, assert that herein Paul arrived at the ultimate purpose in writing the epistle to the Romans, which was to make Rome the strategic base of his future missionary effort in the western part of the Roman world. After reading this climactic statement of the main design of the letter, it may be used as a guide in interpreting the previous parts—something the first recipients could not do when they first heard it read in their assembly. They could only do so on the second time over. The following summarizes, in several propositions, what Paul seems to have said and relates it to the *going* and *sending* mission of world evangelism, as related to his time.

A NEW MISSIONARY VENTURE WAS ABOUT TO BE LAUNCHED

Paul was going to transfer his missionary activity to Spain. There was even a hint of this in Luke's report. For, not long after he wrote the epistle to Rome, while he was still in the midst of the three year campaign at Ephesus, "Paul purposed in the spirit to go to Jerusalem after he had passed through Macedonia and Achaia, saying, 'After I have been there, I must also see Rome'" (Acts 19:21).

Reasons had already been given. Those he summarized by claiming that he had run out of space for his effort in the East: there was "no further place for [him] in these regions" (Rom 15:23). His intention was therefore to "go . . . to Spain" (15:24). The schedule, as far as he could determine it, was first to go to Jerusa- lem and then to go to Spain by way of Rome: "Therefore, when I have finished this, and have put my seal on this fruit of theirs, I will go on by way of you to Spain" (15:28). Of course, as every reader of Acts 21-28 knows, Paul lost all personal control of his travels and work for several years. When he finally got to Rome it was under guard as a prisoner of the Empire. Whether he ever reached Spain is not known for certain, although there are strong local traditions in various parts of Spain that he did. Those are credited sufficiently in Spain today that "in the early 1960's several Spanish communities celebrated the 19th cente- nary of the arrival of the Apostle Paul in Spain, and in 1961 the Spanish postal authorities issued a 1-peseta commemorative stamp showing El Greco's Apostle Paul with the text: XIX CENTENARIO DE LA VENIDA DE SAN PABLO A

ESPAÑA."[1] Early Christian documents support the tradition of Paul's missionary travel about the Empire later than the two years of Acts 28:30-31 and therefore after his release from the Roman prison (*Epistle of Clement of Rome to the Corinthians* (A.D. 96), *The Canon of Muratori* (c. A.D. 170), the *Apocryphal Acts of Peter*, Chapter 3).[2]

THE MISSIONARY PARTY HAD ALREADY BEEN FORMED.

This can be assumed by correlating certain statements in Romans with data of the later chapters of Acts. The Christians of Macedonia and Achaia (Athens and environs in Greece) had given money for the relief of those believers of the mother church of Christendom at Jerusalem who were in poverty and oppressed (Rom. 15:26). This was a duty (he used the word "debtors" *opheiletai*, v. 27, KJV) of the Gentile believers. He was about to carry this gift personally to Jerusalem, but he was apprehensive that the anti-Gentile sentiments of the Jewish Christians at Jerusalem might prevent him from delivering it. He asked the Roman believers to pray they would receive it (15:31). He was also apprehensive that he might come to harm from the jealous non-Christian Jews of Palestine (15:31). All this appeared in the reports of the book of Romans. Paul was not traveling alone because Acts 20-28 is reported in first person plural—the well known "we" device. Evidently Luke stayed with Paul right on through the two years of imprisonment at Caesarea and the voyage to Rome (see Acts 27:1; 28:1). It seems safe to suppose that other of the well-known associates of Paul, veterans of the eastern campaigns, were to join him at Rome. The tradition, however, is that his companions were two young believers of Rome and that they sailed with him from Ostia (*Acts of Peter*, chapter 3).

THE PRINCIPLE OF UNIVERSAL CHRISTIAN SUPPORT IS ASSUMED.

There is first of all the cooperative collection itself, to which Paul alluded. He argued that Gentiles have a special duty in this regard: "They are indebted to them. For if the Gentiles have shared in their spiritual things, they are indebted to minister to them also in material things" (Rom. 15:27). This principle could extend to support of missions in distant places where the ordinary believer cannot go. It links neatly with the question, "And how shall they preach unless they are sent?" (10:15) and with the argument given in 1 Corinthians 9:7 for support of apostles and other missionary "professionals": "Who . . . serves as a soldier at his own expense?"

THE PERSONAL, PRACTICAL MISSIONARY APPEAL IS STATED.

This is, perhaps, the *raison d'etre* of the epistle. Paul selected Rome and the Roman church as base for his new missionary thrust. He had just expressed his

1. Otto F. A. Meinardus, "Paul's Missionary Journey to Spain: Tradition and Folklore," *The Biblical Archaeology* 41 (June 1978):63.
2. Ibid., pp. 61-62.

long deferred desire to come "to you [Romans]" (Rom. 15:23) and now Paul plainly, if indirectly, placed his mission before their Christian consideration:

> Whenever I go to Spain—for I hope to see you in passing, and to be helped on my way there by you, when I have first enjoyed your company for a while. . . . I will go on by way of you to Spain. And I know that when I come to you, I will come in the fulness of the blessing of Christ. Now I urge you, brethren, by our Lord Jesus Christ and by the love of the Spirit, to strive together with me in your prayers to God for me. (Rom. 15:24, 28-30)

Paul wanted their *friendship;* he called it "company" (v. 24). Then he desired their *material support* (surely more than an escort) saying "[I hope] to be helped on my way there by you" (v. 24).

C. K. Barrett has formulated the meaning of "to be helped on my way there by you" very well. He concluded a survey of the evidences:

> Thus the expression seems to have been almost a technical term with a well-understood meaning among missionaries. Paul is hinting that he would like the church of Rome to take some responsibility for his Spanish mission, so that he can start work in the west with their moral support at least, and possibly with some contribution from them in assistance or funds. If this is so, we can see a special reason why he took pains to give the Romans a clear and fully argued statement of his position [chapter 1-14]. They might be prejudiced against him by misrepresentations. It was a matter of practical moment to him that they should understand and accept the doctrinal basis on which his missionary preaching rested.[3]

C. E. B. Cranfield said *kai huf humēn propemfthēnai ekei,* "to be helped on my way there by you," means "active help toward the carrying out of the proposed mission . . . more than a mere farewell accompanied with prayers and good wishes." A footnote states *"propempein* was used to denote the fulfillment of various services which might be required by a departing traveller, such as the provision of rations, money, means of transport, letters of introduction, and escort for some part of the way. It became a regular technical term of the Christian mission."[4] Examination of the following occurrences of *prompempō* in the New Testament establishes that it is here and elsewhere the precise term New Testament missionaries used for provisions by the churches for the means of support of the missionaries: Acts 15:3; 20:38; 21:5; 1 Corinthians 16:6, 11; 2 Corinthians 1:16; Titus 3:13.

The offering for the poor believers at Jerusalem, in which the Romans had no part, would surely further incline them to see the propriety of giving money to pay for Christian efforts outside their local congregation. This aspect of his advance publicity, like mention of money by missionary publicists today, may be only a broad hint, understandably so in each case.

3. C. K. Barrett, *A Commentary on the Epistle to the Romans,* p. 229.
4. C. E. B. Cranfield, *A Critical and Exegetical Commentary on the Epistle to the Romans,* 2:769. He cited Herodotos 1. 111 and 3. 50; Xenophon *Anabasis* 7. 2. 8; 1 Maccabees 12:14; and the *Epistle of Aristeas* 172.

He also desired their *prayers*. He was specific about prayer for the reception of his mission on the detour to Jerusalem and for physical safety there. Though he did not specifically mention prayer in connection with his great project in Spain, it cannot be doubted that they did think about it and that once in Rome he intended to spell this out fully.

The early church was convinced that Paul's appeal to Caesar was successful, and, being freed again, he entered on another rather lengthy ministry of "itinerant evangelism." Many modern scholars have been convinced that 2 Timothy and Titus come from this later period. The greatest of the early church historians, Eusebius, wrote that "after pleading his cause, he is said to have been sent [note the word "sent" in connection with the theme of this essay], again upon the ministry of preaching, and after a second visit to the city [Rome], he finished his life with martyrdom."[5] If this is true, then the book of Romans may be the first bit of successful *foreign* mission propaganda.[6]

5. Eusebius *Ecclesiastical History* 2. 22.
6. C. H. Dodd, *The Epistle to the Romans,* p. 224.

PART 4

JESUS' POST-RESURRECTION
SAYINGS

18

Ascension Day and Easter Evening

(Acts 1:8; John 20:21-23; Luke 24:44-47; Mark 16:15-16)

It is plain that Jesus said much to His disciples about their going out into the world to preach and about the world's response to their effort.

Jesus also sent out the twelve and the seventy. Yet the studies thus far have not uncovered any words of Jesus to the *direct* effect that one group of disciples (say a congregation, denomination, or missionary society) ought to enlist, send, and support another group of disciples in the manner of modern foreign missions.

It has already been pointed out that Matthew produced his gospel after Christians of the time had become deeply involved in a zealous mission of worldwide evangelism for about fifteen years. Irenaeus, bishop of Lyons in the late second century, said Matthew published his gospel while Peter and Paul were preaching at Rome.[1] When was that? Most authorities suggest a date of A.D. 61 to A.D. 63. That date is advanced because of evidence in Acts and in the epistles.

An earlier date is ruled out because Acts clearly indicates that Paul did not visit Rome until he arrived there a prisoner of the Empire at about A.D. 61. According to Acts 28:30, he stayed there two years, during which time he was allowed, under detention, to come and go and to reside in his own rented quarters. He was thus free to preach publicly in Rome. If indeed Peter was in Rome at the time, as Irenaeus suggests he was, he, too, would have been free to preach. Matthew could well have been written during the period of joint ministry in Rome by the two apostles.

A later date is ruled out by evidence from Titus, 2 Timothy, and Romans. In Titus, there is no mention of imprisonment, and Paul announces definite-sounding plans (3:12). In 2 Timothy, on the other hand, Paul speaks of imminent death (4:6), and the epistle as a whole is completely different in tone from the earlier prison epistles. Since evangelicals generally place Titus and 2 Timothy after Paul's initial imprisonment in Rome, the implication is that Titus speaks of a period of freedom following Paul's house arrest in Rome, while 2 Timothy speaks of a second imprisonment, one much harsher than the first (2 Tim. 1:15-18;

---

1. Irenaeus *Against Heresies* 3. 1. 1.

4:16). The harshness of this second imprisonment in Rome makes it unlikely that Paul was free to preach in Rome. That leaves the period between imprisonments. Did Paul preach in Rome then? It is unlikely that he did. Romans 15 and long tradition suggest instead that Paul engaged in missionary activity in Spain, Macedonia, Asia, and Crete. After that, he must have been accused, arrested, and imprisoned at Rome, where he was executed A.D. 67 or 68. Peter shared a similar destiny at about the same time. Paul was beheaded at the site of St. Paul's Church outside the wall of Rome and Peter was crucified at the site of St. Peter's Cathedral in the Vatican quarter. That *is* the ancient tradition, and considerable Protestant feeling to the contrary, it is fair to say that archaeological excavation of the sites and recent objective studies support it.

It is utterly in keeping with that construction of history that Matthew should compose a gospel, selecting especially those anecdotes, sayings, and addresses that provide the most specific dominical support for a Christian mission of world evangelism. In it he arranged the materials strategically and climaxed the treatise with the most *explicit* statements of Jesus in support for such a world mission to be found in the New Testament: Matthew 28:16-20. Each of the gospels relates portions of Jesus' post-resurrection talks to the disciples on the subject of the mission, and there is an important flashback in the first chapter of Acts. Before examining Matthew's closing words, attention will first be given to the other accounts, reserving for final study the most specific and complete of them all.

JESUS' PREDICTION ON THE DAY OF ASCENSION (Acts 1:8)

"But you shall receive power when the Holy Spirit has come upon you; and you shall be My witnesses both in Jerusalem, and in all Judea and Samaria, and even to the remotest part of the earth" (Acts 1:8).

Strictly speaking, this sentence is a statement of fact, not a command or commission at all. Perhaps if the word is used loosely it might be called a "mandate." It is a statement of future fact. Call it either promise or prediction.

In His very last moments with the eleven (see vv. 2, 4 and 6), the main interest of the Lord was understandably in the inauguration of the new age of witness, by the special descent of the Holy Spirit "not many days from now" (v. 5). This discussion will not dwell at length on that event, but that is not to suggest that it is unimportant. The focus is on information about the mission itself, yet all must acknowledge the mission would have been and is powerless without fulfillment of the promise of Pentecost.

At this moment of parting tenderness, Jesus did not command the apostles what they *must* do, or even *should* do, but simply stated what they were *going* to do—be witnesses. Granted, there is a certain aura of the imperative about such statements by persons of great authority. However, there is nothing of the atmosphere of Sinai in this or any other passage in the New Testament relating to the mission of world evangelism.

"And you shall be My witnesses," or "witnesses unto me" (KJV). Precisely how the genitive "My," is to be taken—whether Christ was what their witness was about or the master of the witnesses—is unimportant. Christ was Lord of those men and they were to witness about Him. The primitive preachment (the *kēr-ygma*) was about Him. The book of Acts uniformly demonstrates that the content of the witness was to be "of my teaching, actions and life, what ye all have yourselves heard and seen."[2] The most succinct summary is Peter's witness to Cornelius (Acts 10:34-43). Peter did not emphasize teachings. He reported nothing of Jesus' teaching and certainly said nothing at all of "what Jesus did for me," nowadays often considered pure Christian witness. Peter spoke to Cornelius only of who Jesus was and what He did, the story of redemption. Paul's sermon at Antioch of Pisidia is much the same (Acts 13). The summary of C. H. Dodd is correct:

> God brought Israel out of Egypt, and gave them David for their king. Of the seed of David Jesus has come as Saviour. He was heralded by John the Baptist. His disciples followed Him from Galilee to Jerusalem. There He was brought to trial by the rulers of the Jews before Pilate, who reluctantly condemned Him. He died according to the Scriptures, and was buried. God raised Him from the dead, according to the Scriptures, and He was seen by witnesses. Through Him forgiveness and justification are offered. Therefore take heed.[3]

The book of Acts shows that "you shall be" means not what the apostles might occasionally have done but what they uninterruptedly *became:* "My witnesses."

When and where they were to be Christ's witnesses is specified more exactly than at first meets the eye. There is something in Acts 1:8 nearly impossible for any smooth translation to convey: "Both in Jerusalem, and in all Judea and Samaria, and even to the remotest part [literally, end] of the earth." RSV omits "both" (in KJV, NASB, and ASV) as does NEB. And thereby hangs a tale and the most overlooked point of the passage. The English language has the word *both,* an adjective and noun designating something common to two (a pair of items, as for example, "both men and women," or "both summer and winter"). English has no such word to designate something common to a series of three or more items. The KJV, ASV, and NASB editors chose slightly to misuse "both" to join "Jerusalem, Judea and Samaria, and the remotest parts." RSV and NEB "solved" the problem by simply skipping an important small Greek word altogether, since there is no equivalent in English and something like "not only in Jerusalem but also in all Judea and Samaria and into the remotest parts," is awkward.

The tiny Greek word is *te.* Grammarians call such words particles. English could use such a useful term as *te,* for it unites as many items in a series as are there, usually joined by "and" *(kai).* So something true of Jerusalem is true also of Judea and Samaria, and the remotest parts. Jesus is not prophesying stages in the spread of Christianity but places of witness. It should be simultaneous witnessing. While not peculiar to Acts, *te* is used there 150 times, more than in all the rest of

2. H. A. W. Meyer, *Critical and Exegetical Commentary on the New Testament,* 4:28.
3. C. H. Dodd, *The Apostolic Preaching and Its Developments,* p. 29.

the New Testament. A clear case of *te* to introduce a series occurs only five verses later (1:13, KJV). Again, for want of an equivalent term, in most versions translated "both," it introduces the names of the eleven apostles "staying" in an "upper room." All eleven are named and most of the names are connected by *kai* (and). Thus in Acts 1:8 the force of the *te . . . kai . . . kai* construction is that disciples were simultaneously and in some equivalent manner to be Christ's witnesses in Jerusalem, Judea and Samaria, and to the remotest parts. As *disciples,* they do not cease to be *witnesses* in one place when some of them happen to move on to another. Progress from the center outward took place all right, and the places named anticipate that, but that is not the point of Jesus' declaration. There is to be a *continuing witness* wherever Christians go and are allowed to stay. This is what the passage means. They soon after went everywhere preaching the gospel—even before the epilogue to Mark's gospel was written. "And they went out and preached everywhere" (Mark 16:20; cf. Acts 11:19-22). When the salt lost its savor it was soon fit only to be cast out and trodden under foot. Medieval Islam, for example, did not usually declare Christianity unlawful in the lands it conquered. It only became difficult, especially economically, to remain Christians. Christendom simply died in most Muslim lands. There are scarcely any Christians at all today in the Islamic lands of North Africa where in the second to sixth centuries there was a strong Christian population. And no places on earth are more resistant to renewed evangelism.

Among the sayings of Jesus about the coming mission of world evangelism, Acts 1:8 is unique and special. He meant that the witness must continue without diminution or interruption in every place Christianity became established. The salt must never lose its savor. The light must never be hid under a bushel. Wolves in sheep's clothing must be exposed. Discipline must be exercised in order that the table of the Lord never become extinct or the table of devils!

The apostles had just asked (Acts 1:6) about restoration of "the kingdom" to Israel. They still had no vision of the mission of evangelism that Jesus had hinted at and had spoken of at length on two occasions (Matt. 10, 13). Acts 1:8 was His answer. Apparently they still thought of the witness as only to Jews scattered throughout the world, as many writers have noted. Their continued lack of understanding revealed how necessary Pentecost really was and the importance of the later revelations to Peter and Paul reported in Acts 9-11 and several of Paul's epistles.

REPETITION OF THE APOSTLES' COMMISSION ON EASTER EVENING
(John 20:21-23)

In the evening of the resurrection day, Jesus made His first appearance to a group of disciples—about six weeks before the time of Acts 1:8. John reported the following:

> Jesus therefore said to them again, "Peace be with you; as the Father has sent Me, I also send you." And when He had said this, He breathed on them, and said to them,

"Receive the Holy Spirit. If you forgive the sins of any, their sins have been forgiven them; if you retain the sins of any, they have been retained." (John 20:21-23)

Is there something like a special authorization for churches to send some of their members out as missionaries in these words? If so, what exactly did Jesus mean? If there is such an authorization or commission here as popular exhortation often assumes, it is in these words, "As the Father has sent Me, I also send you."

Those words were not the first in the Johannine account to introduce the missionary theme and a coming mission of world evangelism. In John 1:1 world evangelization was introduced as Christ having come into the world as "the Word" (John 1:1) and as the "true light" (v. 9). John the Baptist, a man sent from God, bore witness of the light and Christ was the true light coming into the world to enlighten every man. John's entire gospel is an evangelistic tract. F. N. Davey has written of it, "The result of putting it into the hands of learned students, whether of the great religions of Asia or of Judaism, has not seldom been their conversion to the faith of Christ. It has spoken authoritatively alike to those drawn to mysticism and to those schooled in philosophy."[4]

The occasion in John 20 was Jesus' first resurrection appearance to the assembled apostles. Those men were to be the foundation on which the Lord would build His church (Matt. 16:18; Eph. 2:20). If, as Luke 24:33-36 may indicate, there were other disciples present, there are important reasons why the passage relates primarily to the apostles and only through them to the multitude of disciples then and now. This will be discussed in the next paragraphs.

The double pronouncement of peace (John 20:19, 21) served the immediate practical need of the persons present. They had all forsaken Him and fled (Mark 14:50). One had denied Him and another had betrayed Him and perished forever. The two "shaloms" assured the ten apostles present that they were still His select men. The notions that the first was a "hello" and the second a "good-bye" or that the first was addressed to non-apostles and the second to apostles are only conjecture. The context (vv. 19-20) indicates simply that after the first pronouncement they were very glad that He said the words again to quiet them and to reassure them. After all, things like that are done frequently in times of meeting and parting from loved ones, and repetition is the most common way known of making an idea emphatic.

Verse 22 is more difficult. It seems almost cryptic: "He breathed on them, and said to them, 'Receive the Holy Spirit.'" Promises of their being endued with the Holy Spirit began early in John and they referred to an enduement of all Christian believers. Yet this, like the twofold pronouncement of peace, seems to be special for the apostolic group present. A thoughtful comparison of John 15:26-27 with 16:13 and 17:9-20 should be proof that there is a sense in which almost all the gospel following John 12 has primary application to the apostles. Pentecost was to be for everyone; this pronouncement was for the ten (Judas and Thomas being

4. F. N. Davey, "The Gospel According to St. John and the Christian Mission" in Gerald H. Anderson, ed., *The Theology of the Christian Mission*, p. 85.

absent). Pentecost was yet nearly seven weeks in the future. Those numerous interpreters who insist that this was a symbolic act are surely correct. It is not a Johannine Pentecost—a literary duplicate of the Acts 2 account put here for some obscure theological reason[5] or as an earnest of Pentecost. It is nothing other than a historical Easter evening event. There was a great need at that moment among the apostles and those who looked to them for leadership. The passion, death, burial, and resurrection of the Redeemer were history. Ascension and Pentecost remained to fully inaugurate the new era. So the "Spirit of life in Christ Jesus" (Rom. 8:2) of the new age was now communicated to the leaders of the group. They had a difficult, short-term task to complete. They had to patiently tarry in Jerusalem for another week and then proceed together to Galilee to spend a short time with the risen Christ among a larger group of disciples. Then for about a week after His ascension they were to wait quietly and prayerfully (Acts 1:14) at Jerusalem until "the day of Pentecost had come" (Acts 2:1). For those momentous but painfully tedious days they needed a quality of staying power that even the strongest of them had not yet demonstrated. To enable them, Jesus imparted a "Holy Spirit" (John 20:22, *pneuma hagion*), the power of a new life from the risen Savior. This was necessary to create in them the proper conditions for reception of the Holy Spirit in the special way He came at Pentecost. The Spirit conferred was Christ's Spirit, the Holy Spirit as dwelling in Him.

In a parallel way it had been necessary that the Holy Spirit descend upon the Savior, Himself, at the baptism. He then needed "a special gift . . . to qualify Him for His work, and crown the long development of His peculiar powers. . . . We are in the habit of attributing the wisdom . . . grace . . . miracles to His divine nature. But in the Gospels these are . . . attributed to the Holy Ghost. . . . His human nature was enabled to be the organ of His divine nature by a peculiar gift of the Holy Ghost."[6] The conferral of the Spirit in John 20:22 might be conceded to have been a preliminary to Pentecost in the same sense that the descent of the Spirit at Jesus' baptism was preliminary to the mighty work of the Spirit of God in the resurrection some years later (see Rom. 8:11). The words are reminiscent of Genesis 2:7 where God breathed life into the newly formed man, constituting him a living being. Regarding this Easter Eve conferral, B. F. Westcott observed: "The relation of the Paschal to the Pentecostal gift is therefore the relation of quickening to endowing. . . . The characteristic effect of the Pentecostal gift was shown in the new faith by which the disciples were gathered into a living society."[7]

The words about forgiving and retaining sin (v. 23) have been puzzling to all generations of Christians. Note the similarity of language to Matthew 16:19 in which Jesus, speaking to Peter, said, "I will give you the keys of the kingdom of heaven; and whatever you shall bind on earth shall be bound in heaven, and whatever you shall loose on earth shall be loosed in heaven." This similarity does not prove that they relate to the same subject, or, if they do, in the same way.

5. R. E. Brown, *The Gospel According to John*, vol. 29a, *The Anchor Bible*, pp. 1038-39.
6. James Stalker, *The Life of Christ*, pp. 41-42.
7. B. F. Westcott, *The Holy Bible . . . Commentary*, 2:295.

Neither can criticism (literary or redactional) prove that the two reports are of the same event arranged to suit the authors' purposes.[8] Peter's privilege was personally to open the door of gospel access to Gentiles, even against his own wishes, as earlier pages of this book noted. Many think this is what Jesus was speaking of in Matthew 16:19. I judge them to be correct. It became the privilege of the apostles of old (and after them of thousands of others) to proclaim the divine terms of forgiveness of sins by the gospel and with that also to proclaim divine judgment on unbelief, itself eventually an unpardonable sin (see John 3:36). To preach the glad tidings of gospel forgiveness is inherently to announce eternal judgment and divine wrath also. For to reject the gospel leaves the sinner more a "child of wrath" (see Eph. 2:3) than he was before. This is part of the message of any disciple on a mission of world evangelism.

There is also an unmistakable reference here to acts of church discipline, exercised first by apostles (Acts 5:1-11; 1 Cor. 5:1-6) with Spirit-inspired discernment. The churches would later, with less striking power but full right, do the same.[9]

Jesus, of course, was the first to proclaim the forgiveness of the new age, as He did at Nazareth (Luke 4:16-21). Sometimes He declared a particular person's sins forgiven (Matt. 9:2), though not without repentance. He sometimes declared sins not forgiven, i.e., "retained" (Matt. 23:14). Apostles proclaimed redemption and forgiveness, as Acts frequently reports. In matters of discipline of church members, they had power not seen on earth since their day as the story of Ananias and Sapphira shows (Acts 5). Believers today have only power to *announce* redemption and to *declare* forgiveness if people will repent, for the Lord's discernment of the hearts of men (John 2:24) is lacking.

In the most crucial sentence of the passage as far as the sending of evangelists on a mission is concerned, Jesus said, "As the Father has sent Me, I also send you" (John 20:21; essentially the same in KJV and RSV). It is striking that among the five accounts of Jesus' post-resurrection instructions regarding the world mission this is the only one that employs the word "send." It requires careful attention.

If anything among the Lord's post-resurrection sayings is a formal commission of some sort, this is. It is the first. It is not a formal command, but it does announce a mission to be fulfilled. But who is to complete the mission? Who are the sent ones of "I also send you"? There are only two main views. The first is the common assumption that all Christian believers are referred to. This view is not usually defended but when it is, attention is called to the fact that John 20:19-23 seems to be parallel to Luke 24:36-43 and that two disciples who were not apostles seem to have been present (Luke 24:13-35). These two would have shared in the commissioning, it is said. And, since the assembled group are called "disciples" (John 20:20) and apparently distinguished from "the twelve" (v. 24), non-apostles must have shared in the whole occasion. So everything Jesus said

---

8. Brown, p. 1040.
9. See J. H. Bernard, *A Critical and Exegetical Commentary on the Gospel According to St. John,* 2:680.

applied equally to all. These evidences are often thought to be final and sufficient even by respected Bible scholars. It is also thought to be important to a biblical basis for missions.

There are, however, scholars of first rank, who insist that whoever may or may not have been present on the occasion, the whole sentence, "As the Father has sent me, I also send you" "primarily had reference to the original choice of the twelve 'apostles' [a word meaning sent ones]."[10] It has reference to "the Father's relation to Christ and Christ's relation to the *apostles,* not to the general body of disciples."[11] Evidences cited follow.

1. The words seem intended to prompt the hearers to recall who they were (apostles) and their original call to the office (Matt. 10:1-2, 5; Mark 3:14). This is a constant theme in John. The word for "send" in the two references is *apostello* from which comes *apostle.*
2. John 20:21 is parallel to and no doubt consciously shaped by John 15:9, "As the Father has loved Me, I have also loved you," and 17:18, "As Thou didst send Me into the world, I also have sent them [past tense, already done] into the world." In both these passages the apostles and *only* the apostles are involved. Because of the mentioned parallelism of 20:21, it would follow that the "sent" ones are still that same group—the apostles.
3. In a unique sense Christ Himself was the pre-eminent Apostle (*apostolon,* Heb. 3:1) of God the Father who sent *(apesteilen)* Him (John 3:17; cf. 20:21). In a similar sense the twelve only were apostles ("sent ones") of Christ. At the Last Supper, speaking to the twelve as apostles and to no others in any primary sense, He said, "He who receives whomever I send receives Me; and he who receives Me receives Him who sent Me (13:20). J. H. Bernard said of these passages, "Language of this kind is addressed in the Fourth Gospel to the apostles *alone;* and it is difficult, in the face of the parallel passages [15:9, 17:18] . . . to suppose that in this verse, and here only, the evangelist means us to understand that the . . . commission was given to all the disciples who were present, alike and in the same degree." Bernard continues, conceding that "it is quite just to describe this verse as 'the Charter of the Christian Church' (Westcott) but the Charter was addressed in the first instance to the leaders of the Church."[12]
4. It is apparent that the earliest Christian writers to address this matter regarded John 20:20-23 as addressed primarily to the apostles. There is no want of dominical authority for proclamation by every believer of Christ's Lordship and forgiveness of sin through Him. Yet the early writers did not find that authority in words like those of John 20:20-23. Justin Martyr (110-165) wrote as if aware only that apostles were present. Speaking of John 20:20-23, Justin

10. Bernard, 2:675.
11. Ibid., p. 676.
12. Ibid.

explained how Christ's resurrection fulfilled Psalm 22: "He stood in the midst of his brethren the apostles who repented of 'their flight from him when he was crucified, after he rose from the dead, and after they were persuaded by Himself that, before His passion He had mentioned to them that he must suffer these things, and that they were announced beforehand by the prophets, . . . as is made evident in the memoirs [four gospels] of the apostles."[13] Origen (185-254), in what may have been the first effort at systematic theology, said explicitly that the expression "Receive the Holy Spirit" was addressed specifically to "his apostles." Origen argued: "But in the New Testament we have proofs in abundance, as when the Holy Spirit is related to have descended upon Christ, and when the Lord breathed on his apostles after the resurrection and said, 'Receive the Holy Spirit.' . . . and that the name of the Holy Spirit must be joined to that of the unbegotten God the Father and his only-begotten Son."[14] Cyprian argued for the dignity and authority of Peter and of the other original apostles and, through them, of the church: "Christ said to Peter alone, 'Whatsoever thou shall bind on earth . . .' and again, in the Gospel, when Christ breathed on the apostles alone, saying, 'Receive ye the Holy Ghost. . . .' "[15]

5. "The twelve" and "disciples" are employed in verses 24 and 25 in such a way as clearly to indicate that, in this passage, only the apostolic group is involved in verses 20-25. "But Thomas, one of *the twelve,* called Didymus, was not with them when Jesus came. The *other disciples* therefore were saying to him, 'We have seen the Lord' " (John 20:24-25, ital. added). "Apostles" and "disciples" are interchangeable terms in this passage.[16]

It seems clear, then, that John 20:21 is a reiteration of the apostle's commission, not a fresh announcement of the church's commission. It is for contemporary Christians in the sense that the apostles fulfilled their mission and it is carried on today. Yet it is an error to research this passage as if a thorough exegesis of it might provide particular guidance to missionaries and mission boards. Jesus' guidance should be sought in the great texts, such as Matthew 10 and 13, wherein He truly addressed the church's mission, not in this text meant primarily for the apostles.

A recent collaboration by a prominent evangelical Methodist scholar and a respected Baptist professor (neither with the slightest tinge of sacerdotal opinion) cannot be set aside as special pleading for apostolic succession or priestly privilege. They comment on verse 21:

13. Justin Martyr *Dialogue with Trypho the Jew* 106, *The Ante-Nicene Fathers,* 1:252.
14. Origen *On First Principles,* p. 30.
15. Cyprian *The Epistles of Cyprian* 74. 16, *The Ante-Nicene Fathers,* 5:394. In Cyprian's treatise *on the Unity of the Church* he made the same points again *(The Treatises of Cyprian* 1. 4, *The Ante-Nicene Fathers,* 5:422). I am indebted to J. H. Bernard for calling attention to these patristic sources (Bernard, 2:677).
16. The heading to John 20:19-23 in the *New King James Version* is "The Apostles Commissioned."

Jesus now reiterated their commission as *apostoloi,* as "sent ones." He had done so earlier when they were sent forth to preach (Luke 9:2; cf. 10:1). Later he said they were appointed to "go and bear fruit" ([John] 15:16). In his prayer he affirmed, "As thou didst send me into the world, even so sent I them into the world" ([John] 17:18). Now the commission is more formal and more final. Apparently the commission was given only to the ten apostles (cf. [John 20:] 24); this seems implied by the note that Thomas, "one of the twelve," was not present (JHB, II, 677). The formal bestowal of "peace" is preliminary to the formal commissioning.[17]

B. F Westcott's approach was different from that outlined here, yet he argued at length that the twelve apostles' commission is none other than the commission that Christ, the Apostle of the Father, received in the first place.[18] There is not so much a parallel between His commission and theirs (and ours) as identity. Westcott's view has been shared by many scholars since he wrote in 1880, though most recent writers seem to feel obliged to honor his argument by both misunderstanding and belittling it. They are too contemporary in fearing that someone will snatch the Great Commission, seemingly unaware that if a "greater commission" is seen in the New Testament, only good can come of it.

The Father *sent* the Son to be the Savior of the world. The Son completed redemption and appointed apostles, "sent ones," to convey a "witness" to the world that the Savior had come. The witness is continued by reporting what the Father did, what the Son did, and what the apostles recorded in the Scriptures. There is but one mission and commission. It was the Son's mission and commission. Christians are His servants in His commission. In this sense it is possible to say with Paul: "Now all these things are from God, who reconciled us to Himself through Christ, and gave us the ministry of reconciliation, namely, that God was in Christ reconciling the world to Himself, not counting their trespasses against them, and He has committed to us the word [message] of reconciliation" (2 Cor. 5:18-19).

Years would pass before the disciples perceived anything like the full length and breadth and height of redemption. Meanwhile all the disciples in the room immediately took up where they left off with their Lord on the night of betrayal. They began to benefit from new life, new insights, and new power even before Pentecost after that Easter evening and Jesus' statement, "Receive the Holy Spirit." Over the next several years they would venture out into the world and preach everywhere (see Mark 16:20).

They would carry on Jesus' own mission, the one promised to Abraham's seed, rooted in biblical history, celebrated by poets, and predicted by prophets, then carried into effect by the incarnation, passion, death, resurrection, and ascension of the second Person of the Godhead. This is the meaning of "My witnesses," "in His name" and similar language in connection with the mission.

17. George Allen Turner and Julius R. Mantey, *The Evangelical Commentary: The Gospel Accounts According to John,* pp. 396-397.
18. Westcott, p. 294; "special additional note on chapter xx. 21," p. 298.

FURTHER ENLIGHTENMENT ON THE MEANING OF SCRIPTURE, THE FUTURE MISSION, AND IMMEDIATE ACTION
(Luke 24:44-47)

Luke 24:44-49 falls at the end of a lengthy account of how Jesus appeared to two disciples from Emmaus who then hastened to a gathering of the eleven and several other disciples at a room in Jerusalem. Perhaps everything from verse 44 onward, certainly verses 48 and 49, belongs to a later occasion. The command to "tarry in Jerusalem" (v. 49) clearly belongs after the intervening excursion to Galilee (Matt 28:7, 10, 15; Mark 16:7) and return to Jerusalem again. F. Godet has observed that Luke, "having reached the end of he first part of his history [the gospel of Luke], and having the intention of repeating those facts as the point of departure for his second [The Acts of the Apostles], thought it enough to state them in the summary way."[19] The word "then" (v. 45) "may embrace an indefinite space of time."[20] I. Howard Marshall has stated that "Luke has consciously telescoped his story. . . it is probable that he is here summarizing what Jesus told his disciples over the period of the resurrection appearances.[21]

The verses now to be quoted, Luke 24:44-47, probably belong, as does John 20:21-23, to the evening of the day of His resurrection.

> Now He said to them, "These are My words which I spoke to you while I was still with you, that all things which are written about Me in the Law of Moses and the Prophets and the Psalms must be fulfilled." Then He opened their minds to understand the Scriptures, and He said to them, "Thus it is written, that the Christ should suffer and rise again from the dead the third day; and that repentance for forgiveness of sins should be proclaimed in His name to all the nations, beginning from Jerusalem. (Luke 24:44-47)

Again, this study will not be a general exposition but a focus on the ideas of going and sending in the Christian mission of world evangelism. It is contrary to the form and meaning of the passage to declare it a commission in any formal sense. It rather presents the scriptural information and argument from which the duty of a mission of world evangelism is to be inferred. If there is any mandate here, it is in the form of facts rather than of command. "If the accent so far has been on what the Scriptures prophesied concerning the Messiah, now there is a switch to the prophecy [not command] of the preaching of the gospel to all nations. . . . The disciples are implicitly [not explicitly] called to undertake this task."[22]

The first fact concerns the finished universal redemption in Christ. It is redemption predicted in the whole of the Old Testament—"the Law. . . . the Prophets and the Psalms" (v. 44). Rightly viewed, all of the Old Testament is truly messianic—by preparation, by extension, by promise, by indirect and typical

---

19. F. Godet, *A Commentary on the Gospel of St. Luke*, 2:358.
20. Ibid.
21. I. Howard Marshall, *The Gospel of Luke*, p. 904.
22. Marshall, p. 903. See also his defense of the non-imperative nature of the passage, p. 906.

prediction, and even by direct personal reference to Messiah.[23] Only thus can this passage and Luke 24:25-27 (ital. added) rightly be explained: " 'O foolish men and slow of heart to believe in *all* that the prophets have spoken! Was it not necessary for the Christ to suffer these things and to enter into His glory?' And beginning with *Moses* and with *all the prophets,* He explained to them the things concerning Himself in *all the Scriptures.*" Also, "then He opened their minds to understand the Scriptures" (v. 45). They were thus given to understand something: according to the Old Testament Scriptures, "it is written, that the Christ should suffer and rise again from the dead the third day" (v. 46). It takes a Christian heart fully to understand it, yet all Christians do regard the Old Testament as essentially a Christian book.

Every messianic prediction of the Old Testament, with every type or inference, has been rejected by some learned unbeliever. Yet Jesus insisted that the promised redemption had already occurred. The perfect tense of the word in Greek for "it has been written," indicates that the Old Testament is connected with the present state of affairs.

This leads to a second fact. The same Old Testament Scriptures require "that repentance for forgiveness of sins should be preached in His name to all the nations, beginning in Jerusalem" (Luke 24:47). It is not necessary, therefore, to regard prophecies in the gospels of a future mission of the church to the Gentiles as being an invention of the church read back into the time of Jesus and placed on His lips by tendentious writers of the gospels, as some recent New Testament critical authors assert they were.[24] Luke 24:27 is part of a larger Greek sentence beginning with "And He said" at the beginning of verse 46. Everything following *houtōs gegraptai* ("thus it is written") through *ta ethnē* ("the nations") is part of a compound infinitival sentence within the larger sentence. More literally: "Thus it is written, the Christ to suffer and to rise from dead (ones) on the third day, and repentance and forgiveness of sins unto all the nations to be preached in His name." It cannot be denied that in Jesus' exposition of the Old Testament, preaching to the nations was as much a part of Old Testament prediction as the passion and resurrection. Jesus made a special point of it (Matt. 12:18-21, for example).

The mandate is derived, therefore, from a new understanding of the Scriptures. It was an understanding that led to much preaching. The word "[to] be proclaimed" is the aorist passive infinitive of *kēryssō,* root source of the much-bandied-about word *kērugma* (preachment). "God," says Paul, chose "through the foolishness of the *[kērugma]* to save them who believe" (1 Cor. 1:21). Jesus intended that proclamation would be the primary mode of Christian expansion.

Later on, in the book of Acts, whenever a missionary preached a sermon to Jews he specifically declared Jesus as Messiah and Savior, proved by recourse to the Jewish Scriptures. Of striking importance is the fact, pointed out in an earlier chapter, that Paul's argument for a Christian mission to Spain relied almost

23. Robert Duncan Culver, *The Life of Christ,* pp. 18-24.
24. See Marshall, p. 904.

entirely on appeal to the Old Testament, showing that repentance and remission of sins should be preached to the nations. And, if so, the believers at Rome ought to help *send* him (Paul) to do the preaching (Rom. 15). Again, observe that in the very first Christian sermon, Peter preached repentance and remission of sins to "Jews, . . . devout men, from every nation under heaven" (Acts 2:5). Apparently Peter as yet had no awareness that "all the nations" of Luke 24:47 included Gentiles as such. God had to shatter Peter's ingrained Jewishness (Acts 10-11) to get him to understand fully Jesus' words (Luke 24), much less the Old Testament, on the subject of world evangelism.

A Last Look at the "Easter" Commission (Mark 16:15-16)

These verses are within the longer ending of Mark, regarded by most textual scholars and editions of the Greek New Testament as not original with Mark, but as a later addition. The Bible Societies' 1966 edition of the Greek New Testament rejects it as lacking sufficient evidence. Westcott and Hort assert in notes on Mark 16:9-20 in their *The New Testament in the Original Greek* that Mark 16:9-20 contains "important matter apparently derived from extraneous sources." The manuscript evidence for this view (common among scholars of every theological persuasion) is convincing. "The earliest Greek, versional and patristic evidence supports the conclusion that Mark ended his Gospel at Ch. 16:8."[25] Thus Mark's report of the "commission" is cited with some reserve. Jesus' post-resurrection predictions of a future mission of world evangelism are not dependent upon it. Whatever its textual status, whether a genuine part of the gospel of Mark or not, Mark 16:15-16 has the flavor and sense of the other accounts:

> And He said to them, "Go into all the world and preach the gospel to all creation. He who has believed and has been baptized shall be saved; but he who has disbelieved shall be condemned.

Two strong features of this report are emphasis on *preaching* as the normal mode of disseminating the message and upon *the whole creation* as the scope or field of the coming mission of world evangelism. The logic of Romans 10:14-15, "And how shall they hear without a preacher? And how shall they preach unless they are sent?" is but a short step from the language of Mark 16:15.

---

25. William L. Lane, *The Gospel According to Mark*, p. 601. He supports this statement in a competent summary at the end of his book (pp. 601-11).

19

The Great Commission

(Matt. 28:19-20)

Pulpit logic has always struggled with this text. It seems to say that all believers must go to all the nations to make disciples, if "go ye therefore" is to all believers. The strict force of such a reading is usually avoided by adding: "And if you can't go yourself, send someone else," or "Go unless you are called of God to stay," or "All must go, but there are many ways of going. Your going may be to witness to a member of your family at home." Who has not heard these struggling efforts with this text? But the English text does not say to send anyone anywhere. It only says, "Go and make disciples." If everyone does not go, are those who stay disobedient? Obviously not. Surely a better understanding of the passage is available.

This passage is a formal announcement of a mission to the nations. There is a strong imperative in it, something missing in the Luke, John, and Acts accounts. Jesus set up the occasion ("Go to Galilee; I'll meet you there!") for the announcement. Apparently He deliberately waited until His authority to command (v. 18; see also vv. 10, 16) had been fully exhibited by virtue of the resurrection and until the right occasion had been created. It is no wonder that these verses have made a great mark on the evangelical Christian conscience.

Before examining the commission verses, several questions must be addressed.

1. Who was present at the meeting on the mountain of Galilee? Though Matthew mentions only "the eleven disciples" some of the most judicious commentators agree "the eleven come forward as representatives of the entire band of disciples and not the select apostolic college of the Twelve."[1] "Some doubted" (v. 17) almost demands the presence of others than the eleven, several of whom had now seen Jesus a number of times and could scarcely have doubted the reality of His resurrection or the propriety of worshipping Him. Likewise the "five hundred brethren at one time" of 1 Corinthians 15:6 could likely have been collected only in Galilee at this early date. It is easier to understand this

1. John Peter Lange, *Commentary on the Holy Scriptures*, p. 555. Editor Schaff in agreement.

as the church's commission if it is regarded as being delivered to a large assembly of disciples.

2. Was the promise, "I am with you always" to the eleven only or to all disciples? Roman Catholic theologians and certain Anglicans (e.g., Wordsworth) have held that it applies only to the apostles and their successors. The "with you" then has special reference to the power of their successors to rule the church, to "bind . . . and . . . loose" (Matt. 16:19), and to "forgive . . . [and] retain . . . sins" (John 20:23). But it was another famous Anglican exegete who pointed out that in directing them to teach future disciples "to observe that all that I commanded you" (Matt. 28:20) the words are turned to "*the* UNIVERSAL CHURCH—to be performed, in the nature of things by her *ministers* and *teachers.*"[2]

3. What is the extent of the "all authority" (v. 18) given to Christ? Jesus' assertion of "all power" seems to refer to the power of deity assumed by Him at His resurrection and ascension and has regard to the human nature only, since as regards His divine nature "all power" had been His always.[3] On the other hand, it may be a simple personal assertion of His eternal power and Godhead as the Son of Man. This is the force of a suggestion by several writers that there is reference to Daniel 7:14.[4] What is important is that the power of the almighty Lord is with the disciples in their mission to make more disciples everywhere and always.

4. There are other matters of differing opinion, though without direct bearing on the mission. To take the most important, the phrase beginning "In the name of," does not mean that Father, Son, and Holy Spirit is a single three-fold name of the Godhead. The sentence is eliptical: "in the name of the Father and [in the name of] the Son . . ." H. A. W. Meyer explains why this must be true. Precisely, the reading is not "in the name" but "into *[eis]* the name." The person being baptized becomes thereby a *public* Christian believer, a disciple by public action. He is pledged "to a faith which has for its object the Being designated by that name."[5]

The apostles had known from the beginning that they would be going somewhere on a mission of preaching. Shortly after constituting twelve disciples as apostles (Luke 6:13), Jesus sent them throughout Galilee (Matt. 10:2-5; Mark 3:13-14). Throughout these studies thus far, the apostles (sent ones) have been Christ's apostles only. They were sent by Him whose special witnesses they were to become. They were not sent by churches. Even in Paul's case, initiative for the various missions came from no congregation. He was not an apostle of the church

2. Henry Alford, *The New Testament for English Readers*, p. 217.
3. R. C. H. Lenski, *An Interpretation of St. Matthew's Gospel*, p. 1170. See also Lange, 1:556-57.
4. Literature on the subject is enormous. See "The Origin of the Son of Man Christology," by Howard M. Teeple, *Journal of Biblical Literature* 84 (September 1965):213-50; also Karl Adam, *The Christ of Faith*, pp. 130-42.
5. H. A. W. Meyer, *Critical and Exegetical Commentary on the New Testament*, 2:302 and note.

at Antioch even though he had a special relationship with that congregation.[6]

The elements of the commission of Matthew 28:19-20 come to focus in four Greek verbal forms, rendered "Go . . . make disciples . . . baptizing . . . teaching." It is important to observe that only one—"make disciples"—is a finite, imperative verb. "Make disciples" presupposes but does not govern "go" grammatically. "Make disciples" governs "baptizing" and "teaching," but not in the same way, for "teaching" is dependent on "baptizing."[7]

Poreuthentes ("Go . . . and") is a nominative, plural, masculine participle, first aorist of *poreuomai*, a deponent verb meaning "to pass from one place to another, to go." ("Deponent" means passive in form but active in meaning.) It is *not* an imperative form and as an aorist participle would naturally be rendered either "having gone" or "as you go." It is inflected in agreement with the understood subject of the imperative verb ("make disciples") that immediately follows. According to Arndt and Gingrich,[8] "the aorist participle of *poreuomai* [go] is often used pleonastically to enliven the narrative . . . the idea of going . . . is not emphasized." Arndt and Gingrich cite thirteen New Testament examples, eight of which are from Matthew, though 28:19 is not one of them (see 9:13; 11:4; 18:12; 21:6; 22:15; 25:16; 27:66; and 28:7). There is no equivalent English idiom. The meaning of the Greek expression is not, "Go! Do!" but, "Do such and such," with the "having gone" or "as you go" presupposed. Even if the expression were omitted, the meaning would not be changed. In Matthew 9:13 (ital. added), for example, where *poreuomai* is followed by *mathetē* (to be a disciple) the rendering is "*go and learn* what this means, I desire compassion. . . ." To obey does not mean to go anywhere at all, but simply to start doing better immediately. A similar idiom is James 5:1 (KJV), "Go to now, ye rich men, weep and howl." Present day English might reverse the idiom and say, "Come now, ye rich men. . . ." Neither *go* or *come* adds to the idea of the imperative "weep." It is simply part of the address to the listeners or readers.

H. A. W. Meyer calls attention to the fact that in making disciples of all nations Jesus did not say specifically "whether it was or was not necessary that they [the Gentiles] . . . become Jewish proselytes [on the way to becoming Christians], though He certainly meant that it was not necessary; and hence, because of this omission, the difficulty which the apostles had at first about directly and uncondi-

---

6. What is meant to be an apostle is discussed at length by Robert Duncan Culver, "Apostles and the Apostalate in the New Testament," *Bibliotheca Sacra* 134 (April-June 1977):131-43.

7. Much of the following discussion on "go," "baptize," and "teach" is based on Robert Duncan Culver, "What is the Church's Commission? Some Exegetical Issues in Matthew 28:16-20," *Bulletin of the Evangelical Theological Society* 10 (Spring 1967):115-26. It was later published by *Bibliotheca Sacra* (July 1968). Both the data and the arguments have since been employed by several other writers. Dr. George W. Peters has formally incorporated a sizeable part of the article in his textbook *A Biblical Theology of Missions*, pp. 173, 182-84. Also see J. Herbert Kane, *Christian Missions in Biblical Perspective* p. 46. The purpose of the article was to relate Matthew 28:19-20 to the Christian mission.

8. William F. Arndt and F. Wilbur Gingrich, trans. and eds., *A Greek-English Lexicon of the New Testament*, p. 692.

tionally admitting the Gentiles."[9] In Meyer's time the rationalist writers, David Hume, Karl Credner, and Carl Heim had cited the story of Peter and Cornelius in Acts 10 and 11 as proof that there had been no dominical commission to preach to all the nations. So Meyer added that "Jesus' omission to say on what basis, if any, other than repentance, faith and baptism they were to be admitted to Christian discipleship explains sufficiently why the later revelation (Acts 10-11) was necessary."[10] It should also be added that "disciple" has always been inter-changeable with "Christian by profession."

The third verbal form, *baptizontes* (baptizing), is a nominative, plural, mascu-line participle, present active of *baptizō*. It is, like *poreuthentes*, in agreement with the finite imperative verb *mathēteusate*. It is not imperative in form, though because of its dependent position and relationship to the imperative verb that controls it, it is in a position to convey an imperative idea nevertheless, as shall be seen.

Didaskontes (teaching) is to be analyzed exactly the same as the preceding, except that it is derived from *didaskō*, meaning to teach. It is also in agreement with *mathēteusate*, yet is grammatically and syntactically connected with *bapti-zontes* as dependent, not strictly coordinate as is sometimes assumed. The justifi-cation for this statement is the absence of *kai* (and), the coordinating conjunction. That is, the "teaching" is associated with the "baptizing," not merely subsequent to it.

A certain structural relationship clearly emerges. There is only one basic element in the commission—*mathēteusate panta ta ethnē*, "make disciples of all the nations." Presupposed by this basic command is the fact that Christian believers should already be deployed on the scene of their missionary labors—*poreuthentes*, "having gone," or, "as they go." Two activities will be involved in making disciples of the nations, not successively but somehow contemporaneous-ly, *baptizontes*, "baptizing," and *didaskontes*, "teaching."

The critical commentaries, i.e., those on the Greek text, present a reassuring consensus on these basic facts of exegesis. Not that every one of them consulted presented all these points, but that they do not essentially disagree; rather, they supplement one another.[11]

More recently, Dr. Cleon Rogers, in a well-conceived and carefully documented article,[12] has argued that because Hebrew, Greek, and English idiomatic use of imperatives and participles are not the same, sometimes a participle in the

9. H. A. W. Meyer, *Critical and Exegetical Commentary on the New Testament,* 1:527.
10. Ibid.
11. The commentaries consulted included many of the best, recognized exegetical authorities. In my article, "What Is the Church's Commission? Some Exegetical Issues in Matthew 28:16-20" (see note 7, above), there are several pages of technical discussion of the grammatical points summa-rized above. Not all the commentators or grammarians are quoted that were consulted, for they duplicated one another. Karl Barth has written from a quite different point of interest. See "An Exegetical Study of Matthew 28:16-20," in Gerald H. Anderson, ed., *The Theology of the Christian Mission.*
12. Cleon Rogers, "The Great Commission," *Bibliotheca Sacra* 130 (July-Sept. 1973):258-67.

position of *poreuthentes* must be translated as an imperative. Thus in Rogers's opinion the word in Matthew 28:19 should read in English, "Go ye."

Rogers's argument is significant, for if it is correct it would be difficult to say other than that in Matthew 28:19 Jesus was commanding all the disciples to witness in foreign lands. Yet it is not conclusive, for Rogers does not dislodge the evidence presented earlier in this chapter, especially the evidence Arndt and Gingrich have developed concerning the pleonastic use of the aorist participle of *poreuomai,* evidence which indicates that Matthew 28:19-20 cannot be interpreted to mean that all disciples should go abroad. It is true that all are instructed to make disciples of all the nations, but it is only an inference and not a command of Matthew 28:19 that some must be sent to the nations that have no witness. Matthew's account does require that Christians already among the nations—and they are almost everywhere—be such witnesses that they make new disciples. The instructions of Matthew 10 tell them what to expect personally as they witness, and Matthew 13 tells them what to expect by way of results in the lives of their hearers. Romans 10 provides a logical argument for both going and sending, while Romans 15 provides scriptural arguments for the same. The whole Bible reinforces the mandate for missions.

SUMMARY AND CONCLUSION

The last words of Jesus in Matthew, the parting promise of verse 20, are not only a fitting climax but an unmistakable promise of the presence of Jesus Christ in the witnessing church through the Holy Spirit. "Lo, I am with you always, even to the end of the age." That promise of the continuing presence of the Savior is of a piece with Luke 24:49: "Stay in the city until you are clothed with power from on high," and Acts 1:8: "You shall receive power when the Holy Spirit has come upon you; and you shall be My witnesses." Those promises refer to a truth laid out plainly in the New Testament: the church was constituted a witnessing body by the effusion of the Spirit at Pentecost: "And they were all filled with the Holy Spirit and began to speak" (Acts 2:4). Paul said they (and all believers) were "all baptized into one body" (1 Cor. 12:13). They have all, so to speak, been speaking in Christian witness ever since. The witnessing Spirit (Rom. 8:16; 1 John 5:7) caused witnessing to Christ's finished work of redemption to be a law of the very nature of the newly constituted assembly. Herein lies the true foundation of energy for going and sending in the Christian mission. It is part of the essence and being of the church.

The doctrine of the Spirit's presence and power in the witnessing church has had a large place in recent missionary and theological literature. It is impossible, probably, to say anything new about it. It is nevertheless precisely the point upon which this study must end. Out of that large literature there is one book that furnishes words to summarize the argument of this book: Henry R. Boer's *Pentecost and Missions.*

Boer builds on a teaching found often in recent writings on the theology of missions: there are two divine mandates for mankind. The first is for the entire race, announced at the creation of man and reaffirmed after the Flood: "Be fruitful and multiply, and fill the earth; and subdue it; and rule over the fish of the sea and over the birds of the sky, and over every living thing that moves on the earth" (Gen. 1:28; cf. Gen. 9:1-2). According to Dr. George W. Peters, this "first mandate" was to populate the earth and to subdue it. It "was spoken to Adam as representative of the race."[13] "The second mandate [the mission of world evangelism] was spoken to the Apostles as representatives of the church of Jesus Christ, involving the whole realm of the gospel" carried forward by preaching and the related things that missionaries do.[14]

Boer, who rightly finds the effusion of the Spirit at Pentecost and the duty of witness as central to the constitution and nature of the church, commented on those two mandates and the relation of their execution by believers to the command of God (first mandate) and of Christ (second mandate). This quotation is somewhat lengthy because the extract conveys the theme of this book with superb accuracy and where the emphasis in mission theology must lie. The quotation begins with the first mandate.

> Although we have before us here a command, it is no less plain that we are dealing with more than *simply* a command. It would be better to say that the command we find in Gen. 1 and 9 is a divine and therefore *organic law* which enters into the very fiber of man's being, which penetrates and permeates his entire constitution. It is of the *nature* of man to be reproductive, to subdue the earth, and to rule over the animals that inhabit it. This command is obeyed, the law is observed, by all men everywhere and at all times. Awareness of it is not at all necessary in order to obey it. Men observe this law because their nature, their whole being, drives them to obey it. . . . It is only when men try to evade or escape the law of their natural being that this law becomes a command for them. Then they must be confronted with the command in order that via obedience to the objective imperative they may be brought again to a normal observance of the law of their life. The difference between command and law . . . is . . . that command has objective but no subjective force, whereas law has both. . . . A divine law. . . although it has an external origin, carries within itself its own effectuation. . . . Understanding command and law in this sense, it may be said that God alone can make laws, and man can only give commands.[15]

The men who carried the faith to places where Christ's name had not yet been pronounced in faith—Paul, Ulfilas, Augustine, the Moravians, Brainerd, Carey, Judson, and all the rest—did not do so primarily because they felt guilty that they had not yet carried out some "commandments contained in ordinances" (Eph. 2:15). They had, to the contrary, drunk deeply of the living water and become aware of an inner compulsion to do all they could to be witnesses of Christ, listening first carefully to *all* the instructions, inferences, and arguments of Scripture. They began in the Spirit and certainly did not finish in the flesh. Wrote Robert E. Speer,

13. George W. Peters, *A Biblical Theology of Missions,* p. 166.
14. Ibid., p. 167.
15. Boer, *Pentecost and Missions,* pp. 121-22.

Men who assent to the missionary enterprise on the strength of the last command of Christ alone, or primarily, will give it little support, and their interest in it will soon become as formal as the ground on which it rests. The spirit of Christianity is higher than legalism, and it is of the spirit of legalism to press injunctions of courses of action where the underlying principles of action are unseen or unfelt. The men who have done the work of God in the world are men in whom the Spirit of God was at work, and who would have done God's work even in the absence of expressed legislation.[16]

The analogy between the impulse to multiply the race by procreation and the impulse to win men to Christ by evangelism has some limits. The church has not found it in herself to be nearly as vigorous in evangelism as the human race has been in propagating itself. Procreation goes on and hardly even pauses, while evangelism, beyond the realm of professing believers and their families, seems almost to die out for long periods.

For happy results even the procreative impulse needs moral and rational direction and all the practical assistance society can give it. Society is right now paying the fearful penalties that have come from turning over the relationship of the sexes to natural impulses. The dynamic of propagation is only *furnished* by the inner nature of mankind; it is not properly *directed*.

Similarly, the presence of the Pentecostal effusion of the Spirit of God, perpetual throughout the present age, effectual in every true believer, must be trusted to furnish the motive power of missionary evangelism. Yet, the fires of evangelism dampen quickly without careful tending. Energetic promotion of the mission by everyone who finds it even slightly in his heart and mouth to confess Christ is required.

An aspect of the parable of the four soils and the seed may help to enforce this final thought: A frightful waste of good seed appears to be a necessary part of the missionary effort. Gospel seed falls in large amounts on waysides where it never germinates, on shallow rocky soil, and on good earth already loaded with seeds of weeds. No permanent fruit comes of it. Yet, the sower has faithfully done his best and will not lose his reward. The abundant crop of grain produced in the fields of good soils justifies energetic, lavish scattering of seed. Even a cup of cold water given in Jesus' name has some effect for advancement of the kingdom of God and will not fail to be rewarded. The Savior has given His word.

16. Robert E. Speer, *Missionary Principles and Practice*, pp. 9-10, as quoted by Boer, p. 123.

Appendix A:

Notes on Recent Critical Interpretation of Jesus' Parables

One hears frequently today that great advances in the study of the parables of Jesus have been made in recent times. Indeed many books and articles have been written on the parables in this century. The Society of Biblical Literature has held seminars on the parables as part of its meetings. Let us take notice of this surge of interest and explain how it does or does not affect our understanding of Jesus' sermons and parables in relation to the Christian mission of world evangelism.

Until the time of the Enlightenment (eighteenth century) Christian understanding always accepted the gospels' own testimony and the testimony of the early church about the time of their writing and the identity of the authors. The gospels were considered apostolic and authentic, which is to say that they were viewed as accounts written by members of the circle of twelve (Matthew and John) or by one under immediate sponsorship of an apostle (Mark by Peter) or by one associated with an apostle and whose gospel was received by an age of the church supervised by apostles (Luke). One of the earliest post-New Testament Christian testimonies called them "memoirs of the Apostles."[1]

No dependence of one gospel author upon another gospel author or mutual dependence on a third source was felt necessary or appropriate. Luke's assertion that he researched sources who were eyewitnesses from the beginning was taken at face value, and the other gospels were held to be eyewitness accounts.

Such a view of the gospels was in keeping with Christ's explicit promise to the apostles during their last evening together (John 13:7; 16:12-13) of a divine enablement to recall, to understand, and to explain the events of His career (words and deeds). Throughout most of the history of Christendom those assurances from the Lord's most tender moments with the twelve had been regarded as true, as have been the penultimate words of the gospel of John. John was the youngest of the apostles and thus prepared his account some fifty to sixty years after the death of Christ. Just before the close of his gospel he made the strongest

1. Justin Martyr *Apology* 1, 66-67.

possible assertion of the truth of what he had written: "This is the disciple who bears witness of these things, and wrote these things; and we know that his witness is true" (John 21:24).

Since the Enlightenment, writers of every degree of scholarship and devotion (or lack of either) have sought to penetrate the approximately three decades before the three synoptic gospels (Matthew, Mark, Luke) were written. They have sought information about sources (written or oral), occasion, and motives for writing. Since there is scarcely any information except the gospels themselves and several early epistles of Paul, those materials have been examined, combed, sorted, distilled, and re-distilled. Certain theoretical conclusions (hardly scientific results) among several prominent theoreticians have emerged. These have achieved sufficient attention that certain tentative results are widely—if not firmly—recognized by a circle of writers who write largely for one another and their students and the libraries that deposit their books for later writers of scholastic theses.

In this school of opinion generally it has been held that Mark's was the first gospel to be written (and indeed it may be true, though the same data has been turned upside down to "prove" that Matthew or Luke was first). There is said to have been another "source," German *Quelle*, hence Q., which existed as contemporary with Mark but earlier than Matthew or Luke. It is asserted that when Matthew and then Luke composed their gospels they employed Mark and Q as sources. This is said to account for the materials common to Matthew and Luke but not in Mark. Finally, since Matthew reports things not in Luke or Mark, and Luke things not in Matthew or Mark, two other sources have been proposed: a source for Matthew called M, and a source for Luke called L.

Those who are interested in such theories can and do confidently refer to "the four sources" of the synoptic gospels—Mark, Q, M, and L. This is the *Four Document Theory*. If one wishes, he may assume divine guidance in use of these sources, hence divine inspiration, and many do so. Or one may suppose that three authors or groups of unknown authors simply did their fallible best with what they had. It is then up to the enlightened reader to judge their words rather than to be judged by them. Those not enamored of such theories wonder why, in that age when hundreds of eyewitnesses were still living, and when, as is well known, the actual words of Jesus from the mouths of people who heard Jesus speak them were treasured far more than the written word, writers should have turned to something called Q, M, or L as sources for their permanent records. They suspect that such documents as Q, M, or L may never have existed outside the minds and writings of literary critics. Certainly no bona fide copies have ever turned up, though considerable documentary remains have been preserved from that epoch.

More recently it has been proposed that during the decades A.D. 30-60 the churches circulated various small units, oral and written, about Jesus. These pieces regarding His career were in various forms: miracle stories, parables, legends, sayings, prayers, and short stories, all used in liturgy, devotion, and instruction. As the years passed, the material was embellished and worked over to meet the changing constituency (Jewish dominance to Gentile dominance) and outlook (soon return of Christ to later) of the church. These pieces were possessed in the churches like beads in a coffer until Mark furnished a narrative framework for the units, putting "the beads" on the string of his narrative.

In such an explanation of the development of the gospel record, the church ("the creative community") is seen as not only having preserved some of the essence of what Jesus said and did, but also as having created much (or most) of it. It is assumed that similar processes occurred when Matthew (employing Q and Mark and M) and Luke (employing Q and Mark and L) put their gospels together. The theory goes by the German name of *Formegeschichte* (history of forms) or Form Criticism.

Other theorists, noting that interpreters have long discerned different theological emphases in each of the gospels, have applied studies of ancient literary *genre* to their perusal of the gospels. Such work is a refinement of the Form Criticism just mentioned and is called *Redaction Criticism*. It lays emphasis on the theological purposes of the authors of the gospel record.

Why this discussion of the various explanations of the gospel accounts? How do these matters relate to interpreting sermons and parables of Jesus? To answer, more must be observed concerning the theories advanced by modern critics.

The theorists all have shifted authority away from Scripture to an unknown or even hypothetical Jesus of history. That shift has affected the way they have viewed the parables. Jülicher, Dibelius, Dodd, Bultmann, Jeremias, Kümmel, and their lesser colleagues and disciples have regarded the parables of the present gospels as several steps removed from the dominical words of Jesus.

It is therefore not certain what such writers have meant when they have affirmed faith in historic Christian doctrines. W. G. Kümmel, one of the clearest writers, at least, closed his *Promise and Fulfillment* with orthodox-sounding affirmations. Yet he had just affirmed that Christ was mistaken in teaching that there would be a *parousia* of the Son of Man within the lifetime of people then living. Kümmel felt he could not expunge this embarrassment by critical methods.

Kümmel came to such contradictory conclusions because he saw the gospel record as being essentially distorted. In *Promise and Fulfillment* he tried to determine what the essential message *(kērygma)* of Jesus was, and what its value was, then and now. He focused on the proclamation of the kingdom of God, showing what other leading teachers and writers who shared his presuppositions said. He assumed the synoptic gospels (including of course the parables) were two stages removed from the actual words of Jesus. The first stage was the stage of tradition in the early church before the written gospels when the church modified the reports of "things seen and heard" to support what they then believed and did. These modified traditions appeared in the gospels. The second stage comprised the modifications made by the writers themselves in the traditions to conform to their own ideas about what should or should not be true. The result, Kümmel asserted, was that the gospel accounts were tendentious, that is, they were twisted to prove a point. In Kümmel's opinion, the various critics should sort out the layers until they learn what Jesus *really* said. Only then would they be able to construct a theology on the basis of the *true* message of Jesus, relieved of the overlay that reflected the biases of the church of about A.D. 60 and of the writers and their sources: Mark, Q, M, and L. Kümel said: "In the *oldest* tradition of Jesus' message, to be ascertained by critical methods, we meet with the Jesus whose *historical* message alone confirms the correctness of the apostolic message. To set forth this oldest message is therefore not only a historical task, but one that is theologically indispensable, and no hermeneutic mistake."[2] In other words, we must all become committed adherents to and masters of Form Criticism before being qualified theologians.

Jülicher, to take the earliest of these authors, held that the parables as Jesus spoke them related wholly to incidents or issues contemporary with Jesus and His audience. Any application to men today was secondary. Other authors have held that the parables (along with about everything else Jesus presented regarding the kingdom of God or the kingdom of heaven) were related to the coming of the Son of Man to judge the world. Schweitzer held that Jesus expected to usher in this coming *parousia* in His own person and failed in the mission. Still others have held that an eschatology realized among the hearers then was what Jesus meant. In the impact on the world of the powers of the world to come in the hearts of men who heard Jesus there was a kind of inaugurated eschatology, the coming of the kingdom. The church proclaimed this for a while, but shortly added the apocalyptic parts of the gospels (Matt. 24, Mark 13, Luke 21) when there was no second coming. The parables of the kingdom were likewise modified to suit.

All these writers seem to have been saying in slightly different ways that, as Gentiles came into the church, the tradition (including parables) was modified to meet the new constituency, and that as the *parousia* delayed, the tradition was modified to meet new conditions. Some have spoken of how, during this period of thirty years or so, the church (that is "the creative community,") reshaped the traditions now enshrined in the gospels.

Almost every author of the type discussed in this appendix has denied that Jesus had any specific foreknowledge of a future church and the long age of its existence. Passages directly applicable to the church they have viewed as being the work of "the creative community," i.e., the first generation of Christians, and of the redactors. Passages such as Matthew 16:13-28, wherein Jesus plainly spoke of a future church that would come into existence after his death and resurrection, they likewise have assigned to "the creative community" or have placed in doubt. They have made such denials partly because their theories about His message and the manner of its incorporation in the gospels forbade any other position and partly because they seem to have had few strong convictions about the deity of the Lord and were thus doubtful of His foreknowledge.

What can be said of scholars who take such positions? Their sincerity and hard work should not be questioned. They have scoured the meager materials available for reconstructing those nearly blank three decades of history. No doubt they have made some valuable insights concerning the parables. Also, they have

---

2. W. G. Kümmel, *Promise and Fulfillment*, p. 105.

written of their devotion to Jesus. One writer, for example, has movingly reported that once the gospels were stripped of accretions and tendentious modifications the reader found himself listening to the veritable voice of the Son of Man Himself.

This much seems certain. Outside of the limited number of persons who read their books for professional reasons, few have found the critics' work interesting or convincing. Matthew 13 conveys much more of the ring of truth just as it reads than the Matthew 13 that emerges after the crew of critics has stripped the chapter of alleged accretions and tendentious changes. The critics themselves seem to have grasped how empty their work was. The foreword of a 1978 history of interpretation of Jesus' parables ended on this melancholy note: "The appearance of this volume will do much to stimulate the round of advances and will contribute to its own obsolescence. Such is the reward of productive scholarship."[3]

The writer was correct in judging the lasting power of the work he was evaluating. It would not endure. But he did not pinpoint the cause of that lack of vitality. It is not the crowding of new theories that will condemn their work to early obsolescence, but their work's lack of a truly Christian sense of religious authority.

3. Robert Funk, introduction to *The Parables of Jesus: A History of Interpretations and Bibliography*, by Warren S. Kissinger, p. vi.

Appendix B:
Reflections on Interpreting Parables

A biblical parable is generally understood as a story told to teach some moral, lesson, or doctrine. Usually only one teaching is the burden of each parable. The prophet Nathan's apparently fictitous story of the little ewe sheep and his point, "You are the man" (2 Sam. 12:7, see also vv. 1-5) is an example. It is worth noting, however, that though the lesson was very simple, Nathan used many more words to elaborate the point and to drive it home to David than he employed in the parable itself. It was all so very realistic that David at first thought it was a true report of injustice in his kingdom and he was about to put judicial process in motion.

Jotham's parable of the bramble (Judges 9:7-15), however, is not a believable story. It is not only fictitious but fabulous. The trees go out to make a king over themselves. The olive tree, the fig tree, the grape vine, and the bramble speak as if human. There is a central thrust, "get rid of Abimelech," but almost everything the trees say and do has rather specific parallel and application to affairs in the ancient city of Shechem. The story is part fable (speaking animals and plants) and part allegory (a story in which the various elements each stand for something).

The pithy comparisons of the book of Proverbs are called parables, too (Prov. 1:6), and the strange taunting song against the king of Babylon, in which the earth sings, trees talk, and shades in the realm of the dead make speeches, is also called a parable (Isa. 14:3-11). Further, while the Hebrew Bible uses a variety of terms for these things, the Septuagint (ancient Greek translation) often employs *parabolē* (parable), as the foregoing references from Proverbs and Isaiah show. These passages come across in the New Testament allusions and quotations as *parabolē*. So our rather specific word *parable* becomes an indefinite designation of several different kinds of stories, riddles, similitudes, and the like.

There is therefore no strict basis in the language of Scripture to classify the parables of Jesus under any common technical term. Jesus' parables are, however, much closer to the single-idea type (Nathan's parable) than the allegory-fable type of Jotham or the complex imagery of the taunt song of Isaiah 14.

As far as can be determined, there is little, if any, disagreement about the above-mentioned assertions among New Testament scholars today. Until the Protestant Reformers, the parables were commonly expounded as allegories. Calvin was the first important teacher to break severely from that habit of interpretation and truly sought the lesson or doctrine Jesus was teaching by looking steadfastly at the parable in its context. His comments are still valuable today.

The great scholarly expositors of the nineteenth century, several of whom have been cited in this book, treat Jesus' parables as similitudes—a certain truth corresponds to a point made by a story—not some part of it but the whole of it. This is the general rule. Sometimes more than one truth may be taught, but if so it is plain. There may be other elements of instruction present but they are subsidiary to the main lesson.

Some parables are very simple—a seed that grows to harvest wholly by "automatic" powers and processes. There is nothing the farmer can do but wait. The lesson is *patience*. There is apparently no other lesson, though patience is much more than a word and several pages have been written about it in this book. Other parables have several parts and if the parable teaches one truth, that truth has "parts" or "features." Such is the similitude of the seed and the four soils. Several parables predict the course of future events—the rejection of the Savior by His people, the gathering of Gentiles into the church and even the destruction of Jerusalem by the Romans. These are close to outright allegory. Two of these follow one another in the narrative of Passion Week: the householder and the faithless husbandmen (Matt. 21:33-46); the king and the reluctant wedding guests (22:1-4). Of course, liberal scholars will employ their critical tools to expunge any such future plans of Jesus from the "authentic tradition." Joachim Jeremias has "discovered" ten ways by which the creative church and the redactors modified and embellished the original parables and sayings of Jesus.[1] These modifications and embellishments may be detected, it is said, by finding any parts identical to distinct features of either Judaism or the church of about A.D. 60. What is left is said to be authentic. Other criteria are employed but this is the chief one.

Yet the more moderate of the liberal critics acknowledge that the "authentic kernel" sometimes contains allegorical elements. A. M. Hunter, who is certainly moderate and generally helpful, commented: "We are asserting that no aesthetic scruple would have prevented Jesus [from] using allegory if and when it suited his purpose. . . . A good working rule would be this. When interpreting, don't try to eliminate everything allegorical . . . and so trim them into pure parables. On the other hand, never allegorize to the point which mars the one lesson, or warning, or challenge, which the parable was meant to convey."[2]

The parables are not mere pleasant tales to illustrate sermons to cultivated audiences. They were delivered in an atmosphere of sharp conflict. After one of them one segment of the crowd was so incensed they sought to have Jesus arrested (Matt. 21:45-46).

---

1. Joachim Jeremias, *The Parables of Jesus,* pp. 23-114.
2. A. M. Hunter, *The Parables Then and Now,* p. 24.

However much or little the disciples understood, Jesus clearly declared to them that His words would be fully understood only after the effusion of the Spirit upon them. They were supposed to explain them further to us and we are therefore in a much better position than the first audiences. Some principles that good interpreters use are as follows:

1. Expect to find the unknown conveyed by the known. This is true of all communication to some degree. All abstract ideas are conveyed by use of language figures of one sort or another. Think of how the words *image, imagine,* and *imagination* are used.

2. The chief point of comparison is to the whole parable. The point cannot be understood until the end. When Jesus says, "The kingdom of heaven is like," the comparison (similitude) is not simply a net or leaven or a grain of mustard seed but the whole story of a net, leaven, or a grain of mustard seed. Hear Jesus out before you make up your mind.

3. Expect the point of the parable to be a truth that challenges the reader to some change of life, some act of repentance or faith. The people of Jesus' day, who were amused or entertained but not challenged, missed the point. Some who did see the point were only angered. Only a few truly understood and believed. Jesus' parables were not democratic media of mass appeal. He never got elected to anything except a cross!

4. Do not expect every detail to have specific meaning. Most details serve only as vehicles for the story. There may be elements of allegory (multiple symbolism), but the parables remain essentially parables (again think of Nathan's parable). In a true allegory such as Bunyan's *The Pilgrim's Progress* or the modern fantastic tales of Lewis, Williams, or Miller every detail such as the Slough of Despond has a precise and obvious counterpart in the Christian's life. None of Jesus' parables is quite like that.

5. Expect that often the main point will be spelled out plainly by the gospel author. Luke, for example, informed his readers clearly that Jesus spoke the parable of the pounds in order to correct the notion "that the kingdom of God should immediately appear" (Luke 19:11, KJV). If Scripture speaks with authority Luke can hardly be set aside for the learned opinions of Dodd, Jeremias, or Bultmann.

6. Sometimes the main point is clearly conveyed by the historical setting. Both scribes and Pharisees, Luke says, had grumbled because Jesus warmly welcomed tax-gatherers and sinners to hear Him (Luke 15:1-2). Immediately Jesus spoke three parables (the lost sheep, the lost coin, and the prodigal son) comparing joy on earth over finding lost things to the joy of heavenly beings "over one sinner who repents" (vv. 7, 10). The father's words to the brother of the prodigal son convey the same lesson: "But we had to be merry and rejoice, for this brother of yours was dead and has begun to live, and was lost and has been found" (v. 32). The lesson is plainly *joy,* not forgiveness, as the nearly uniform exegesis of liberal Protestant theologians would have it.

7. Like Paul Harvey's famous "The Rest of the Story" and good yarns everywhere, the point of the parable usually comes at or near the end. Think of the

three parables just cited from Luke 15. In each of the three, the joy that the scribes and Pharisees missed and which God, heaven, and the angels have over sinners who repent comes at the very end of the parable.

8. Sometimes Jesus rather clearly explained what certain parables meant and expected the disciples to gain sufficient insight thereby to interpret similar parables given on the same occasion. This was the case with the eight parables of the kingdom that have been studied (see Matt. 13:51-52; cf. vv. 18-23 and 36-43).

Selected Bibliography

Adam, Karl. *The Christ of Faith*. Translated by Joyce Crick. New York: Pantheon, 1957.

Albright, W. F., and Freedman, David Noel, gen. eds. *The Anchor Bible*. 44 vols. Garden City, N.Y.: Doubleday, 1970.

Alford, Henry. *The New Testament for English Readers*. Chicago: Moody, n.d.

Allen, Roland. *The Spontaneous Expansion of the Church: And the Causes which Hinder It*. London: World Dominion Press, 1927.

Anderson, Gerald H., ed. *The Theology of the Christian Mission*. New York: McGraw-Hill, 1961.

Arndt, William F., and Gingrich, F. Wilbur, trans. and eds. *A Greek-English Lexicon of the New Testament*, by Walter Bauer. 2d ed. rev. Chicago: U. of Chicago, 1979.

Balke, Willem. *Calvin and the Anabaptist Radicals*. Translated by William Heynen. Grand Rapids: Eerdmans, 1981.

Barrett, C. K. *A Commentary on the Epistle to the Romans*. New York: Harpers, 1957.

Barth, Karl. "An Exegetical Study of Matthew 28:16-20," in *The Theology of the Christian Mission*. Edited by Gerald H. Anderson. New York: McGraw-Hill, 1961.

Bernard, J. H. *A Critical and Exegetical Commentary on the Gospel According to St. John*. Vol. 29:2. The International Critical Commentary. Edinburgh: T & T Clark, 1928.

Boer, Harry R. *Pentecost and Missions*. Grand Rapids: Eerdmans, 1961.

Brown, R. E. *The Gospel According to John*. Vol. 29A. *The Anchor Bible*. Edited by W. F. Albright and David Noel Freedman. Garden City, N.Y.: Doubleday, 1970.

Calvin, John. *Calvin's Commentaries: A Harmony of Matthew, Mark and Luke*. Translated by A. W. Morrison. 3 vols. Grand Rapids: Eerdmans, 1972.

————. *Institutes of the Christian Religion*. 2 vols. Translated by Henry Beveridge. Grand Rapids: Eerdmans, 1964.

Cranfield, C. E. B. *A Critical and Exegetical Commentary on the Epistle to the*

Romans. Vol. 32:2. The International Critical Commentary. Edinburgh: T & T Clark, 1979.

Culver, Robert Duncan. "Apostles and the Apostolate in the New Testament." *Bibliotheca Sacra* 134 (April-June 1977):131-43.

————. *The Life of Christ.* Grand Rapids: Baker, 1976.

————. "Were the Old Testament Prophecies Really Prophetic?" in *Can I Trust the Bible?* Edited by Howard F. Vos. Chicago: Moody, 1963.

————. "What Is the Church's Commission? Some Exegetical Issues in Matthew 28:16-20." *Bulletin of the Evangelical Theological Society* 10.2(Spring 1967):115-26.

Cyprian. *The Epistles of Cyprian in The Ante-Nicene Fathers.* Vol. 5. Edited by Alexander Roberts and James Donaldson. Grand Rapids: Eerdmans, 1975.

————. *The Treatises of Cyprian in The Ante-Nicene Fathers.* Vol. 5. Edited by Alexander Roberts and James Donaldson. Grand Rapids: Eerdmans, 1975.

Dahood, Mitchell. *Psalms.* Vol. 16-17a. *The Anchor Bible.* Edited by W. F. Albright and David Noel Freedman. Garden City, N.Y.: Doubleday, 1970.

Davey, F. N. "The Gospel According to John and the Christian Mission," in *The Theology of the Christian Mission.* Edited by Gerald H. Anderson. New York: McGraw-Hill, 1961.

Dodd, C. H. *The Apostolic Preaching and Its Developments.* London: Hodder and Stoughton, 1950.

————. *The Epistle to the Romans.* London: Hodder and Stoughton, 1949.

Edersheim, Alfred. *The Life and Times of Jesus the Messiah.* 2 vols. Grand Rapids: Eerdmans, 1967.

Ellicott, Charles John, ed. *Ellicott's Commentary on the Whole Bible: A Verse by Verse Explanation.* 8 vols. Grand Rapids: Zondervan, 1954. Vol. 6: *The Four Gospels.*

Encyclopedia Britannica. 11th ed. (1910-11), s.v. "John Huss."

Eusebius. *Ecclesiastical History.* Translated by C. F. Crusé. 2d ed. revised & corrected. Philadelphia: Rev. R. Davis & Brother, 1833.

Fife, Robert Herndon. *The Revolt of Martin Luther.* New York: Columbia U., 1957.

Funk, Robert. Introduction to *The Parables of Jesus: A History of Interpretation and Bibliography.* Metuchen, N.J.: Scarecrow Press, 1979.

Glover, Robert Hall. *The Progress of World-Wide Missions.* Revised and enlarged by J. Herbert Kane. New York: Harper & Row, 1960.

Godet, F. *A Commentary on the Gospel of St. Luke.* Translated by E. W. Shalders and M. D. Cusin. 3rd ed. New York: Funk & Wagnalls, 1890.

————. *A Commentary on the Epistle to the Romans.* Translated by M. D. Cusin. Translation revised and edited by T. W. Chambers. Grand Rapids: Zondervan, 1956.

Haldane, Robert. *Exposition of the Epistle to the Romans.* 5th Edinburgh edition. New York: Robert Carter, 1847.

Hendriksen, William. *Matthew: New Testament Commentary Series.* Grand Rapids: Baker, 1973.

Hunter, A. M. *The Parables Then and Now.* Philadelphia: Westminster, 1971.

Irenaeus. *Against Heresies.* Translated by F. R. Montgomery Hitchcock. *Early Church Classics.* Vol. 1. London: Society for Promoting Christian Knowledge, 1916.

Ironside, H. A. *Expository Notes on the Gospel of Matthew.* New York: Loizeaux Bros., 1948.

Jeremias, Joachim. *The Parables of Jesus.* 2d ed. rev. New York: Scribner's, 1972.

Kane, J. Herbert. *Christian Missions in Biblical Perspective.* Grand Rapids: Baker, 1976.

————. *Understanding Christian Missions.* Grand Rapids: Baker, 1974.

Kittel, Gerhard, and Friedrich, Gerhard, eds. *Theological Dictionary of the New Testament.* Translated by Geoffrey Bromiley. 10 vols. Grand Rapids: Eerdmans, 1964.

Kümmel, W. G. *Promise and Fulfillment: The Eschatological Message of Jesus.* Naperville, Ill.: Alec R. Allenson, 1957.

Ladd, George Eldon. *The Gospel of the Kingdom: Scriptural Studies in the Kingdom of God.* Grand Rapids: Eerdmans, 1959.

Lane, William L. *The Gospel According to Mark.* Grand Rapids: Eerdmans, 1974.

Lange, John Peter. *Commentary on the Holy Scriptures.* Edited by Philip Schaff. Grand Rapids: Zondervan, n.d.

Latourette, Kenneth Scott. *A History of the Expansion of Christianity.* 7 vols. New York: Harper & Row, 1937.

Laurenson, L. *Messiah the Prince, An Outline of Matthew's Gospel.* Edinburgh: J. K. Souter, 1924.

Lenski, R. C. H. *An Interpretation of St. Matthew's Gospel.* Columbus, O.: Wartburg Press, 1943.

Marshall, I. Howard. *The Gospel of Luke: A Commentary on the Greek Text.* Grand Rapids: Eerdmans, 1978.

Martyr, Justin. *Dialogue with Trypho the Jew,* in *The Ante-Nicene Fathers.* Vol. 1. Edited by Alexander Roberts and James Donaldson. Grand Rapids: Eerdmans, 1975.

————. *Apology.* In *Saint Justin Martyr* by Thomas B. Falls. New York: Christian Heritage, 1948.

McClintock & Strong's Encyclopedia of Biblical, Theological and Ecclesiastical Literature. Reprint. Grand Rapids: Baker, 1970. S.v. "Savonarola."

Meinardus, Otto F. A. "Paul's Missionary Journey to Spain: Tradition and Folklore." *The Biblical Archaeologist* 41 (June 1978):61-63.

Meyer, H. A. W. *Critical and Exegetical Commentary on the New Testament.* 11 vols. New York: Funk & Wagnalls, 1884.

Origen. *On First Principles.* Koetschau's text of *De Principiis,* translated by G. W. Butterworth. New York: Harper & Row, 1966.

Owen, J. J. *A Commentary, Critical, Expository and Practical on the Gospels of Matthew and Mark.* New York: Scribner's, 1866.

Peters, George W. *A Biblical Theology of Missions.* Chicago: Moody, 1972.

Pink, A. W. *The Prophetic Parables of Matthew 13.* Swengel, Pa.: Bible Truth Depot, n.d.

Roberts, Alexander and Donaldson, James, eds. *The Ante-Nicene Fathers*. Grand Rapids: Eerdmans, 1975.

Rogers, Cleon. "The Great Commission." *Bibliotheca Sacra* 130 (July-September, 1973):258-67.

Sauer, Erich. *From Eternity to Eternity*. Grand Rapids: Eerdmans, 1954.

Schaeffer, Francis. *The God Who Is There*. Downers Grove, Ill.: InterVarsity, 1968.

Scofield, C. I., et al, eds. *The New Scofield Reference Bible*. New York: Oxford U., 1967.

Stalker, James. *The Life of Jesus Christ*. New York: Revell, 1949.

Stier, Ewald Rudolf. *Die Redendes Herrn Jesu*. 6 vols. Barmen: n.p., 1843-48.

Strack, Hermann L. and Billerbeck, Paul. *Kommentar zum Neuen Testamentum aus Talmud und Midrasch*. 6 vols. Munich: C. H. Beck, 1978-79.

Teeple, Howard M. "The Origin of the Son of Man Christology." *Journal of Biblical Literature* 84 (September 1965):213-50.

Tertullian. *Apology*. Translated by T. R. Glover. Cambridge, Mass.: Harvard U., 1960.

Thomas, David. *The Genius of the Gospel: A Homiletical Commentary on the Gospel of St. Matthew*. London: Dickinson and Higham, 1873.

Turner, George Allen, and Mantey, Julius R. *The Evangelical Commentary: The Gospel According to John*. Grand Rapids: Eerdmans, n.d.

Vos, Howard F., ed. *Can I Trust The Bible?* Chicago: Moody, 1963.

Warren, Max. *I Believe in the Great Commission*. Grand Rapids: Eerdmans, 1976.

Westcott, B. F. *The Holy Bible . . . with an Explanatory and Critical Commentary*. Edited by F. C. Cook. 13 vols. London: John Murray, 1899. Vol. 2 of the New Testament, *John—Acts*.

Whitcomb, John C. *An Analysis of Evangelical Missions and Evangelism in the Light of the Great Commission*. Winona Lake, Ind.: BMH Books, n.d.

Index of Subjects

Index of Persons

Index of Scripture

Moody Press, a ministry of the Moody Bible Institute, is designed for education, evangelization and edification. If we may assist you in knowing more about Christ and the Christian life, please write us without obligation: Moody Press, c/o MLM, Chicago, Illinois 60610.